Big Sky, Big Parks

Big Sky, Big Parks

AN EXPLORATION OF
YELLOWSTONE AND GLACIER NATIONAL PARKS,
AND ALL THAT MONTANA IN BETWEEN

EDNOR THERRIAULT

TWODOT®

ESSEX, CONNECTICUT
HELENA, MONTANA

An imprint of Globe Pequot, the trade division of
The Rowman & Littlefield Publishing Group, Inc.
4501 Forbes Blvd., Ste. 200
Lanham, MD 20706
www.rowman.com

Distributed by NATIONAL BOOK NETWORK

British Library Cataloguing in Publication Information available

Library of Congress Cataloging-in-Publication Data
Names: Therriault, Ednor, author.
Title: Big sky, big parks : an exploration of Yellowstone and Glacier
    National Parks, and all that Montana in between / Ednor Therriault.
Other titles: Exploration of Yellowstone and Glacier National Parks, and
    all that Montana in between
Description: Essex, Connecticut : TwoDot, [2023] | Includes bibliographical
    references and index. | Summary: "A travel guide to Glacier and
    Yellowstone National Parks, blending history, culture, and local flavor.
    An entertaining travel companion and a useful resource for those
    visiting the two national parks, and the vast chunk of Montana that
    connects them"— Provided by publisher.
Identifiers: LCCN 2022061599 (print) | LCCN 2022061600 (ebook) | ISBN
    9781493064755 (paper ; alk. paper) | ISBN 9781493064762 (electronic)
Subjects: LCSH: Glacier National Park (Mont.)—Guidebooks. | Yellowstone
    National Park—Guidebooks. | Glacier National Park (Mont.)—History. |
    Yellowstone National Park—History.
Classification: LCC F737.G5 .T46 2023 (print) | LCC F737.G5 (ebook) | DDC
    917.86/5204—dc23/eng/20230203
LC record available at https://lccn.loc.gov/2022061599
LC ebook record available at https://lccn.loc.gov/2022061600

CONTENTS

Introduction vii

Glacier National Park **1**
1. Welcome to Glacier! 3
2. Chasing the Plows on Going-to-the-Sun Road 11
3. The Phoenix of Glacier Park 18
4. What Happened to the Whitehead Brothers? 25
5. Waterton's Bison Return After Trial by Fire 34
6. Above It All 41
7. Stalking the Untamed Mushroom 48
8. A Forgotten Hero in Glacier Park 65
9. History on Display at Marias Pass Memorial Park 71
10. Growing Up Glacier 79

Yellowstone National Park **87**
11. Welcome to Yellowstone! 88
12. Grand Loop Road: Yellowstone's Asphalt Heart 97
13. The Pack Is Back 114
14. Yellowstone Is an Active Volcano: But How Active, Exactly? . . 123
15. Fort Yellowstone to the Rescue 137
16. Lost (and Found) in Yellowstone 145
17. Danger and Comfort: Seeing Yellowstone "The Wylie Way" . . . 161
18. Uncle Tom's Trail . . . of Terror 169
19. Some Like It Hot 175
20. Yellowstone's Latest 500-Year Flood 183

The Montana Swath **191**
21. See, Rock City! 192
22. The Little Shell Tribe, the "Newest" Nation in Montana 207

23. Remembering Butte's Own Disneyland 216
24. Where the Buffalo (and Others) Roam 224
25. Ladies and Gentlemen, the Virginia City Players 231
26. Montana's State Parks: Like National Parks, Only Smaller . . .240
27. Buffalo Soldiers: Winning the West on Two Wheels 249
28. World Museum of Wildlife Is Truly World Class 258
29. Lewis and/or Clark Slept Here. 265
30. Hungry Horse Dam, the Flathead Valley's Hidden Jewel 273

Acknowledgments 280
Further Reading 282
Index 284
About the Author 298

INTRODUCTION

In 1915, 5 years after Glacier National Park was designated, a group of businessmen centered in Great Falls formed something called the Yellowstone-Glacier Bee Line Highway Association. They identified thirteen Montana roads that created routes between Yellowstone and Glacier, and set about creating promotional opportunities for business along these routes, hoping to capitalize on the tourist traffic between the parks. They gave the roads their own colorful symbols, applying names like Roosevelt Highway, Vigilante Trail, and the Custer Battlefield Highway to give them a patina of historic significance. As its name implied, the Y-G Bee Line, running 346 miles from Gardiner to Browning, provided the quickest, most direct route between Montana's two national parks. My question is: Why?

If you're ever going to take your time driving between national parks, Montana is the place to do it. More than any of the large, square-cornered states in the American West, Montana fires the imagination. Big Sky Country has a kind of burnished glow, a buckskin mystique that makes it somehow a little more special—a Wild West with the emphasis on "wild." The third biggest state in the Lower 48, its vast open spaces still hold the promise of the undiscovered and the unspoiled, places not yet dimmed by the shadow of a Sonic or Starbucks.

Each year 12 million people come to Montana seeking adventure or solitude, or both. And the Treasure State welcomes them with open arms. In fact, tourism drives much of the state's economy, second only to agriculture. That Montana is home to two of America's most popular national parks just sweetens the deal, and the state enjoys a symbiotic relationship with them both. Visitors to Yellowstone and Glacier spend about half a billion dollars annually in Montana while falling under the spell of our state's abundant charms. It's no big secret that Montana is full of bucket list sights and experiences—as a vacation destination, it's a no-brainer.

Yellowstone and Glacier National Parks are separated by a few hundred miles, but with enough time and some careful planning it's possible to visit both during a trip to Montana. A successful "double dip" vacation requires you to set realistic expectations. You won't be able to take in everything that both parks have to offer (there are people who spend their entire lives exploring the parks, and haven't come close to seeing it all), but you can enjoy a trip that produces so many indelible memories of Glacier, Yellowstone, and western Montana that you'll be eager for another visit to Big Sky country before you're finished unpacking your suitcase back home.

◆～◆

Yellowstone was the world's first national park, and it is one of America's biggest. In the contiguous United States, only the Grand Canyon and Death Valley occupy more national park real estate. It's hard to wrap your head around just how big 2.2 million acres is. Rhode Island and Delaware could fit within its borders, although such a move would be prohibitively expensive. Most of the park lies within Wyoming, but Yellowstone slightly overlaps Montana and Idaho, as the park was established in 1872 before the Montana and Idaho territories were carved into official states. Montana gleefully claims and promotes Yellowstone as its own, which feels legit since three of the park's five gateway communities are located in Montana, including West Yellowstone, its busiest entrance.

Half the world's geysers are in Yellowstone, most of them in the area of the park that sits atop a 34-by-45-mile caldera, a collapsed supervolcano that last erupted 630,000 years ago. While some believe that it's long overdue for another eruption, in geological terms let's just say this won't be something to worry about while in Yellowstone. One thing that probably *will* blow while you're in Yellowstone is your mind. The bizarre natural formations and thermal features of the park, with its roaring geysers, bubbling hot pools, and steaming rivers, inspired early mountain men like Jim Bridger to describe the area mostly in terms of hell on earth, leading to a lot of devil-themed nomenclature. Indigenous peoples regard it as a sacred place—not a home of "evil spirits" to be feared and avoided, despite the condescending claims of many early white explorers/exploiters. One band of the Shoshone, the Tukudeka, or Mountain Sheepeaters, even lived full-time on the Yellowstone plateau, cleverly using its superheated waters to help craft bows, tools, and clothing from the plentiful bighorn sheep that were central to their culture.

During Yellowstone Park's first decade, it wasn't just its animals that ran wild. In 1886 the US Army established a post in Mammoth Hot Springs to provide some protection for the park from poachers, vandals, and others who were exploiting Yellowstone's resources. Lacking proper funding and manpower, though, they were woefully underequipped for the endeavor. The idea of a handful of soldiers on horseback or skis patrolling a couple million acres of wilderness, mountains, and open prairies was laughable, but for 30 years the soldiers at Fort Mammoth served as Yellowstone's guardians.

We have a much greater understanding of the delicate balance of Yellowstone's ecology now, but still it seems like every year we read about some numbskulls taunting death by trying to pet a buffalo or risking being boiled alive by leaving the boardwalk and sauntering onto the brittle crust of an off-limits thermal area. The spectacular nature of Yellowstone contains an inherent risk, but visitors who respect the unforgiving reality of its more dangerous terrain and inhabitants are rewarded with the thrilling sights and experiences that will resonate for a lifetime. There's nowhere in the world like Yellowstone.

❧

And then there's Glacier, Yellowstone's younger brother. Butting the Canadian border about 400 miles northwest of Yellowstone, Glacier National Park is a super-sized collection of everything the Northern Rockies have to offer. In some ways Yellowstone's slightly less popular sibling, Glacier averages around 3 million visitors per year compared with Yellowstone's 4 million, but turnstile counts are meaningless in reflecting the outsized, rugged beauty of Glacier. Established in 1910, Glacier comprises a million acres of skyscraping peaks, emerald mountain lakes, and towering waterfalls, as well as some of the most impressive wildlife you can find in North America. In 1932 the park was incorporated with Waterton Lakes National Park north of the border to create Waterton-Glacier

International Peace Park. Early visitors likened it to the Swiss Alps, and much of the architecture echoes that comparison.

While occupying fewer square miles than Yellowstone, Glacier is actually the older—much older—brother to its volcanic counterpart. Tectonic plates colliding more than 150 million years ago along the western edge of North America piled up, creating jagged mountains with billion-year-old layers of rock on top. It was only 15,000 years ago since the last ice age—not a lot of time in geological terms—that the receding inland sea and the massive glaciers of several ice ages carved out the last mountain peaks and valleys in Glacier, leaving behind hundreds of crystal clear alpine lakes and rivers that flow jade green with glacial silt.

The park's namesake ice fields haven't fared so well. Scientists have estimated that out of eighty significant glaciers extant about 500 years ago in what is now Glacier Park, only thirty-two remain. Climate change is a culprit, but so are the unpredictable dynamics of weather and precipitation. Unless there's another ice age right around the corner, Glacier's glaciers may eventually disappear.

Of course, there is so much more to Glacier National Park than glaciers. Like Yellowstone, the park is home to a variety of impressive and highly photogenic wildlife. Moose, elk, mountain goats, bighorn sheep, wolves, mountain lions, and of course grizzly and black bears all thrive in the lush forests and steep terrain. These aren't docile zoo animals, obviously, and signs throughout the park issue warnings in several languages not to approach wildlife. Evidently it's not obvious to all. Run-ins with large animals in Glacier are rare, but they do happen. Grizzly attacks are the ones that usually generate the headlines. Due to ignorance, foolishness, and sometimes just bad luck, some of these encounters are fatal. But don't worry—the chances that you'll be eaten by a grizzly bear while visiting Glacier National Park are slimmer than Monday's paper. In fact, more people die each year by falling off a mountain trail while trying to get a rad selfie for their Instagram. As in Yellowstone, visitors sometimes fail to show a healthy respect for the park's dramatic terrain and its wild inhabitants.

Another mistake made by many people who visit Glacier and/or Yellowstone during a trip to Montana is thinking they can see all of either park in a day or two. Anyone who has been to Yellowstone in August can tell you that it will take an entire day, for instance, just to find a parking space within walking distance of Steamboat Geyser. In Glacier, driving the length of Going-to-the-Sun Road, even riding in a tour bus, is another all-day activity. You can do it in 6 hours, traffic notwithstanding, but again: Why?

These vast areas may seem quite manageable on a map, but the popular features and hiking trails of Montana's national parks are mostly separated by large, roadless wilderness, not arranged conveniently together like the rides at an Orlando theme park. Once you accept the idea that you won't be able to take it all in during a lifetime, let alone a 3-day weekend, you'll be able to pick and choose a few must-see spots and avoid disappointment by planning accordingly.

⌁

The question, "What's your hurry?" applies to traveling between Glacier and Yellowstone. It can be done in under 7 hours, but those who cruise control their way from one park to the other might just miss out on the best part of their whole vacation: all that Montana in between—the Montana Swath, we'll call it. There are hundreds of possible routes you can choose to plunge right into the real Montana on the road between Glacier and Yellowstone, and none of them is a wrong choice. As spectacular as Montana's national parks can be, the rest of Montana is no slouch. For instance, it's nearly impossible to get to Glacier Park without passing through at least one of Montana's Indian reservations. Seven reservations across the state are home to twelve tribal nations. Tribes host several events throughout the year which are open to nontribal members, and it's a terrific opportunity to participate and learn more about Montana's Native American culture. The Indigenous peoples who inhabited the land for at least 13,000 years before the first European settlers crossed the plains into the Northwest are a big part of Montana's history, and in many cases their stories are only just now being learned outside the tribe. Attending a powwow on a fine Montana summer evening could be the most fulfilling experience of your entire vacation. While you're there, make sure you pick up an Indian taco. It's a hefty, messy pile of taco ingredients heaped onto a puffy mat of crispy fry bread, a tasty Indian staple.

A fry bread recipe is a major source of familial pride, a closely held secret handed down for generations.

Which brings us to the most important component of any road trip: the food. As you travel through western Montana you'll find several mouthwatering treasures that are unique to the area, and some of them are available only during certain times of the year. You'll want to know where and when you can pick up these strictly Montana treats, from the bison jerky made by M&S Meats on Flathead Lake, to the incredible corn on the cob grown at Benson's Farm in Missoula. (Hint: You'll know it's ready for picking when they unfurl their corn flag.)

On your journey between the parks you'll brush up against a wealth of Montana history, some of which is still happening today. Just west of Yellowstone, the twin "living" ghost towns of Virginia City and Nevada City are buzzing with activity through the summer. Virginia City even has its own theater troupe that has been entertaining audiences with their professional productions for more than half a century. Their plays are so engaging that you might forget about all the hangings and brutal murders that went on in the town's gold rush heyday.

Dozens of Montana's county and pioneer museums are bursting with fascinating secrets of the state's wild and wooly history. You can also dig much deeper into Montana's past by following the Dinosaur Trail, a series of museums and research facilities dedicated to studying and displaying the fossils of dinosaurs like T-Rex and Triceratops that once roamed the area.

Lewis and Clark buffs will enjoy the historic sites scattered through the Montana Swath, from Traveler's Rest in the Bitterroot Valley, where the Corps of Discovery bivouacked for several days, to William Clark's name etched into the sandstone of Pompeys Pillar near Billings. Dozens of Montana's natural features are named after the intrepid duo, including the Clark Fork, the river that runs through downtown Missoula. On hot summer days the slow-moving river is usually jammed with hundreds of people floating lazily on rafts and inner tubes. Locals call it the "tube hatch."

Really, the most important thing you can bring when you come to Montana to explore Glacier and Yellowstone is plenty of time. During the peak summer months in the parks, expect lines for bathrooms, trailheads, and most services, and know it will take longer to travel from one attraction to the next. Still, there are ways to avoid many of the slowdowns. The vast majority of visitors you'll see in both parks might as well be on a monorail. The heaviest crowds, the fleets of tour buses, and the highest anxiety levels will all be massed at the big, sexy attractions like Artists Point on the Grand Canyon of Yellowstone, or at Glacier's popular Logan Pass Visitor Center near the peak of Going-to-the-Sun Road. With a little knowledge and effort, as you'll find in this book, you can split off that well-worn path and explore areas of the parks that most people don't bother with. Or you can rise with the sun and get to the popular features like Old Faithful before the big crowds have even started arguing about what to have for breakfast, or wait until the shadows grow long to visit the Trail of the Cedars in Glacier.

And don't forget—you're out west. Everything's bigger and farther away. If a Montanan says, "It's just down the road," they might mean a hundred miles. Set some realistic expectations for each day in the parks: two or three major spots to visit, or maybe one long hike, leaving some time for spontaneity. It took you a lot of time, effort, and expense to get here; you want to be able to relax, breathe deeply, shake off the stress, and just hang out and take it in. And you don't want to be in a hurry on the road. Whether you're new to Montana, or just visiting from a different part of the state, keep your ears and eyes open, and have your antennae up. Get off the interstate and take those back roads and state highways. That's where the most beautiful drives are. Stop at a roadside stand and buy a sack of sweet Flathead cherries. Drift through a ghost town or two. Spend a couple hours with the dinosaurs in Bozeman's Museum of the Rockies. The wonders of western Montana are right there waiting, and they are spectacular. If you allow yourself the time to get to know the Last Best Place while visiting Glacier and Yellowstone, you may discover what that Big Sky mystique is all about. Who knows, you might even wind up falling in love with Montana and never leave.

It's happened to a lot of us.

GLACIER NATIONAL PARK

1

Welcome to Glacier!

[Note: Visitation numbers have surged in the last few years, and as of the 2023 summer season, you'll need a vehicle reservation to access all entrances to Glacier National Park. These tickets must be purchased in advance. More information is available at recreation.gov.]

BABB

BABB IS YOUR SIGNPOST TO MANY GLACIER ROAD, WHICH TAKES YOU TO the park entrance along Lake Sherburn, down to the village of Many Glacier. It's the only road into that area which is not connected to Going-to-the-Sun Road, and it's closed in the winter. As gateways go, Babb is more of a missing board in the fence. It's a pleasant enough area, but, as Gertrude Stein famously said, "There is no there there." It's the proverbial wide spot in the road, but people do love the area, and the few businesses there are notable.

For a lot of knowledgeable visitors, a trip to Glacier Park's east side isn't complete without a meal at the legendary Two Sisters Café just south of Babb proper. Chef Beth Higgins, New Orleans–trained, has been whipping up fresh, locally sourced dishes since she and her sister Susan opened the Café in 1993. It's a big, rowdy, moderately priced restaurant that occupies an upper spot in Glacier Park's gastronomical hierarchy.

The Cattle Baron Supper Club is another destination restaurant that happens to be located in Babb. It's on the spendy side, but like Two Sisters, is a must-stop for many park visitors. It's even worth the drive from Saint Mary, if you're in the mood for a hubcap-sized steak and a frosty huckleberry margarita.

Babb is the outpost, the last chance for American commerce before you enter Canada, 10 miles due north at Piegan. As you approach the Piegan crossing, you'll see a sculpture of a couple of tribal warriors, keeping watch over that entrance to the Blackfeet Nation. The herd of bison across the street serves as another reminder that this land has been occupied for thousands of years. For a more direct route to Waterton Peace Park (and a prettier drive), take MT 17 west to the Chief Mountain border station. Of course, a passport is required.

Accommodations-wise, there is the usual smattering of Vrbo and airbnb properties, and a couple of interesting options. One is the Chewing Black Bones Campground on the shore of St. Mary's Lake, 3 miles south of Babb. Some may find the open-field campground loop off-putting, but its location on the lake makes for a great panorama. It's a Native-owned, RV-oriented park with hookups, showers, and bathrooms, and a great day-use area with picnic shelters and a tipi village with a dozen or so traditional tipis.

The only other overnight option is Thronson's Motel, right next door to Thronson's General Store. It's a throwback, a blockish, two-story affair that offers spare and comfortable rooms as well as a handful of rustic cabins. It's the perfect kind of lodging for people who are more interested in a clean place to sleep, shower, and shave (really, who shaves on their vacation?) before spending every possible minute exploring the park, and don't need their lodging to be a big part of the experience.

SAINT MARY

At the eastern terminus of Going-to-the-Sun Road, Saint Mary is one of the most stunning visual treats among Glacier's gateway communities. The snow-painted peaks of Red Eagle, Mahtohtopa, and Little Chief Mountains seem to rise straight up out of the lake to the southwest. Directly across the water from St. Mary Village, Napi Rock and Single-shot Mountain dominate the skyline, dramatic evidence that the plains to the east have come to an end. The views are just one of the perks of the Village, which fills up quickly every summer. Its five-story lodge and outbuildings offer 127 guest rooms, and this tourist ecosystem has pretty much everything you'll need—a restaurant, espresso shop, gift store, and outdoors gear shop. It really is a perfectly located hub for a multiday vacation in the park.

A wide variety of lodging can be had in or near Saint Mary, from a $20-a-night airbnb room to the luxury-soaked accommodations at the Great Bear Lodge in St. Mary Village. One interesting new development is the collection of tiny homes near the park entrance. These one-car-garage-sized dwellings have a surprising level of comfort packed into their clever, environmentally conscious designs. They're not the cheapest, but one unit will sleep four people who need just a clean, comfortable place to crash between hiking and touring days.

One of the great finds in St. Mary is the Park Cafe and Grocery. Unlike the store in Babb, you can buy beer and wine at the grocery while you gas up, as well as odds and ends like auto supplies and some camping needs. Right next door the Park Cafe serves up decent diner fare, but the star of the show is their homemade pie. For 60 years they've been dishing up strawberry rhubarb, peach raspberry, and of course, huckleberry.

The historic Ranger Station at Saint Mary is another favorite among Glacier aficionados. Built in 1913, just 3 years after the park's inception, the cabin is in the National Registry of Historic Places. Its design follows the National Park Rustic style that was initiated by architect Robert Reamer when he built the Old Faithful Inn in 1903. It's the park's first administrative building, harkening back to a simpler time in the park when its overseers had a smaller footprint—especially when compared to the grand visitor center nearby.

East Glacier

One of my favorite things about the East Glacier area is surely the least favorite of many visitors. If you're traveling on MT 49 between Two Medicine Road and Saint Mary, Looking Glass Road appears to be the most direct route. On the map. In real life, it is a white-knuckle thrill ride. The road is paved, but it's notoriously difficult to maintain, leaving it in various states of degradation. Asphalt patches look like a losing battle, as the potholes proliferate too quickly for the road crews to keep up. It's a narrow, serpentine road full of hairpin turns and entire sections that seem to be finding their own level. It is quite a roller coaster ride, and the driver will have to keep their eyes glued to the ever-changing road surface. Of course, not everyone likes a roller coaster. But when the road swoops down into stands of quaking aspens here and there, with their leaves shimmering in the wind like thousands of tiny jazz hands, it's a drive that has a charm all its own.

East Glacier is the first community you'll encounter coming in from Browning, and it's bisected by the Amtrak line. Many passengers will disembark the *Empire Builder*, cross the road, and check into the magnificent Glacier Park Lodge. It was built in 1913, one of the original Great Northern lodges constructed to serve rail passengers, mostly coming in from the eastern seaboard. Although the lodge sits a tantalizing 1.5 miles outside the park border, the East Entrance at Two Medicine is a 7.7-mile drive.

East Glacier village is a fun mix of low-budget lodging, decent-to-great restaurants (including Serrano's, perhaps the best food in the park),

Just south of East Glacier on US 2, you'll see a pair of Blackfeet guardian sculptures created by tribal member Jay Laber. There is a pair of mounted guardians at each of the four directions. AUTHOR PHOTO

kitschy tourist attractions (handmade Harry Potter wands, anyone?) and a lovely hostel, Brownie's. The hostel is situated above an outstanding bakery of the same name, which serves up killer treats like quiche, huckleberry muffins, and baked Amish oatmeal bars.

East Glacier west of the tracks feels pretty groovy, a funky little community with a hang-loose vibe like you might encounter at a ski village. Visitors are staying in motels, cabins, lodges, even tipis. From here you can access the park at the aforementioned Two Medicine entrance, or north on US 89 to St. Mary, and Many Glacier via Babb. Otherwise, to gain entrance to the park you'll have to drive south around the lower end of the park on US 2 to West Glacier. It's a gorgeous 60 miles, though, and it's a worthy way to see a lot of the park without actually being in the park.

West Glacier/Coram/Hungry Horse

This is a good time to ask, what constitutes a gateway community? While West Glacier is the most popular entrance, the community that serves the park is really a loose collection of small towns you'll pass through if coming in from Kalispell or Whitefish to the west, or Bigfork or Polson from the south.

Just east of Columbia Falls is **Hungry Horse**, which came into being not so much to serve park visitors, but as the base of one of the largest dam projects in the Northwest. Its eponymous reservoir is created by a spectacular, 564-foot-high concrete arch dam on the South Fork of the Flathead River, completed in 1953. Hungry Horse offers plenty of lodging and tourist-oriented business, but it's not all Glacier Park–themed. It's more of a northwest Montana mix of huckleberry treats, ski and snowmobile rentals, and other outdoor pursuits like hunting and fishing. And in case you forget the town's true origins, there's the Dam Town Tavern as a reminder.

Martin City is a tiny burg up Badrock Canyon that served as a kind of bedroom community for workers on the Hungry Horse Dam. Its location at the edge of two Montana wilderness areas make it a great place to camp and see wildlife. Other than a couple of rough 'n rowdy western saloons (one of which hosts an annual barstool race down the snowy main street), there's not much in the way of retail.

Coram, 15 miles south of West Glacier, is smack in the middle of the most family fun–oriented stretch of highway leading into the park. The first thing to trap tourists is the Amazing Fun Center, the name of which sounds like it was translated from a foreign language. The complex features a bumper boat pool, a two-story maze, an eighteen-hole miniature golf course, and a go-kart track. You want a zipline? Glacier Highline has you covered with dozens of treetop rope courses, Tarzan swings, and other attractions to keep the kids out of your hair for a few hours.

West Glacier has the commercial infrastructure to support the crowds you might imagine at the park's busiest entrance. As with St. Mary, as soon as you enter the park you'll be on Going-to-the-Sun Road (GTSR). Remember, as of the 2023 summer season, every main entrance to the park will require not only a park pass, but also a vehicle registration ticket. More information is available at recreation.gov.

At first blush, West Glacier seems to be a sea of RVs, and it definitely caters to the home-on-wheels crowd. But it's a robust little town that feels more outdoors-oriented than its counterpart at Yellowstone. Fly shops, rafting trips, kayak rentals, golf, the list goes on. However you want to propel yourself around the area, regardless of the season, even if you want to hold down a couple of trees with a hammock, there is probably a West Glacier business that offers the gear and/or experience.

Of all the gateway communities surrounding Glacier Park, West Glacier seems to enjoy the most comfortable symbiosis. It's all about the park here. It serves the upscale traveler as well as the vacationing family on a budget, but doesn't feel like it belongs to any particular economic strata or social demographic. Kalispell, 33 miles away, has the closest major airport to the park, which brings a large segment of international visitors, and streams of tourists from both US coasts. It makes for a truly eclectic mix of people, and you'll frequently find yourself hearing half a dozen foreign languages being spoken within earshot.

West Glacier is also full of the classic alpine architecture reminiscent of Swiss chalets, a nod to Glacier Park's nickname, America's Switzerland, an early marketing sobriquet applied by the Great Northern Railroad. Once you enter West Glacier, you feel like you're already humming with that national park vibe.

Polebridge

Remote. Rustic. Rewarding. These are words used frequently to describe the park's Northwest Entrance. As it's not connected to Going-to-the-Sun Road, Polebridge has become more of a backup plan for those who want to see the park but didn't score a ticket to its main attraction. Polebridge is not easy to get to. There is no gas station here. Large tour buses cannot negotiate the road. Cell service is nonexistent. There is no electricity.

But there's also a negative side. There's always a long line at Polebridge Mercantile, where people queue up all day every day to buy a huckleberry bear claw, the most famous pastry in all of Glacier Park.

Honestly, if you're more geared to visitor centers and park villages, this is probably not the gateway community for you. First off, it is a relatively long and somewhat uncomfortable drive out of Columbia Falls. North Fork Road runs along the North Fork of the Flathead River (MT 486), and most of it is washboarded and perforated with kidney-bruising potholes. The 35-mile journey takes about an hour. By my calculation, I believe your average speed will be 35 mph. Once you get there you're just a few miles from the check-in hut on Bowman Lake Road. Bowman Lake is one of the most beautiful lakes in the park and to its north is Kintla Lake, equally beautiful and maybe even less visited.

During the summer you'll see a surprising number of vehicles in Polebridge, but it never gets as crowded as, say, Apgar Village near West Glacier, or St. Mary on the east side. It's a there-and-back road, and with no gas station there, it obviously takes forethought and some commitment, and that alone cuts down on the crowds.

Ben Rover, a popular Forest Service cabin, typically is booked out a year in advance. It's perfectly situated right on the river just a short walk from the Merc. It has no electricity or running water but there's a well and a vault toilet outside, and propane lanterns and a wood stove inside. It sleeps up to eight people comfortably and just seems to be a perfect fit for the surrounding wilderness. It's downright cushy compared to how the homesteaders had it at the time the area was settled.

Polebridge is a tiny, unincorporated area for people seeking independence and solitude. But when a local needs help, it becomes a community.

Just under 200 people live there full-time, and during the hard winter months that number drops to maybe a dozen.

Among Glacier's gateway communities, Polebridge is regarded with the affection reserved for three-legged dogs and winless football teams. It lacks the access and facilities of the other, sexier towns around the park, but people who continue coming back to Polebridge tend to love it as "their" spot, their own little corner of Glacier. The Merc has been standing for over 100 years, and hasn't changed much in that time. They offer cabins for rent out back, and it sits next to the Northern Lights Saloon, which has a small restaurant and occasional live music. These joints offer a stop for tourists and a bit of a communal hub for the locals, but people don't drive 35 miles up a crappy dirt road for a bear claw. Polebridge isn't for everybody, and they kind of like it that way.

2

Chasing the Plows on Going-to-the-Sun Road

EACH YEAR AROUND MID-APRIL, MONTANANS TURN THEIR THOUGHTS to . . . taxes. Sorry. Once that unpleasantness is out of the way, they start showing the symptoms of spring fever. Although there will likely be at least a couple more serious snow dumps, most ski areas have shut down for the season, snowmobilers have winterized and garaged their sleds, and plows get to work clearing away the snow on Going-to-the-Sun Road. The park receives anywhere from 10 to 15 feet of snow per winter, and as the snow melts off the mountains, the road acts like a gutter, piling up the white stuff so crews are typically pushing through 10- to 15-feet-high drifts. Sometimes it's a bit more, as in 2018, when crews measured the Big Drift, just east of Logan Pass, at 80 feet of snow. Think about that next time you complain about having to shovel your driveway.

Cars aren't allowed on the road until it's completely clear, and that date is as unpredictable as the weather. In 2022, thanks to late storms and avalanches slowing the progress of the plows, GTSR had its latest opening on record, July 13. From then until Labor Day, bikes are forbidden from the road during peak hours—it's just too narrow to share with motor vehicles. But until then, as long as the plows are still pushing toward Logan Pass, the asphalt belongs to bikes and hikers.

There aren't many roads in the United States that can claim a spot in the National Register of Historic Places and have also been named a National Historic Civil Engineering Landmark, and the chance to bike up to the top of the Crown of the Continent draws hordes of cyclists to GTSR every year. What was once almost unknown outside of western Montana's cycling community has bloomed into a popular event, thanks largely to the advent of e-bikes. Battery-powered cycles are rented from dozens of businesses in Glacier's gateway communities, making the spring cycling adventure available to just about anyone. And that, according to many of the more experienced and capable cycling enthusiasts, is the problem.

Coming in from the West Entrance, the distance from Apgar to Avalanche Lake trailhead is about 13 miles. From there it's another 13 miles to Logan Pass, assuming the plows have cleared the entire road. While many bikers ride the first half, which is mostly flat road running along Lake McDonald, traffic can get congested on the weekends so most take advantage of one of the shuttles that run between the two points. Cars are not allowed past Avalanche during plowing season, so that's where the real ride begins. How far up you can go depends on several factors: weather, snowpack, avalanche danger, and other environmental considerations. Coming up from St. Mary on the east side is less steep, but the west ascent is by far the more popular. It's not a particularly difficult ride, more of a slow-motion gran fondo. Still, the last 12 miles are an uphill slog at a 6 percent grade. A cyclist must be in fairly good shape to do it. Well, until recently. More on that in a minute. The point is that a spring ride up GTSR is a unique event. It's certainly not a race—this isn't about beating a stopwatch, it's about watching the scenery.

About a mile from Avalanche there's a scenic pullout called Red Rock Point, offering a sweet overlook of the taupe- and rust-colored boulders crowding the rushing waters of McDonald Creek. The contrast between the rocks and the water, which is the color of avocado flesh due to the glacial silt it carries, is striking. Six miles beyond that is the west side tunnel, one of two tunnels on GTSR (the east side tunnel is on the other side of Logan Pass). The 192-foot-long tunnel will give riders a chill as they pass through, but after several miles of uphill pedaling on a clear spring day, this will probably be a welcome sensation. The "refrigerator effect" of the ambient temperature cooled by the surrounding snow isn't an issue for most riders as they're pumping uphill, generating heat and burning calories. The problem is riding through that cold on the way down at

A throng of cyclists waits to be shuttled to the Avalanche Trailhead, where they'll begin their ride up Going-to-the-Sun Road on a spring day before the road is completely plowed and open to motor vehicles. AUTHOR PHOTO

30 mph or more. More accurately, the problem is people embarking on GTSR in the spring being unprepared for the conditions that they'll face. On its face it might seem like a casual ride, especially with the help from an e-bike. But the reality is that the consequences of unforeseen events or conditions for an ill-equipped and unprepared cyclist could be deadly.

Ed Stalling lives in western Montana, where he's retired from a career that included several stints working for the Forest Service, and a handful of posts in a few national parks. He's also been part of several search and rescue operations. His outdoor experience is extensive, and he still enjoys hiking, biking, and camping in national forests throughout the West, year-round. With his wife and partner in adventure Lori, he's ridden up Going-to-the-Sun Road in the spring several times, seeing old friends each year from the cycling fraternity, sometimes even overnighting near the top on a full moon ride. But no more.

"I think what changed it is e-bikes," he told me. While he welcomes the idea that the powered bikes open up access for people with different abilities, he's turned off by the sudden appearance of massive throngs of neophytes making their way up a road that used to be uncrowded and mellow, and pretty much everyone who made the ride was an experienced cyclist and outdoors enthusiast who knew what they were doing. "It was always a Montana bike community thing," he says. "It was like old home week. There was never a parking issue, there was never a crowd." And it was never a closely guarded secret, he adds, although it was almost exclusively local riders who could keep an eye on developing weather and avalanche conditions and the progress of the plows, and then choose their time to go. In the last few years that's all changed. Pandemic lockdowns and subsequent travel restrictions had many Americans turning their travel plans inward, swelling the crowds in the national parks. Still, it's not the crowds that bother Stalling the most. It's the inexperience of the riders creating more potential for disaster.

"You're talking about being in the high country of Montana, above the treeline. And it's a time of year when tourists think it's summer or spring, say early June, but in the high country it's still like February. People leave in shorts and a shirt, maybe a windbreaker, and get up there and a blizzard comes in and they're like, 'what the f***?' I've literally recovered bodies of people who have died from hypothermia. I know how real it is. All they did was get wet when it was 34 degrees, and couldn't get to warm clothes in time."

As the ride occurs during spring melt, the road is going to be wet, and not just at the obvious spots like the Weeping Wall or other roadside waterfalls. Mountain ranges tend to have their own weather systems, and the jagged peaks of Glacier are certainly no exception. What starts out as a beautiful spring morning with temps in the 50s or 60s near Lake McDonald could quickly change to a cold, wet afternoon that could drench riders who are near the top of GTSR, with water coming from the road and the sky. Avalanches are another real threat, and it seems every year there are cyclists who get stranded on the wrong side of a slide that blocks the road, trapping them, sometimes necessitating rescue by helicopter. The exploding popularity of the spring ride coupled with its participants' lack of experience and backcountry knowledge will surely result in an increase in the number of dangerous situations, Stalling feels. As with everything else in our post-COVID world, there aren't enough workers to keep up. Rangers don't patrol GTSR in great numbers as it is, and they will become spread even thinner as the biking hordes continue to grow in size. It's a recipe for disaster that will result in more tragic accidents, or perhaps the Park Service will severely limit access to the road, or end this spring ride altogether. As it is, riders aren't allowed beyond the Loop, 8 miles up from the Avalanche trailhead, until late into the season, even as the road above has been cleared away. Avalanche danger is usually given as the reason, but it could also be that rangers are trying to keep riders safe from themselves.

Caroline Keys, a teacher and musician from Missoula who considers herself a casual biker, has made the trek a few times and, like Stalling, she worries about the safety of those who are lulled into a sense of protection by riding an e-bike. On her most recent ascent, in 2022, she estimated that as many as 85 percent of the riders were on a powered bike. It's not as if people are riding scooters up the hill. The Park Service allows only pedal-assist bikes—not fully powered rigs—with motors no bigger than 750 watts, or one horsepower. Still, the advent of e-bikes has completely changed the face of the spring ride up GTSR. "I'm super happy that technology makes such a beautiful thing accessible for people of more abilities," she said, "but when you're huffing and puffing [on a regular bike] and somebody goes by with a milkshake in their cupholder . . . I can see that argument."

Keys spent several seasons working for the Glacier Boat Company, giving tours of the park's breathtaking bodies of water, ferrying visitors between hotels and trailheads. Her love of the park is obvious, and her knowledge of its terrain has been earned over decades of exploring. She adores the spring ride up GTSR. "The e-bike thing can be a real polarizing deal," she admits, but she's also glad more people are given the chance to enjoy such a unique experience that provides an entirely different perspective on Glacier than touring in a car. "It's nice to have the whole road to yourself, without automobiles. Part of the glory and luxury of it is, wow, there's no cars. You can just ride all over the place." Also, by the time bikes are allowed to start pushing up the road as far as the plows have gone, the days are starting to get longer. "You can just dilly dally as much as you want because you're never going to have to worry about sharing the road with traffic. You could take all 14 to 16 hours of daylight to do that ride if you want to. It's just great."

Another bonus of moseying, she adds, is the opportunity to stop frequently and inspect some points of interest in detail, something you can't do with hundreds of vehicles rolling past within inches of you. One of her favorites is the clusters of stromatolites visible just outside the eastern end of the west side tunnel. These fossils of blue-green algae are from some of the earliest life forms on Earth, dating back billions of years. To climb off your bike and get up close and personal with something like that, well, it's one of the endless experiences that make Glacier Park special.

Another Glacier feature encountered by many cyclists is, of course, bears. Grizzlies and black bears are just starting to come out from their winter dens about the time the road opens to cyclists, so riders must be prepared. Bear spray is a must, and it's important to maintain a safe distance, although a lot of the time a bear will pop out of the underbrush and step onto the road, close enough to a biker that they can smell each other. "Bear encounters are an entirely different thing when you're on a bike than in a car," says Keys with a laugh. "That's always interesting."

Preparation and knowledge will help cyclists avoid many of the pitfalls that can occur on the spring GTSR ride. While most take their time going up, stopping for snacks and rests while enjoying the panoramic beauty at a relaxed pace, the descent is a different story altogether. And it's where many riders can be ambushed by hypothermia or frostbite. As mentioned earlier, the road is wet. Not a big deal when you're crawling uphill in low gear, but when riders go whipping down that grade at 30 miles an hour and the afternoon air has grown chilly, it's a serious situation. Keys shared a story of a friend who rode up wearing sandals, and in a desperate attempt to keep their toes from freezing off on the way down, wrapped their feet in aluminum foil from the sandwich they'd had for lunch at the top.

Even on a warm, sunny morning, bikers who tackle GTSR in the spring must be prepared for anything. Stalling, who has pretty much seen every scenario in his years making the ride, points out that there aren't any pre-ride inspections going on at Avalanche or Apgar, so it's up to the cyclists to be prepared. "You get a flat tire, your derailleur breaks, your chain breaks—any mountain biker knows how to fix a chain in the woods, otherwise you're not going to get home." He also hates to see riders surprised by getting drenched on the way down. "Anybody who bikes in Montana in the spring knows that you have extra clothes for the descent."

—~—

Word is out on the plow-chasing ride up GTSR in the spring, and one can only hope that its fast-growing popularity won't ultimately lead to its demise. Veterans of many ascents and full moon rides come down on both sides of the e-bike controversy, but everyone can agree that the ride will never be the same. It's impossible to predict what the future holds for this one-of-a-kind experience as the National Park Service (NPS) navigates the challenges presented by the expanding crowds drawn in by the advent of power-assisted bikes. The fact remains that for cyclists, whether pumping a mountain bike up the hill, snaking their way around the hairpin turns on a sleek road bike, or leading a family of all ages astride rented e-bikes, the chance to traverse the Crown of the Continent on one of America's most breathtaking roads without the presence of cars can provide endless memories and stories. Some sober preparation and thorough planning can help ensure that all the stories are happy ones.

3

The Phoenix of Glacier Park

IT WAS ONE OF THOSE SPLENDID AUGUST DAYS IN GLACIER, IF YOU LIKE it warm. The Northern Rockies were baking in a stretch of hot, dry days that flirted with the 90-degree mark. The only flaw was the wildfire smoke. Late summer in Montana usually means smoke, and the air was hazy and gray as the particulate-laden smoke from forest fires across Idaho, Oregon, and California blanketed the West. Montana was under a Stage II fire restriction, and Glacier had already seen its share of fires as it did every summer. Most of these blazes burned in remote wilderness that was too rugged to access, and unless they were threatening any structures, they usually were left to run their course. Stewards of Glacier's million acres of wilderness understand the role of fire in regenerating the forests.

On this Thursday in 2017, darkening clouds stacked up as the day wore on, and late that afternoon a massive thunderstorm rolled across the park, zapping the mountains and forests with more than 150 lightning strikes, igniting dozens of fires. That in itself wasn't unusual, but because of the persistent heat, most of the rain evaporated before it reached the ground. The fuels in Glacier's tamarack and lodgepole pine forests were bone dry ready to burn with the smallest spark.

One of the fires reported was a 100-acre blaze burning in the Sprague Creek and Camas Creek drainages, in the western part of the park near Lake McDonald. Spot fires were popping up along Sprague Creek Trail, the most popular route to Sperry Chalet. While park authorities did not consider the historic chalet to be threatened at the time, the trail itself was the main supply line to the backcountry lodge. Out of caution, the forty-two guests staying there were asked to evacuate. A post on Sperry's

"What's Happening" blog from August 12 lauds the guests for their efforts: "On Friday we successfully evacuated all guests from Sperry Chalet, most of them departing via the Gunsight Pass Trail. And I gotta say, I am really impressed with the wherewithal of Sperry Chalet guests. Can I just brag a little about the incredible effort this group made, crossing two mountain passes and the continental divide on a long and strenuous evacuation route. Well done!" The blog entry closes with a hopeful note. "We are currently optimistic that Sperry Chalet may have an opportunity to re-open this summer. For now we have to wait and see what this fire does. As with all endeavors in the wilderness, Mother Nature is making the rules up as she goes along."

By August 18 the Sprague Fire, now roaring across the face of Brown Mountain, was becoming a problem. Mother Nature was flexing her muscles, and the fire had grown to more than 500 acres, demanding the attention of fire crews. Firefighters worked to save the historic Mount Brown Fire Lookout tower by wrapping the wood structure with fire-protective material. Within 3 days the fire expanded to 1,189 acres and was racing across Lincoln Ridge just south of the Sperry Chalet complex.

One hundred firefighters worked to protect the Sperry Chalet with sprinklers, a portable pond, and a helicopter providing water drops on the hot spots. Several trails in the area had already been closed, and the Sprague Fire continued to grow. Crews hoped that the thinner vegetation along the ridge, along with the cooling weather, would help slow the pace of the blaze. The reality was that it probably would burn until the first snowstorm of the season arrived to smother it.

Lake McDonald Lodge closed on August 28, as smoke conditions had reached the point of being unhealthy for workers and visitors. Crews continued to control spot fires and thin out fuels from the path of the Sprague Creek fire, but high winds and dry conditions pumped the inferno to over 2,000 acres. By August 31, four helicopters were dropping water on the raging fire as determined firefighters worked to protect the chalet. When the fire swept into old-growth areas to the north and east of Sperry Chalet the blaze doubled in size to 4,000 acres, nearly surrounding the property. Just after 6:00 p.m. firefighters saw smoke coming from underneath the eaves of the chalet. They hit the

The original Sperry Chalet, pictured here just after it was built in 1915, is a popular backcountry chalet that can be reached by foot or horseback only.

roof with hoses, but the windows blew out, spewing smoke and flames. The fire had reached the building.

Glacier Park's Sperry Chalet, a National Historic Landmark which had stood for more than 100 years, was consumed by fire. All that was left standing were a smoking pile of embers and the scorched rock walls at either end of the building.

——◦——

Sperry Chalet was built over two seasons, beginning in 1912, just 2 years after Glacier National Park was established. Northern Pacific Railway president Louis Hill decided to create a series of nine chalets and lodges that would be scattered through the park, each about a day's horseback ride from the next. First to be completed was the Belton Chalet, conveniently located across the street from the West Glacier Depot where visitors debarked from Great Northern's new passenger line. The Glacier Park Hotel Company, a subsidiary of the railroad, enlisted architects Cutter and Malmgren to design a set of lodges that would resemble Swiss chalets, in keeping with Great Northern's marketing image for Glacier: America's Switzerland. Sperry was completed in 1914. The main hotel building was a commanding, two-story dormitory made from rubble obtained from a nearby quarry and pine trees harvested from the surrounding forest. The huge, coarse rocks gave the building a rustic feel, and fulfilled the desire of the burgeoning National Parks system to give their structures the appearance of belonging in the settings in which they were built. Sperry Chalet's design and location are so natural and unobtrusive that some say it appears to have risen out of the earth. A large set of letters crafted from narrow logs that read "GNRy" was attached to the building beneath the gable. It stood for Great Northern Railway—perhaps the lowercase y was added to head off any confusion that this might be a remote hideaway for Guns N' Roses.

As Sperry was unreachable by road, all other materials, supplies, and equipment were brought in by horses and mules. Its location on the lip of a glacial cirque provided a stunning, panoramic view into the heart of Glacier Park. By the 1920s automobile travel began to bring more visitors to the national parks, and Sperry Chalet soon took its place as the most enchanting of Glacier's backcountry chalets. Its history includes several evacuations due to encroaching forest fires, and it was closed during both the world wars. The Great Depression also took its toll on visitor traffic. In 1932 only 112 guests stayed at Sperry the entire season.

The chalet has seen several improvements and renovations over the years. The deck and balconies were replaced in 1978-79, and the entire complex underwent a complete restoration in 1996. A restroom building with plumbed sinks was added in 2008, making it easier for guests to wash up.

Karl Olson happened to be at the chalet in 2017 just a couple of weeks before it was destroyed in the Sprague Fire. He was back home in Missoula, still enjoying the afterglow from his trip when he learned the beloved chalet had burned. "We were having post-Sperry dinner and drinks in Missoula, debriefing when we heard the news," he said. Fires to the northeast had already prompted the closure of the trail from Jackson Glacier Overlook on Going-to-the-Sun Road while he and his friends were there. Although particulate from the smoke is plainly visible in his vacation photos, Olson said his party wasn't too concerned about the fire. "They got it under control while we were at Sperry. When they opened the Jackson trail we thought it would be fine for the rest of the summer." He had made his first visit to Sperry Chalet 20 years earlier, when he and his partner enjoyed a memorable adventure. "It was easy to get rooms then," he said. "We fell in love with it."

He is only one of thousands of Glacier Park visitors who have fallen under the spell of Sperry Chalet during its century of use. Some believe it is the ultimate experience not just in Glacier, but in all the country's sixty-three national parks.

It's not surprising, then, to know that even before the Sprague Fire was brought under control, plans were set in motion to rebuild the cherished chalet. The four other structures at Sperry had been saved, including a kitchen and dining hall, a maintenance building, and the restroom building. By mid-September, the Glacier National Park Conservancy, the park's fundraising arm, had received a huge outpouring of support from individuals asking what they could do to help. The secretary of the interior announced that rebuilding the chalet would be a priority, and by

October an environmental assessment had been completed and helicopters were bringing in construction materials. The scorched but solid stone walls were being shored up as the husk was being prepared to survive the winter. In 2 years, the chalet was rebuilt around the original stone walls to meet current building codes with modern techniques and construction methods, while preserving the look and feel of the original building. The interior features cedar tongue-in-groove paneling in keeping with the surroundings, and the original propane-powered kitchen and lanterns were replaced with electric versions powered by solar panels. Sperry Chalet was back, and welcoming visitors by the 2020 season.

As glorious and popular as it is, Sperry Chalet is not for everyone. Some national park visitors require more creature comforts than the spartan chalet offers. Rooms are ski lodge spare, with bunks for two to four people, and visitors must be prepared to make a short jaunt across the grounds to the restroom building during the, um, wee hours. While the new chalet does feature some electricity supplied by roof-mounted solar panels, power is used mainly for the kitchen. Flashlights for each guest are highly recommended. Check the website to get full information on accommodations. It's important to note that there are no wall outlets for charging devices, and no Wi-Fi, TV, or phones. A hike up nearby Lincoln Ridge will put you into cell range, but there are many who find the lack of connectivity at the chalet a big fat addition to the plus column.

The "lifeboat mentality" is one of the unique elements of a stay at Sperry. During their time at the chalet, each day's group of guests forms a natural camaraderie. "Sperry Chalet is one of those places where it just feels different because everyone who stays there is a community," Minnesotan Kate Minor told a Great Falls reporter upon hearing the news of the tragic fire in 2017. She and her husband Karl had spent one night of their honeymoon there in 2010. "It felt unlike any other place we've stayed before," she said. "Partly because you have to hike to get there so it's kind of exclusive and attracts a different breed of people." That sense of shared isolation is one of the common feelings people mention in their memories of their Sperry Chalet stay. There's an atmosphere of awe, a humbling reverence toward being surrounded by the majestic beauty of the glacier-carved peaks and alpine forests, away from the noise and congestion of vehicles and rowdy tourists. Alpine-loving mountain goats inhabit the rugged mountain faces of the area, and routinely wander in and out of the complex, providing an extra bit of wildlife experience. On rainy days folks will sit inside the rustic dining hall and read, write, chat, or just sit quietly, absorbing the wonder of their surroundings. A coffee hour after each dinner provides an easygoing opportunity for guests to intermingle. As they drift out onto the balcony to take in a beautiful Glacier sunset, perhaps they'll share some wine from a bota bag that someone has packed in. The civility and friendliness is nearly universal among the guests on any given day at Sperry.

The original chalet may have been reduced to ash, but its replacement more than lives up to its predecessor. Thanks to the efforts of the National Park Service and an army of supporters, this legacy of Louis Hill, a railroad king who balanced a keen business sense with a healthy appreciation of Glacier's wild beauty, lives on. As of this writing a night at the chalet runs about $250 per person—for an outpost that requires its guests to pack in every single bit of creature comforts for their stay, it may seem a little steep, like much of the trail that leads there. For those who pony up, though, the Sperry Chalet's charms are worth every nickel.

4

What Happened to the Whitehead Brothers?

IN THE SUMMER OF 1924, THE CITY OF CHICAGO WAS IN THE DOLDRUMS. Citizens were horrified by a shocking kidnapping and murder committed by a pair of university frat boys named Nathaniel Leopold and Richard Loeb, who wanted to demonstrate their superior intellect by abducting and killing someone, believing they could get away with the perfect crime. They murdered a 14-year-old boy, dumped his body in a culvert 25 miles south of Chicago, and began sending ransom notes to the victim's parents. Their plan unraveled, and within 2 weeks the pair were caught, confessed to the crime, and were sentenced to life plus 99 years in prison. The chill produced that summer by the "crime of the century" wasn't as cold as the icy winter winds that blow across the city from Lake Michigan, but it was close.

Chicago baseball fans had another shadow cast over their summer as their beloved White Sox were on their way to finishing at the absolute bottom of the American League for the first time in their history. Comiskey Park was more like a funeral parlor than a major-league stadium. Just when everybody could use a stiff drink, Prohibition had driven alcohol consumption underground, and Chicago was struggling in the bloody grip of organized crime.

Was it any wonder that a hard-working young man like Joseph Whitehead wanted to get out of town for a couple weeks? The clean-cut, 29-year-old engineer had a good job at the Universal Battery Company—his $400 a month salary enabled him to support his newly widowed mother, his sister, and younger brother William, 22, who was attending MIT in Boston. Perhaps Joe was feeling the weight of his responsibilities, and the hot, grim Chicago summer spurred the need to recharge his own batteries. A few days of fresh air and hiking through Glacier National Park must have been just the tonic he needed. Young William probably jumped at the chance to get a bit of adventure with his big brother before returning to campus for his final year. The Whitehead brothers packed their gear, kissed their mother and sister goodbye, and left Union Station aboard the Great Northern Railroad's newly refurbished *Oriental Limited* in mid-August.

When the boys failed to return on September 1, Dora Whitehead immediately contacted park authorities and reported her sons missing. Chief Ranger James P. Brooks took charge of the case, which would eventually lead to the biggest manhunt in National Park Service history. Everyone from park rangers and veteran trappers to J. Edgar Hoover and President Calvin Coolidge wanted to find out what happened to the Whitehead brothers.

Joe and Bill had gotten off the train at East Glacier on August 17 and checked into their room at the Glacier Park Lodge. "Arrived O.K.," Bill wrote in a letter home. "Had a fine trip, somewhat dusty but not bad. The food was good and the prices reasonable." Joe's reputation as a meticulous planner was borne out in their 2-week itinerary, copies of which were left with his boss at Universal Battery and with his mother. The next morning the brothers took a bus to St. Mary, where they entered the park. From there they chugged nearly the length of St. Mary Lake in a steam-powered tour boat to Going-to-the-Sun Chalet on Sun Point near the southern end of the lake. The brothers bedded down that night in the cliff-top chalet, no doubt feeling that they'd finally arrived at the Crown of the Continent.

Joe and Bill were certainly good sons, writing letters to Dora every day. She'd been agonizing about their trip through Glacier, imagining every calamity that could befall a hiker in the western wilderness. While not seasoned outdoorsmen, these men were not known as risk-takers, and several witnesses later recounted the brothers remarking that, as much as they'd love to explore the more remote areas of the park, they lacked the experience and gear to do so.

They both wore hiking knickers, stout boots, a cotton shirt, a sweater, and sometimes a felt hat—summertime Glacier togs. Carrying light rucksacks and a rope (Dora's idea), they rode horseback over Piegan Pass to the Many Glacier Hotel, where they headquartered for 4 days. It had rained for most of their stay and they were hoping for better weather. They hiked to Grinnell Glacier, Cracker Lake, Iceberg Lake, and a few other modest trails, never failing to describe their exploits in their daily dispatches to Dora, while giving her constant reassurance that her precious boys were taking no undue risks. In a letter dated August 20, Joe wrote, "We are enjoying ourselves very much and taking no chances of injuring ourselves. Don't worry, mother," he insisted, "we won't go into any danger."

Dora knew her sons, and told Ranger Brooks that there was no way they could have befallen some accident by putting themselves into a dicey situation. "They were not venturesome boys, they both had good common sense, were thoughtful and considerate, and devoted to each other and their sister and me."

The last letter Dora received from Joe and Bill was dated August 23, written on Many Glacier Hotel stationery. They were getting ready to leave the hotel, they wrote, and would be heading over the Continental Divide to Granite Park, where they would stay a night in the chalet before embarking on their longest hike yet, a 21-mile trek south along McDonald Creek to the Lewis Hotel (now the Lake McDonald Lodge). They never got there.

Glacier Park's Superintendent Charles Kraebel launched an extensive search effort. Ranger Brooks, who was also an assistant superintendent, obtained the brothers' itinerary from L. C. Mowry, Joe's boss, and he began combing every place on their list for witnesses who may have interacted with the Whiteheads. Meanwhile, Mowry hopped on a plane to Glacier to join in the search. Joe and Bill had been seen walking away from Granite Park the morning of August 24, but investigators could turn up no further sightings. They had simply vanished.

The search continued, with several teams of rangers and volunteers walking every trail between Granite Park and Lake McDonald. Conjecture and rumors swirled—the brothers could have fallen off a precipice into a crevasse, their bodies never to be found. They could have been crushed by a boulder falling down a mountainside. They could have fallen into one of Glacier's many lakes or icy creeks and drowned (they were not swimmers). They could have been attacked and killed by a grizzly bear. The opportunity for a "natural" accident seemed limitless, and as the search wore on without a trace of the brothers, hope was fading.

Not so for Ranger Brooks. "Do not feel alarmed," he wrote to Dora on September 5. "We feel that no harm has befallen them. We have many cases of this kind every year and never any serious accidents." Acting Superintendent Henry W. Hutchings cast a colder eye on the situation. The odds of a couple of city-bred greenhorns surviving in the harsh wilderness of Glacier Park for 2 weeks with no weapons or camping gear seemed remote. He raised the possibility that the brothers might have left the park and, for whatever reason, failed to contact anyone to inform them of their whereabouts. This kind of scenario would likely include foul play. In other words, an "unnatural" accident.

The case quickly garnered national attention, and during the second week of the search, Ranger Brooks received word from Glacier headquarters that President Calvin Coolidge had become interested in the brothers' disappearance. He instructed park officials to "spare no expense" in the search efforts, and Brooks was required to send a dispatch twice daily to apprise the president of the "facts as to the search."

Around this time, Mowry divulged some information about the brothers that led Brooks to question the characterization of Joe and Bill as a couple of meek individuals who cowered at danger and were averse to risky behavior. Mowry had been privy to some conversations between the brothers and some of their Chicago friends. Evidently, they planned on using their rope to lower each other down over cliffs, and also had hoped to go bushwhacking off-trail to some remote, unnamed lakes they'd found on a USGS map, so they could name them. This information contradicted the attitudes they'd expressed in their letters home, and raised more questions about where the brothers might have gone to get themselves into a sticky predicament.

By September 14 the chances of finding the Whitehead brothers were almost nil. Ranger Brooks had to acknowledge the real issues of the expense of hiring extra men, and the shortage of rangers in the east side of the park where fire danger was high and protection was thin. He expressed his concerns in a letter to Superintendent Kraebel, who was already regarding their mission as one of recovery, not rescue. The same day, 3 weeks after Dora's boys had last been seen, Brooks composed a carefully worded missive to Mrs. Whitehead: "Our Rangers are experienced men, imbued with the spirit of going out to accomplish the task assigned to them. When they fail it is because they have exhausted every possible means." They did their best. Stephen Mather, director of the National Park Service, traveled to Chicago the next day to have a long sit-down with the distraught mother, essentially reiterating the sentiments of Brooks's letter.

By this time the Biological Survey (now the US Fish and Wildlife Service) had joined the search, sending veteran hunter-trapper Chauncey "Chance" Beebe to bring his formidable skills to bear in the Glacier mountains. With his tracking dogs and his partner Jim Whilt, who called himself the "Poet of the Rockies," Beebe set up camp on McDonald Creek. The pair spent a month combing the area with the dogs, but had to decamp when the snows came in October.

Keeping the Whitehead brothers' destination in mind, it would seem that the most logical route they would have taken for their last hike would have been heading west out of Granite Park on Granite Park Trail, then hooking around the Loop trailhead on a hairpin turn of Going-to-the-Sun Road to turn southeast, past Packer's Roost, then along McDonald Creek around the east end of Glacier Wall. From there it would have been a pretty mellow walk for the last 10 miles to Lewis Hotel. Since no one knew the exact path they took out of Granite Park that day, it's an educated guess.

This theory got a big boost when some startling information came to light on September 21. Three employees of the Park Saddle Horse Company were returning equipment from a pack trip to the company's base camp, and they encountered two young men on the trail between Granite Park and Lewis Hotel. Jack Jessup had seen two hikers matching the Whitehead brothers' descriptions near the Patrol Cabin on Logan Creek. "When Bob Lyford and I was deadheading," he wrote, "we met to [*sic*] men on the trail from Granit [sic] to Lewis. They look like about 20 years of age . . . that was all the hikers on the trail." The timing and the location would mean that the two men they saw would almost certainly have been the Whitehead brothers. By now the possibility of foul play was being actively considered, and the three packers were quickly investigated and ruled out as suspects. If Jessup was to be taken at his word—and he had no apparent motive to fabricate his story—this would mean that Joe and Bill were seen at just before noon on August 24, 10 miles north of their destination. Not long afterward, the riders in a different horse party were also interviewed. They had ridden from Granite Park to Lewis Hotel along the same trail. They did encounter Jessup and his fellow packers coming the other way, but saw no one else on the trail.

So what happened to Joe and Bill in that last 10-mile stretch of trail? They could easily have covered that distance in a couple of hours. Did they decide to go cross-country and seek out one of the tiny lakes they hoped to name? Were they attacked and dragged off by a grizzly bear that managed the feat without leaving a speck of evidence? What about the foul play angle? The area was a hotbed of rum-runners who brought hooch out of Canada to a thirsty United States that was in the midst of its Prohibition while Canada was ending theirs. "They seem to have disappeared off the face of the earth," wrote Hubert Work, secretary of the interior, to the attorney general, Harry Daugherty. He went on to ask that the FBI be brought into the case. "These young men were . . . guests of the Government in the Park at the time of their disappearance," he wrote, "and to that extent were entitled to all the protection that could be given to them."

In the fourth week of the search, Dora Whitehead offered a $500 reward for any evidence that led to finding her sons. James Hill supplemented that with $1,000 from the railroad for discovery of their bodies. Joe's Masonic Lodge in Chicago kicked in another $200. As with most rewards, this cash incentive prompted a steady stream of spurious reports for years. By this point Dora had settled on the idea that her boys were victims of some nefarious action. "They were the victims of a hold-up somewhere on that trail," she wrote to Superintendent Kraebel in late September. Kraebel had officially ended the search on September

17. A month later, Dora wrote to Kraebel again, with this agonized plea for results:

"My sons were murdered on that trail or some place nearby, or else they were forced to travel against their will. . . . Only six weeks of searching by the Government for two fine American born young men—one of whom gladly gave a year of his life to the service of his country! Isn't he worth more than that? Mr. Kraebel, I want my sons—dead or alive. My two sons were murdered or kidnapped in a National Park and I am pleading with the Government of the United States to find them."

Although the Park's search for the Whitehead brothers had officially ended, the investigation into a possible criminal explanation was ramping up. In November the FBI was brought in, and Director J. Edgar Hoover assigned two field offices to the case—one in Butte and one in Chicago. Interviews with friends, family, park visitors, and acquaintances, as well as a deep dive into the brothers' personal histories, yielded nothing that might lead to the cause of their disappearance.

Dora had not given up hope, and never would. In January she distributed 500 flyers bearing the boys' photos under the bold headline, "$1,700 REWARD For JOSEPH and WILLIAM WHITEHEAD." Joe and Bill are gazing directly into the camera, both wearing round, wire-rimmed glasses, dark hair slicked back, crisp suits buttoned down. These were not frivolous men. Nor did they look like the types who could be seduced into a lifestyle of bootlegging or other crimes. They looked responsible and upstanding. They looked innocent. The flyers helped spur rumors and dead-end leads for years to come, including a few independent searches, but nothing solid ever came in.

Dora and her daughter Edith traveled to the park in July 1925 to retrace for themselves the brothers' assumed route, and to interview park officials and everyone who had worked the case. After three exhausting weeks of their own investigating, Dora and Edith concluded that the boys must have met with foul play, as they just weren't the type to take any risks in such dangerous country. The women returned home to Chicago.

The FBI continued to follow up leads through the rest of 1925, with tips coming in from all over the West. A Whitefish trapper claimed that the brothers had spent the winter holed up in the cabin of an old trapper

$1,700.00 REWARD

For

JOSEPH and WILLIAM WHITEHEAD

Brothers disappeared Sunday, August 24, on the trail between Granite Park Chalets and the Lewis Hotel in Glacier National Park, Montana.

JOSEPH H. WHITEHEAD	WILLIAM A. WHITEHEAD
Age 29.	Age, 22.
Height, 5 ft. 11 in.	Height, 5 ft. 11½ in.
Weight, 175 lbs.	Weight, 155 lbs.
Gray eyes.	Brown eyes.
Dark brown hair.	Dark brown hair.
Ruddy complexion.	Dark complexion.
Wore glasses with dark rims.	Wore glasses with dark rims.

Both wore hiking clothes: gray knickers, gray wool shirts, high, tan laced hiking shoes, soft felt hats. Carried light packs. Both wore sweaters: one gray, the other tan.

Sons of Mrs. Dora B. Whitehead, 3040 Warren Avenue, Chicago.

Notify: Charles J. Kraebel, Supt. Glacier National Park, Belton, Montana.

Dora Whitehead, mother of the missing brothers, had these flyers distributed all over the Glacier area when her boys failed to return home to Chicago on the appointed day. They were never found. NPS PHOTO, PUBLIC DOMAIN in the park, living off snared otter and marten. Another report had the brothers operating a vaudeville show in Bellingham, Washington. They were also allegedly seen running a church service in Proctor, British Columbia. Eve Beebe, the wife of Chance Beebe, the Biological Survey trapper, started telling a wild story about a woman who'd shot Joe and Bill after luring them into a night of drinking in a cabin near Lake Five. All leads were followed up. None ever panned out.

Hoover continued to work the investigation, likely responding to political pressure from the White House. Incoming leads slowed down to a trickle, but Dora kept writing letters to the FBI, the NPS, the White House, and other official entities who had been involved in the case. She remained convinced that her boys had been murdered or kidnapped.

The FBI officially closed the case on March 31, 1926. Their field offices quickly followed suit. Special Agent Dickason from the Butte office acknowledged what was on nearly everyone's mind when he wrote in a 1928 report, "There is absolutely nothing that could be done now." The case had gone cold, and was moved to the "Missing Persons" file. In 1961, Park Superintendent Edward Hummel responded to a routine correspondence from J. Edgar Hoover, informing the director that the Park Headquarters no longer needed any information regarding the disappearance of Joseph and William Whitehead. End of story.

Or was it? Although everyone who was involved in the case is dead, the answer is out there. It may be buried deep in the bedrock soils of Glacier Park. It may rest in the history of a remote Canadian logging camp or the flimsy walls of some bootlegger's hideout where a couple of young Chicago men decided to slip out of the park and begin new lives. More likely, the answer is one that Glacier Park will keep to itself, along with so many other mysteries that lie hidden under its deep glacial waters or in the impenetrable depths of its breathtaking canyons and crevasses. It's been a hundred years since the Whitehead brothers went missing. As time goes by, it's becoming less likely that we'll ever find out what really happened to the two young Glacier Park visitors who vanished without a trace.

5

Waterton's Bison Return After Trial by Fire

THE HOT, CRISPY SUMMER OF 2017 BROUGHT ITS USUAL SHARE OF WILD-fires to the Northern Rockies, including the infamous Sprague Fire that destroyed the century-old Sperry Chalet in Glacier National Park. To the north, wildfires hopscotched their way across British Columbia and Alberta in the region southwest of Calgary, popping up everywhere and triggering the evacuation and closure of several parks located in their heavily forested path. "The protection of all Albertans and communities from the threat of wildfires is a top priority. Because of the hot, dry conditions we're treating this as a very serious situation," said a spokesman for Alberta Environment and Parks. Campgrounds and day-use areas were evacuated, including Chinook Provincial Recreation Area, Livingstone Falls Provincial Recreation Area, and Honeymoon Creek Equestrian Camp. Even before the Sprague Fire in Glacier was declared under control, lightning sparked a new blaze in British Columbia's Flathead area, which quickly ripped across B.C.'s southeast corner near Waterton Park's eastern boundary at Sage Pass and South Kootenay Pass. The Kenow fire had grown to 10,000 acres and had the township of Waterton directly in its crosshairs. The Glacier Park border crossing at Chief Mountain was temporarily closed, and on September 3, Parks Canada began to prepare for the worst, closing all hiking and climbing trails in Waterton Lakes National Park. They also shut down the Red Rock Parkway and all back-country campgrounds, and closed Cameron Lake to all visitor use.

Winds of up to 60 mph continued pushing the Kenow fire east into Alberta, and crews converged on Waterton to try and protect the tiny town. The low humidity, unrelenting heat, and high winds created perfect conditions for the fire to make a big run, which it did on Labor Day weekend. The grasslands around Waterton were torched as the fire continued its march down the Cameron Valley along the Akamina Parkway, and officials called for the evacuation of hundreds of people from the township. As the fire advanced on Waterton, the town's residents buttoned up their properties and prepared for evacuation. Kevin Hicks, who managed the Waterton Lakes Lodge and two other hotels, received word on Friday that he and the hotel staff had 1 hour to close up the hotel and get out. After checking out the last six guests, Hicks and his employees ran around with wrenches, shutting off all the gas. They weren't sure if their hotel would still be standing after the weekend. "It was bizarre, it was quick," he said of the sudden evacuation. "I kind of took a picture in my own head of what it's like now—and what am I going to see after, when I do get to go back?"

Also in the path of the blaze was the historic Prince of Wales Hotel, just outside of Waterton township between Upper and Middle Waterton Lakes. The stately hotel, built in 1927, was already being pelted with embers the size of hockey pucks. Staff had been preparing for the encroaching fire, having closed the doors and sent some 1,800 travelers to alternative lodging. Fire crews had been on-site for days, soaking the building with fire retardant and water pumped from nearby Upper Waterton Lake. Thanks to their heroic efforts, firefighters managed to save the hotel from the blaze, which came close enough to scorch the sides of the driveway leading to the entrance.

The nearby visitor center, a small facility built in 1958, burned to the ground.

Rod and Tracy Leland were still aglow after exchanging wedding vows just a few days earlier on the lawn of his family's Waterton Lakes cabin, but instead of hunkering down in a suite somewhere and living off room service and love, they were cutting brush, clearing out deadfall, and arranging sprinklers on the roof of the cabin. On Friday they had to evacuate. Rod was concerned for the fate of the beloved cabin, of course, but he was confident that their preparation would pay off. "The sentiment amongst our family is that we've done everything we could possibly do," he said. "It's gonna be what it's gonna be."

The Kenow wildfire of 2017 was one of the worst to ever hit the Waterton National Park, the Canadian half of Glacier-Waterton International Peace Park. While the bison in Waterton's Bison Paddock were evacuated (mostly), their pasture was torched. Firefighters managed to save the historic Prince of Wales Hotel, pictured here. WIKI COMMONS PHOTO

Also in danger was the Waterton Bison Paddock, a fenced territory just inside the Pincher Creek entrance on Highway 6 on the northeast edge of the park. Waterton's small buffalo herd, numbering fewer than a dozen animals at that time, had been reintroduced in 1952. The area contained the bisons' summer and winter pastures, and was ringed by a road drivers could take to observe the giant ungulates from their cars. As the Kenow fire continued to spread north and east, roaring through Pincher Creek and Cardston County, the Blood Tribe declared a state of emergency. The East Gate Warden Station was destroyed, along with the Alpine Stables, a trail-riding business. Tribal members and park employees who'd worked hard to establish and maintain the bison paddock program took no chances with the sacred buffalo. They rushed to the paddock and rounded up the herd so they could be loaded onto trailers and evacuated to Saskatchewan's Grasslands National Park. Well, not the entire herd, exactly. One of the herd's two bulls stubbornly evaded capture, running off into the smoke that covered the grazed-out summer pasture. With the fire bearing down, crews abandoned the recalcitrant beast and hoped for the best.

In 1906 there were only twenty buffalo left in Canada. They had been hunted to the edge of extinction, a purge that also destroyed the way of life enjoyed for as much as 20,000 years by North America's Indigenous peoples of the Northern Plains, whose spiritual, cultural, and corporeal lives revolved around the buffalo. After being forced onto reservations after the colonization by European Americans and their French and Scottish trapper/trader counterparts north of the 49th Parallel, the plains tribes worked at reestablishing herds of their all-important resource. The Blood Indians, along with the Kainai, Piikani, and Siksika nations, wanted to bring the buffalo back to its homeland in the Northern Plains. Meanwhile, a Pend d'Oreille Indian from Montana's Flathead Valley named Walking Coyote made some huge strides in that direction. In the spring of 1873 he captured eight buffalo—four calves, two bulls and two cows—from a wild herd east of the Divide. The following spring he brought them back to the Flathead and managed to establish a thriving herd. By 1884 there were thirteen animals, and Walking Coyote found a couple of buyers for his burgeoning herd. Charles A. Allard and Michel Pablo, both reservation ranchers and sons of Indian mothers, agreed to partner up on the herd, and bought ten buffalo. By 1896 the Pablo-Allard herd had grown to an impressive 300 head. When Allard died that year after falling from his horse, the herd was split between his estate and Pablo.

By 1906 Pablo's herd had grown to more than 700. As homesteaders continued to squeeze him out of the valley's rich agricultural land, the Canadian government stepped in, ready to begin the return of the buffalo to its native lands of Alberta and British Columbia. Charles A. Conrad, founder of Kalispell, bought about a third of Pablo's herd and the rest were sold to Canada. The bison would be brought to the railway station in Ravalli, loaded into train cars, and delivered to Buffalo Park in Wainwright,

Alberta. Meanwhile, the herd continued to expand, and it took 3 years to get them all transferred and shipped to Alberta. About 630 buffalo were released into a 200-square-mile enclosure in Wainwright, and the balance were shipped to Elk Island National Park in Lamont. With buffalo hunting severely limited or banned outright, their populations rebounded quickly. By 1938 there were an estimated 18,000 buffalo in Canada, 8,000 of them within Elk Island National Park.

Everything was going swimmingly until about 1950, when the land at Elk Island became infected with the bacillus of bovine tuberculosis. The slow-growing bacterium causes TB in cattle, and can infect other animals—and humans—through inhaling droplets or ingesting infected meat or consuming the raw milk of an infected cow. A portion of the herd was transferred to Wood Buffalo Park in northern Alberta, where they swelled the ranks of the 300 buffalo already there. Others were moved down the Athabasca River drainage, where they're now scattered through the Northwest Territories.

Six lucky specimens in prime condition were chosen in 1952 to inhabit the newly constructed Bison Paddock in Waterton Lakes National Park. Two adjoined pastures would comprise their summer and winter grazing grounds, and the herd would move back and forth with the seasons. Providing tons of hay for a large herd of bison to winter over is an expensive proposition, and the additional financial burden led officials to keep this a "show herd" of around a dozen animals. The paddock was laid out with visitors in mind from the get-go, as it was situated near a promontory where people could park and have a great view of the beasts moving about the prairie below, munching on the fescue grasses, dry wallowing in shallow dirt pits, and just going about their buffalo business.

The location also overlaps some human history. It's located on the remains of a historic path, the Hudson's Bay Fur Brigade Trail. It's one of two routes that were used during the Hudson's Bay Company's heyday, when trappers and traders would move furs and supplies between the company's headquarters in the Coastal and Columbia Districts at Fort Vancouver, and posts in New Caledonia and in Rupert's Land, the territory surrounding the Hudson's Bay drainage. One of the most significant groups traveling the trail was an annual procession known as the

Hudson's Bay Express. It consisted of a party transporting the company's books and profits to their headquarters. It's not to be confused with overnight shipping of your Schutz Fairy Flat Sandals from the retailer now known simply as The Bay.

━◦━

By mid-September the Kenow fire was still burning out of control, but had spared the Waterton township. The visitor center was a mound of smoking rubble, and the East Gate warden station was gone, along with its equipment and vehicles. Several campgrounds had been damaged, and many power lines destroyed, leaving much of the area without electricity. The mandatory evacuation order for Waterton remained in place, and officials said it could be weeks before residents were allowed to return to their homes. Fire crews were being helped by a break in the heat, and the cooler weather brought some rain showers that helped them slow the growth of the blaze. Thanks to the tireless efforts of the firefighting crews, no homes or businesses in the township were lost. The Bison Paddock and its fencing did suffer some damage. The summer pasture, which had already been heavily grazed, was scorched, as was the winter range. It would be years before the grasses could recover and the bison could be returned to the area.

But what became of the fugitive bull, the 10-year-old tough guy who evaded capture and was left to fend for himself as the Kenow fire raced through the area? He was fine. The day after the fire made its big run, officials located the bull, which had managed to emerge from the ordeal relatively unscathed. Dan Rafla, human-wildlife conflict specialist with Parks Canada, said the bull probably survived by sticking close to the small chain of ponds that stretch across the Paddock grounds. Also, since the grasses had been mostly consumed by the herd over the summer, there wasn't much left to burn. The bison's biggest threat during the fire's run was probably the heavy smoke and its lung-clogging particulate. "It was probably a stressful, intense experience, in the dark with a lot going on," Rafla said. "The following day, he was fine. We got him moving to make sure there weren't any burns or scorch marks." Once he was deemed healthy, the bison was moved to a herd managed by the Piikani

Nation. Parks Canada frequently donates bison to the Piikani to help avoid inbreeding in their own herds, so it's likely that the smoky bull was living with other bison he'd already known.

It would be almost 4 years before any bison could be reintroduced to the grasslands of the Bison Paddock. In February 2021, a group of six bison yearlings from Elk Island—four females and two males—were released by members of the Kainai Nation into the winter pasture. After spring snowmelt they would move into the summer pasture, which was now fully recovered, supporting plenty of native grasses for the bison to munch on. As the animals reacquainted themselves with the land, some found the original wallow sites used by previous generations, even unearthing bones of their ancestors as they rolled onto their backs and writhed in the shallow dirt pits.

The Kenow fire was the biggest and most intense wildfire ever recorded within the park. The combination of high temperatures, strong winds, and low humidity created a blaze so intense that even the topsoil burned away. Nearly 40 percent of the park was torched, and several structures were lost as Waterton Lakes National Park's 2017 season was cut short. The plains bison made it through the fire, as they have for hundreds of thousands of years. Reintroduction efforts are ongoing, thanks to the continuing work of the First Nations, and there are now at least five distinct herds of buffalo ranging free across Canada. The dozen denizens of the Waterton Bison Paddock continue to improve their little chunk of the prairie environment, playing a key role in an ecosystem that includes wildfire as part of its regeneration cycle.

6

Above It All

I live in western Montana, and I'm sure my fellow Montanans will agree that you encounter things here that you just won't see in places like Connecticut, Los Angeles, or, say, Florida. On second thought, check that. Nothing is outside the realm of possibility in Florida.

Not long after I'd moved here from Seattle in the early 1990s, I spent a weekend with a good friend at his parents' house at Seeley Lake, nestled in the Seeley-Swan Mountains. After an evening of revelry (and the attendant adult beverages) I was offered the guest room, a converted garage. It had a comfy queen bed and its own wood stove. Very cozy. My friend and his mother were still gathering empties and straightening up when I came running back into the house in a full panic. No way I was sleeping out there, I said. Not with the devil looking down at me, watching me sleep, waiting to slurp up my soul. My buddy explained that it was not the head of the Prince of Darkness mounted on the wall above the bed. It was a mountain goat. They're harmless, he said. Not interested in stealing your soul. "But that *face*," I said. I slept on the couch.

<center>~~~</center>

As the buffalo is to Yellowstone, the mountain goat is to Glacier. Its image is on the door of every red jammer bus, smack dab in the middle of the Glacier National Park Transportation Company logo. The Great Northern Railway featured the silhouette of the rugged animal in its logo, posing majestically on a crag, gazing off in the distance, presumably at another carload of Glacier visitors arriving via rail from St. Paul. Of course, there is no connection between the shady netherworld and the mountain goat.

Mountain goats can be seen in most areas of Glacier, and in places like Hidden Lake Trail they've become pretty used to people. Like all wildlife in our national parks, they should not be approached. WIKI COMMONS PHOTO BY R. M. RUSSELL

Sure, the goat's wide-set eyes, black as onyx, and its sharp, charcoal-colored horns and pointy ears may suggest a nefarious demon that will haunt your dreams, but mountain goats are mostly harmless, even downright playful at times. And they're perfectly suited for Glacier's high-altitude environment. One thing they are not, though, is goats. Although they look like goats, act like goats, and (probably) smell like goats, *Oreamnos americanus* are more closely related to the gazelle and antelope than to the true goat. Still, when a goat-like creature is so well equipped for the alpine environment in which it thrives, it seems like a minor semantic quibble to object to its name, which is as etymologically as pragmatic as it gets.

It's hard to imagine an animal better matched to its domain than the mountain goat. They love the alpine cliffs, ridges, and outcroppings above the treeline, and they cling to extremely steep surfaces without working up a sweat. These goats can out-leap an NBA power forward, perform contortions and jumps that would put an Olympic gymnast to shame, and have Spider-Man's outrageous climbing ability to help them elude predators and seek food and shelter. Add to that a coat that gets thick in the winter and light in the summer, and you have a superstar mountain crawler that never fails to thrill those who see it in action.

Here's the best part: You're almost guaranteed to see a few of these striking beasts during your time in the park. They do their best to avoid their natural predators like grizzlies, wolves, and golden eagles (the huge raptors will occasionally snatch up a newborn kid while mom has her back turned), but as far as people are concerned—meh. They have become inured to our presence. Certain areas of the park are hotspots for mountain goats, despite the near-constant foot traffic of people. You can pretty much count on seeing a few near Logan Pass, especially on the trail to Hidden Lake. The overlook just beyond that trail is another popular hangout. They tend to hang out on Iceberg Lake Trail as well, and can usually be seen along the Sperry Glacier Trail and on the trail to Gunsight Pass. What brings them to these spots? The same thing that brings you to that second margarita—salt. Mountain goats, like many ungulates, are believed to have a sodium deficiency and spend a lot of their time in mineral-heavy areas with exposed rocks that they will lick for hours on end. They've even been licking the handrails at Logan Pass Visitors Center to get the salt left behind by human sweat.

One of the most popular goat-watching areas in the park is at the very southern tip, at the aptly named Goat Lick overlook on Highway 2. Located about midway between East Glacier and West Glacier, the massive, nearly vertical rock wall on the east bank of the middle fork of the Flathead River is a rich source of minerals that attracts goats from all over the southern half of the park and the Great Bear Wilderness to the west. They are so attracted to that lick that they occasionally will swim across the river to get to it. It's a super popular stopping place for visitors, too, but there is no guarantee that you'll see a single goat there. They are notoriously schedule-resistant. Still, don't forget your binoculars. If you hit the overlook at the right time, say early morning or just before sunset, you may be gobsmacked by the sight of a dozen or more goats scattered across the face of this sheer cliff, looking like so many mountain goat magnets stuck to a refrigerator door.

If you do see a large group like that, you'll be witnessing one of the few times when the males are mixed in with the females with no apparent drama. Females, or nannies, are more aggressive than the males, allowing them to be nearby only during mating season. Even then, they're tolerant at best. They protect their offspring, other females, and whatever territory they happen to occupy. The goats' need for the abundance of minerals at Goat Lick supersedes their normal social hegemony.

The males, or billies, tend to fly solo or in small bachelor groups once they've reached breeding age, which is just after the following year's kids are born. Both genders sprout horns during that first year, and spend a lot of time playing and roughhousing, picking up socialization skills as well as learning how to climb and jump. The nannies bunch up in casual bands of goats, anywhere from two to twenty, that are pretty loose-knit, with yearlings and other nannies coming and going. Males and females are nearly indistinguishable, save for their size and a slight difference in the shape of their horns. Males are usually between 180 and 250 pounds, while females tip the scale at 130–200 pounds. The horns of the male are slightly broader than those of the female, and have a steady curve to them. Female horns are a little straighter, and take a sudden bend toward the tip. The horns are used sometimes for fighting among males when competing over a nannie during mating season, but unlike their bighorn sheep cousins, they don't butt heads. Their skulls are relatively thin, so they'll swing their heads at their opponent, trying to stab a horn into their hindquarters or flanks.

These vegetarians are generalist grazers—when they're not licking up the seasoning salt they can be found in the subalpine range, working their way through wildflower meadows, munching greens across grassy fields, or moving through small wooded areas, eating pretty much whatever plant material they can find. In summer, while they're down from the higher elevations, they like to take advantage of the remaining bands of snow, where they can frequently be spotted stretching out to cool off their fur-insulated bodies. But it's the cliffs, canyon walls, and sheer rock faces where they spend most of their time, clinging so effortlessly to the tiniest cracks and ledges and blowing the minds of so many Glacier visitors. How on earth do they stay up there?

Like I say, these creatures are tailor-made to negotiate their steep stomping grounds. They have relatively slender bodies, allowing them to keep their weight centered closer to the cliff face. Compared to other ungulates, they have fairly short legs, lowering their center of gravity and providing even more stability. Rumors that their uphill legs are shorter than their downhill legs are untrue, and probably repeated mostly by dads. It's their feet, though, that are probably most helpful in providing them grip, strength, and, well, sure-footedness as they work their way across the narrow ledges of Glacier's rock walls and craggy terrain. The hooves of these two-toed animals have a hard outer surface of keratin, the stuff that comprises fingernails and horns, and are slightly flexible, pointy in the front and covered with a rough texture that helps grab the terrain. The pliable, tough pad on the bottom actually extends a bit beyond the edge of the hoof to maximize traction. They can spread their hooves wide, giving them two points of purchase—even gripping a rock or foothold, pincerlike. Their stubby legs have three joints below the super flexible shoulder or hip, allowing further articulation for precise foot placement. They also have two functional dew claws on the back of their legs just above the feet, but unlike the dew claws on a dog which are used mainly to ruin upholstery, these small appendages are used to help grab a surface or slow them down when sliding down a dirt slope. Their keen eyesight, which can detect movement from over a mile away, helps them quickly identify even the smallest footholds as they clamber along a cliff wall.

Maybe "clambering" falls short of describing the deliberate movement these animals display when traversing a steep mountain face. As evidenced by their large shoulder humps and bulky upper front legs, mountain goats are front-heavy. Like a kibble-focused Chihuahua, their rear legs will sometimes come off the ground as they balance all their weight on their powerful front legs. With a delicate grace that belies their bulk, they can swing their rear quarters around, sometimes even overhead, to reposition the rear feet on a ledge, like a gymnast moving along a balance beam. Of course, these moves don't happen along a busy hiking trail. It takes a lot of patience and good optics to look high up in the rocks and spot this kind of behavior.

The goats spend the bulk of their time along the steep rock faces and peaks up to 10,000 feet, beyond the reach of predators. They learn to climb early on—kids have been seen standing upright, hopping and jumping around, and attempting to scale rocks within their first couple days of life. Their training turns into play as they gain confidence and ability. Kids explore their ever-expanding world, mixing it up with play-mates or a rare twin, and mom is never far away. As with most animals, the mother's waking hours are spent seeking and eating food, but while she's consuming alpine grasses, conifer needles, and whatever plants she can find, she always has at least one eye on her curious offspring. While the rambunctious kid will practice climbing the slopes, Mom positions herself so that a slip will cause her kid to fall into her, not off the edge of a precipice. Sometimes the mother herself will become the mountain, letting her kid climb onto her while she's resting.

A mountain goat's fur is especially well designed to match its environment. Next to their skin is a layer of dense, fine wool that provides excellent insulation but allows heat to radiate away in the summer months. In winter, the fur is overgrown by a heavy layer of long, coarse guard hairs. This shaggy coat protects them from the punishing blizzards and subzero weather of Glacier in the winter. The goats will find overhangs, shallow caves, and other protected areas to bed down, but their heavy white fur is warm enough that they can sleep in the open and still survive the harsh winters.

An even bigger challenge in winter is finding enough food. Like many northern mammals, they pack in the groceries in the fall, trying to gain as much fat as they can to help get them through the lean winter months. They'll push through the snow and eat any plants, even dead ones, just to get something in their bellies. When spring comes and the snows begin to melt and blow away to expose fresh grasses and plants, they will frequently move down into the open areas like meadows or wooded areas to feed. Ever vigilant for predators, they'll always have a quick escape route in mind. In spring and early summer they shed their long winter fur, leaving strands of white wool waving like flags on tree branches, protruding rocks, and in the shallow dirt pits they wallow in.

Like every other animal on the planet, the mountain goat is dealing with a changing habitat. Climate change is taking its toll on the park's namesake glaciers. The receding ice fields are driving mountain goat populations into islands of available alpine vegetation, reducing their exposure to other groups of goats, resulting in poor genetic variation. Over the last few years, the pandemic-spurred boom in Glacier's popularity is having an impact on the park's multiple ecosystems. With higher visitor numbers come more vehicles, more pollution, more noise, more trash, and more people edging into the goats' personal space. For now, though, we don't have to worry too much about these crafty, snow-white rock hoppers. They may have a devilish countenance, but they are fairly good-natured—no need to ask, "Why the long face?" The upper reaches of Glacier belong to the mountain goat, and you can see them throughout the park, perched high up on some impossible ledge, calmly surveying their domain and nurturing the next generation of cliff-climbers, safe in the knowledge that very few other Glacier inhabitants have what it takes to get to their lofty position.

7

Stalking the Untamed Mushroom

In the movie *Ghostbusters*, chatty secretary Janine Melnitz is openly crushing on Dr. Egon Spengler, and rattles off a list of her interests with her nasally, New York twang. Then she asks Spengler if he has any hobbies. He looks at her without expression and responds, "I collect spores, molds and fungus." If the reticent ghostbuster ever found himself crawling around the forests of Glacier National Park, he would surely be in hog heaven.

For the newcomer to the world of fungi, Glacier holds a treasure trove of surprising secrets in the hidden world of mushrooms and their fast-growing brethren. From the witches' butter jelly that grows on decaying pine trunks, to the horse's hoof fungus that can be found on living birch trees, there are more than a thousand species of fungi in Glacier, comprising mushrooms, smuts, rust, yeasts, molds, and lichens.

Perhaps the most visible in the wilds of Glacier are the colorful lichens and showy fruiting mushrooms. The *Lactarius* genus of mushroom, for instance, are relatively easy to identify, with their caps looking like an umbrella that's been blown inside-out. Boletes, with their sponge-like flesh, are common throughout the park. You'll also find elfin saddles, puffballs, yellow coral, brittlegills, slippery jacks, and hundreds of other mushroom species that sound like they might have been named by someone who indulged in the magic variety.

Intricate, fanciful, flamboyant or kind of gross, mushrooms are only a tiny fraction of the biological behemoth that produces them. Whether you're hiking through the alpine stands of Douglas firs and Western larch at high altitude, wandering through the wildflower meadows on the east

This *Russula claroflava* mushroom, or yellow brittlegill, is one of hundreds of species of fungus that can be found in Glacier Park. Even the edible ones, however, cannot be harvested within the park. WIKI COMMONS PHOTO BY HENK MONSTER

side of the Continental Divide, or following one of Glacier's many waterways, beneath your feet is an omnipresent web of net-like systems called mycelia. It's the organic material that ties together most plant life on earth. The mycelia send out microscopic tendrils called hyphae, which grow through any food that's available, consuming nutrients and minerals, expanding to form a mycelial mat. All tree roots are enveloped by these net-like mats, which release enzymes into the soil. In a constant give-and-take, mycorrhizal fungi are subsidized by their host organisms. Once the food source runs out or the conditions become untenable, the mycelia go into reproductive mode, shifting their energy from feeding to the creation of mushrooms, their reproductive appendages. And mushrooms don't mess around—they grow fast and relentlessly. They've been known to break through asphalt. Once mature, the mushrooms release spores that are carried through the ecosystem to establish themselves on another hospitable food source. They send out exploratory hyphae, and the cycle repeats.

Fungi are among the first life forms to come ashore from the sea of primordial soup more than one billion years ago. Mycelia have been enjoying a mycorrhizal relationship with plants ever since. At one time fungi were classified as plant life, but since we've learned that they don't produce their own food using photosynthesis, fungi are considered a distinct kingdom, alongside animals, plants, and bacteria. In an environment like Glacier Park, where bacterial action like decay is slowed by the cold temperatures, the work of fungi is crucial to keep things moving along in this complex, interconnected system of living things.

One reason this part of the Northern Rockies is home to such a wide variety of mushrooms is the diversity of habitat. The Divide splits the park into east and west, each with its own ecosystem. Then you add in the different biomes related to altitude—alpine, subalpine, boreal zones, forests, and grasslands—and the range of hospitable fungi habitat is virtually limitless. Just as the park's flora and fauna thrive in their most hospitable environment, fungi also flourish where conditions favor their specific needs. Certain mushrooms will be found only on certain species of trees, which really helps speed up the hunting and identification of these fascinating forest dwellers. As mycology is a relative latecomer to the biological party—even though mushrooms predate other life-forms by hundreds of millions of years—new species are being identified in the park all the time. As early as 1919, just 9 years after the park was designated, sixty-one species of parasitic rusts were collected and reported by Paul C. Standley. They were still being classified as "interesting plants." Another discovery was reported in the magazine *Mycologia* in 1941, when E. B. Mains found examples of the rust *Mesopsora hypericorum* infecting some plants on the trail between Hidden Lake and Logan Pass at an altitude of about 7,000 feet. It was believed to be the first *M. hypericorum* found in North America. You want mushrooms? Glacier is one mighty mycota.

The arrowhead-shaped logo of the National Park Service features mountains, a couple varieties of trees, and a bison. Not a single mushroom. Unless they're already hip to the wild world of mushrooms, most visitors don't come into Glacier Park hoping to bag a photo of a living, breathing pear-shaped puffball. It's the sexy beasts like wolves, grizzlies, eagles, and elk that get all the attention and stop traffic just by showing up near a road. That's a pity, because the world of fungi is as varied, fascinating, and surprising as the other biological kingdoms that populate the park. Armed with the knowledge of where to find mushrooms and how to identify them, you can easily add an extra level of enjoyment to your visit to Glacier. The thrill of spotting a black trumpet chanterelle or happening upon the intricate body of a hen of the woods can be as exciting to an amateur mycology buff as glassing a grizzly bear from a mile away on the slope of a mountain, or standing under the baleful gaze of a bald eagle perched on a snag.

Of course, there are a couple of important points to consider before you amble off into the woods on a mushroom hunt. First off, no foraging is allowed. It is illegal to take anything from a national park, and this includes plants, rocks, animals, and of course mushrooms. Many of the species you'll find throughout the park are edible and quite delicious, including morels, boletes, and chanterelles, but foraging is absolutely verboten. Look, but don't eat.

The other point is rendered moot in Glacier by the first point, but it's worth stating anyway. Obviously, many mushroom species are poisonous. Typically, they have to be ingested in order to make this your last trip to Glacier. But it's probably not a good idea to even touch the ocelot entoloma, torn-capped inocybe, spruce parasol, or the aptly-named death caps.

The other class of mushrooms that lies somewhere between edible and poisonous are the hallucinogenic variety. Again, their collection is prohibited. It could be helpful to note their appearance, though, as once you're outside the park, you may become interested in a burgeoning movement among the medical community that's exploring the use of psilocybes in treating depression, death anxiety, and the psychology of addictions. It's not a new idea, as people have been using mushrooms as medicine for thousands of years. But this resource is gaining credibility in modern science. Researchers are also seeing results in using psilocybin to treat cognitive decline in Alzheimer's patients. The outlook is promising for the increasing use of mushrooms in a therapeutic context.

So, to begin your mushroom hunt, you'll need to know where to look and what to look for. A quality identification guide is *de rigueur*. A couple of great choices are the pocket-sized *Mushrooms: A Falcon Field Guide,*

2nd Edition, by Todd Telander, and *All That the Rain Promises and More: A Hip Pocket Guide to Western Mushrooms* by David Arora, as entertaining as it is informative.

Glacier is a big place, and with a thousand species of mushrooms growing out there, it can seem overwhelming. Fortunately, the locations of many species are highly predictable as they grow only on a certain tree, or require a highly specific environment. The chaga, for instance, typically grows on the side of yellow and white birch trees. Also known as a birch conk or clinker polypore, this black, rough-textured mushroom can grow as big as an ice chest, and has long been used in Asian medicine. Chaga can be found clinging to birch trees around Apgar at the foot of Lake McDonald, and among the forests in the southern half of Glacier. Horse's hoof is another fungus that prefers the birch.

Puffballs are one of the few mushrooms that don't bond with a particular tree, so you can find them throughout the park. Known as gasteroid because their spores are enclosed inside the body, puffballs are represented by several species in Glacier. They don't usually have a stalk or a stem, and just appear to be little fleshy balls sitting on the ground near trees, next to rocks, or in the middle of a trail. The tap of a foot may cause them to split open and release billions of spores. Common puffballs can be found pretty much anywhere, from Bowman Lake to St. Mary. Sculpted puffballs, with their lumpy exterior, have been spotted at higher altitudes like Going-to-the-Sun Mountain.

Probably the most widely recognized mushroom in Glacier or anywhere else is the *Amanita muscaria*, or fly agaric. It's the toadstool-shaped mushroom that features a bright red cap dotted with white spots. Its image in popular culture is nearly inescapable. If you've played the Mario Brothers video game, you've landed on the fly agaric to power up. Smurfs have been known to use them for chairs. Hieronymus Bosch's painting *The Garden of Earthly Delights* features a red mushroom with white spots in the center panel. In 2022, Katy Perry performed a song on *Saturday Night Live* among several giant mushrooms, surrounded by dancers wearing mushroom outfits topped with the distinctive red and white fly agaric caps and brandishing paper fans that read "Eat Me." Did I fail to mention that the fly agaric is also widely known for its hallucinogenic properties?

It is also considered poisonous, although rarely fatal. The scene in Lewis Carroll's *The Adventures of Alice in Wonderland* where the caterpillar invites Alice to take a bite of the mushroom he's sitting on suggests the iconic 'shroom may have inspired the author. As an entheogen used for centuries by shamans of many cultures, the fly agaric has been known in the United States and elsewhere as the "magic mushroom" ever since R. Gordon Wasson wrote about its psychoactive effects in *Life* magazine in 1957, igniting intense interest among the beatnik culture.

The colorful fruiting bodies of the American fly agaric prefer light soils in woodlands under pine, spruce, and birch. They don't seem to be too particular about altitude, as they've been found in Glacier near Quartz Lake, at about 4,000 feet, and near the Grinnell Glacier Overlook, at about 7,500 feet. If you'd like to learn of other locations where it can be found, go ask Alice.

Some of the more heavily used trails in the park can be home to interesting and rare fungi. Trail of the Cedars is an easy, mile-long walk about 5.5 miles east of the Lake McDonald Lodge that sees hordes of people all summer long. It has a real Pacific Northwest feel with its canopy of ancient western red cedars and hemlock, some of them more than 500 years old, and a riot of ferns and moss filling the understory. Halfway along the loop the trail crosses over Avalanche Creek. In the fall, this is a great place to find the orange-yellow fiery agaric and their cousin, the penetrating agaric. Both species feature a wide, shallow cap with gills underneath. The fiery agaric, especially, stands out brightly from its dark green surroundings. They can be found growing on stumps and at the base of large trees, especially oak.

The dense, wet environment of the Trail of the Cedars is also a great place to spot an edible known as the admirable bolete, or bragger's bolete. It has a wide, reddish-brown cap, in striking contrast to the pale yellow or white porous undersurface. This bolete enjoys a mycorrhizal relationship with the hemlock, so look for them around those plants. The admirable bolete is considered edible, although is known to be bland, even for a mushroom. This trait, paired with the fact that the hemlock that supports it may or may not be poisonous, should make it easy to leave these things alone.

The slippery jack may sound like the name of a tavern popular with pirates, but it's a large mushroom that looks like a supersized version of the admirable bolete. There are some big differences between the two, though. The slippery jack tends to grow not in the damp, lush environment of the cedars, but is usually found in clumps of grass under conifers. Also known as the pine bolete, it seems to prefer higher elevations than its smaller cousin. Oh, and it gets its name from the shiny coating of slime on its cap. Eww.

Maybe even more ubiquitous in Glacier Park than mushrooms are another fungus, the lichen. Technically, they're not just a fungus. They are a composite organism, comprising a fungus growing in tandem with algae or cyanobacteria. Their bright colors that draw the eye where they grow on rocks, leaves, tree bark, or even other lichens, are produced by a photo-synthetic component. Some lichens are flat and dry like old house paint, while others, known as jellies, have flower-like bodies and a translucent, gelatinous appearance. If you see some orange-pink weirdo posing as a petunia growing on a tree in the Apgar campground, do not be alarmed. It is an apricot jelly. They're really kind of adorable, and appear in the late summer to early fall.

Recently a couple of "bio-blitzes" were organized in Glacier Park. These information-collecting events teamed up citizen scientists with several experts and researchers in the field of mycology. Their task was to spread out through the park and identify and (with the park's blessing) collect as many samples of fungi as they could. Participants ranged from amateurs who hunt delicacies like morels and chanterelles, to university-based scientists hoping to discover never-before-recorded species in the park. One wild card is that species occupying the park vary throughout the year, as mushrooms are mostly seasonal. Some appear just after spring melt-off, others don't fruit until leaves begin to turn in the fall. Nevertheless, the mushroom hunters of the bio-blitzes helped record important data that indicated not only the presence of more than 150 species of mushroom, but also where they tend to be located.

The relatively dry climate of the Mountain West makes the mushrooms' mycorrhizal relationship with their hosts a crucial component of keeping the vast forests of Glacier healthy and productive. Even though the namesake glaciers are receding because of climate change, the mycelial network just under the surface continues the work of life in Glacier and everywhere else, drawing sustenance from the trees and giving them nourishment in return, while also doing the important tasks of sequestering carbon and producing the wide variety of mushrooms that we're still figuring out how to exploit.

It's something to think about when you're bouncing around Glacier Park. The impressive wildlife, the scenic vistas, the majestic mountains rising up to the clouds—you'll be taking in some of the most breathtaking beauty that nature has to offer. But don't forget to look down, between your boots. That's where the real action is.

Ten Tasty Treasure State Treats to Try

One of the best parts of road-tripping is sampling regional foods you might not find at home. You may be reading this while chewing on a sandwich between slices of bread made with wheat grown in Montana's Golden Triangle, and washing it down with a cold beer brewed with Sonnet hops from the Flathead Valley. Our beef is famous, of course, but locally ranched bison is showing up on more and more menus. Montana is bursting with delicacies for everybody, whether you have a sweet tooth (huckleberry shakes) or are feeling more adventurous (Rocky Mountain oysters). Here is a short and subjective list of Montana treats.

Bison Jerky

Fur traders moving across Canada from Hudson Bay in the 1700s were introduced by the natives to a high-energy food called pemmican, a mixture of dried buffalo meat and berries. It traveled well, and quickly became a popular trade item. Dried buffalo was a staple among Indigenous cultures, helping sustain their people year-round, especially when fresh game was scarce. After the hunt, Indians dried thin slices of the meat for days on wooden racks, giving them a well-preserved protein source. Nowadays obtaining this savory Montana treat is a lot easier—jerky makers do all the work for you! This isn't your run-of-the-mill jerky you see in checkstand packs at your grocery store. This is the real thing. It's dry and tough, but in a good way. For less than $20 for a quarter-pound, you can take home a package of buffalo jerky that has more protein, less fat, and less cholesterol than beef. Several Montana companies produce and sell it, and you can find many of them on the drive between Glacier and Yellowstone. My personal favorite is M&S Meats and Sausage, which has a store in Rollins on the west shore of Flathead Lake, and another location in Polson on the south end of the lake. Once you gnaw a bite, you'll be ready to fend off even your dog's most charming begging routines. It's that good.

Morel Mushrooms

First, a couple of important points: No mushroom should be consumed until its identity has been positively confirmed in a mushroom guide, or by a trusted expert. Second, it is illegal to pick or eat mushrooms—or anything else—in a national park. Okay, now let me tell you about one of nature's most delicious delicacies, the morel mushroom. Western Montana is morel-crazy, and the appearance of these mushrooms after the spring snowmelt generates the kind of excitement you'll see in fly fishermen over the Skwala hatch, or kids swarming on a busted piñata. Montana's forestlands are full of dozens of species of tasty, edible mushrooms, but the morel is widely considered to be the filet mignon of fungi.

They have a distinctive appearance with wavy, vertical fins creating a honeycomb lattice in an elongated, conical cap over a stubby, bulbous stem. Three common groups comprise the morels that are typically found in Montana, usually from mid-April until the weather turns hot in June. The naturals are the first to appear, typically just after snowmelt. They're dark gray or black, usually concentrated in mossy forests. Fire morels are sought in areas the year after a forest fire and also are black or gray but can have a yellow or pinkish hue. The third group are known as river morels, congregating in river bottoms near cottonwoods. They're pale, yellowish, and usually the tallest of the bunch. There are also false morels to beware of, fungi that resemble the real thing, but only true morels are hollow.

They're commonly used in sauces, soups, and other dishes, but morel aficionados, who are known to guard their foraging spots like a fisherman hoards a secret trout hole, will pan fry them in butter with a little garlic.

Jersey Lilly Beans and Sheepherder's Hors D'oeuvres

I'm including this dish even though it is not located on any reasonable route between the parks. But one traveler's "unreasonable" is another traveler's "adventurous," right? The Jersey Lilly Saloon will take you a couple hours out of your way, but there are many Montanans who will swear that these beans are worth it.

The Jersey Lil (as locals call it) in the tiny rail town of Ingomar (population a dozen, give or take), just northeast of Billings on MT 12, is the only place you can get their famous beans. It's the only place in Ingomar where you can get anything. The Jersey Lilly Saloon is the last business left in what was once known as the sheep-shearing capital of the world.

The tender and savory beans they cook up every day still bring the locals from a hundred miles around, and an order of them is quite the production. A generous helping is served up in a small, enameled saucepan, enough to fill bowls for two people. A side plate contains homemade toast croutons, a stack of Saltines, and a tiny Mason jar of hot sauce in case you need a little boost in your beans. The pintos are simmered low and slow until tender, but the seasoning used in the distinctive soup, which has a couple chunks of cured pork for a smoky edge, remains a secret.

The companion dish is straight up weird. Sheepherder's hors d'oeuvres were concocted over a century ago, a nonperishable snack sheepherders could enjoy while out in the field. Stacked on a Saltine are a wedge of orange, a chunk of onion, and a slice of mild cheddar. Trust me, somehow these divergent bits combine to create a satisfying taste. It sounds like a mouthful of train wreck, but somehow it works. One note: The Jersey Lilly has changed hands a couple of times in recent years, so it's wise to double-check that it is operating before you head eastward on that blue highway.

Fry Bread/Indian Taco

Want to start an argument on the reservation? Claim that your auntie makes the best fry bread. It's not like there are a ton of ingredients or a lot of variation. It's usually just flour, baking powder, sugar, and milk. Some recipes may use an egg or lard, but it tends to be a recipe that's handed down unchanged for generations, a source of familial pride and so much more than just a deep-fried disc of dough. What makes each family's fry bread different is something that's beyond the earthly constraints of a kitchen. Love, spirituality, heritage, magic—good luck having that delivered by HelloFresh. The crispy, golden brown pastry topped with honey or powdered sugar is a cultural staple in Indian homes, and they're available at most powwows or multitribal gatherings like Hardin's Crow Fair or Browning's North American Indian Days.

Fry bread didn't exist until Indians were introduced to the wheat flour brought out west by early settlers and explorers. After the tribes were forced onto reservations in the mid- to late 1800s, Indians used government-issued staples to concoct the puffy, fried bread that became known as an Indian specialty. In modern times Indians made fry bread an integral part of their cultural identity—T-shirts bearing the words *Fry Bread Nation* can be seen at some powwows.

For fry bread lovers who want to go savory rather than sweet, there's the Indian taco. It's a fry bread piled with typical taco fillings, sometimes over a base of hot chili. Definitely a modern, cross-cultural take on a portable meal, it's literally a hot mess. And delicious. If you're planning on indulging in an Indian taco at a powwow, make sure you wear a shirt it will look good on.

Benson's Corn

Benson's Farm occupies a rather curious spot in Missoula, sprawled across 20 acres along Reserve Street, the four-lane commercial artery that's the border between urban and agricultural land. When Otto Benson bought the land in 1900 to start raising dairy cows, the streets of downtown Missoula were still dirt, milk was delivered in a horse-drawn wagon, and Reserve Street was a country road that saw more livestock than traffic.

Currently the farm is run by Otto's grandson Bruce, who took over from his dad, Otto the second, who died in 2015 at age 96. Nowadays, their bounty is sold out of the little outbuilding at the entrance to the farm on 7th Street. Their summer produce includes Rainbow Swiss chard, kale, tomatoes, eggplants, and peppers, but it's Benson's corn that is the late summer superstar of western Montana produce. Most years one of the corn fields is planted right alongside Reserve Street, so commuters can gauge the size of the stalks and see how close we're getting to that magic day when the corn-shaped flag is unfurled at the farm's entrance, signaling those four words that Missoulians wait all summer to hear: Benson's corn is in.

The employees at Benson's Farm—as well as the owner, Bruce—make sure their bins of yellow, white, and bicolor ears remain full all day long after they ripen in late August. Locals know: When you see the corn flag flying at the farm entrance just off Reserve Street in Missoula, the corn is in! AUTHOR PHOTO

It's difficult to overstate how good this corn is. It's sweet and firm, with kernels so crisp that when you bite into an ear it sounds like someone's twisting a roll of bubble wrap. It usually ripens in mid- to late August, and that's when they open the produce shed. Three cardboard bins along a front wall offer their three varieties—white, yellow, and bicolor. They generally run two ears for a buck, and you bag your own corn while the people in line behind you begin to salivate. Occasionally Bruce will come in and dump a huge burlap bag of just-picked ears into the bins, and this is when you text somebody at home and tell them to get a pot of water on the boil.

Rocky Mountain Oysters

Here's a news flash for those unfamiliar with this dish: Rocky Mountain oysters are not shellfish. They are bull or calf testicles that have been removed during castration. Anyone who's had their dog neutered only to see him sit on the front porch and lose interest in everything can understand why ranchers do this to feisty calves. They don't want no trouble. Back in the Wild West days, cowpokes on a roundup would take the bovine balls and toss them on a hot iron griddle over the fire. When they exploded, that meant they were done.

Eating organ meats wasn't an original Montana idea, of course. In ancient Rome, the consumption of animal testicles was thought to bring virility and improve sexual performance. In India bull testicles are thought to be an aphrodisiac. While you're in Montana, you may have to muster up a pair to order this dish that's also called prairie oysters, swinging beef, dusty nuts, or cowboy caviar.

Several restaurants across the state serve Rocky Mountain oysters, and there was even a raunchy festival at Rock Creek for a few years that celebrated the culture of cojones. If you're entertaining the idea of trying some, which you should, don't picture yourself eating an apple. They're usually sliced thin or pounded flat like schnitzel (ouch), breaded, and deep fried. The consistency is not unlike chicken liver, and the taste . . . just make sure you're getting the calf glands, not the tougher bull version.

You can find Rocky Mountain oysters near Yellowstone at Stacey's Old Faithful Bar in Gallatin Gateway, the Buffalo Bar in West Yellowstone, and the Old Saloon in the Paradise Valley town of Emigrant. In Billings, the Bull Mountain Grill serves 'em up.

Dixon Melons

When you drive past the tiny hamlet of Dixon, just a few miles west of US 93 North on MT 200, you'll pass the "Famous" Dixon Bar, which has been for sale for as long as anyone can remember, but no one can remember why it's famous. What is famous about Dixon is its melons. It's one of the seasonal foods that gets people excited in western Montana, but the good news is that you don't have to go to Dixon to buy them (nothing personal, Dixon). Most farmers' markets, produce stands, and grocers in the Montana Swath between the national parks sell Dixon melons. For 35 years and counting, three generations of the Hettick family have been working and irrigating 25 acres of land along the Flathead River to produce a thousand tons of melons every year on 50,000 plants. Their flagship is a musk variety bearing the company's name. They also grow watermelons, honeydews, and Sinful and Crenshaw melons. They all taste good enough to seem sinful.

You'll find the Dixon Melon flatbed truck parked at farmers' markets in Polson, Helena, Missoula, and other spots from late summer until the harvest runs its course in early fall (they'll give a heads up on their Facebook page). Get in line and sample a slice off a fresh melon, and you'll immediately start thinking about your return trip to Montana.

Irish Butte Pasty

You don't have to go to Butte to find an authentic pasty, but the farther from the Mining City you get, the paler the imitations you will encounter.

The original pasty (rhymes with "nasty," which it is not, not "tasty," which it is) was introduced by the Cornish miners who emigrated to Butte during its hard rock heyday. The plump, crescent-shaped pastry stuffed with diced beef and rutabagas was the perfect sustenance for the miners who were crowded into elevators and lowered more than a mile underground, from where they would not emerge until the end of their shift. There was no nipping out to Taco Bell at noon for a Chalu parito. The Irish population soon replaced the root vegetable with potatoes, and the Irish Butte pasty came into its own.

The delicious and durable pasty, like most Butte people themselves, could take a punch. Miners would heat their lunch by holding it on a shovel over a fire, then grip it by the thick, scalloped crust that served as a handle. Their filthy hands didn't contact the filling, possibly minimizing the chance of food-borne illness. Once de-pied, the crust was then tossed down into the depths of a mineshaft as a superstitious offering to the spirits of their comrades who had lost their lives in the mines.

Over the years the pasty has evolved a bit, having shrunk in size, and is usually smothered in gravy. Still, it's a meat and potatoes meal that is as Butte as it gets. I happened to be spending time in Butte with a friend in October 2021, and we craved a pasty. When in Rome and all that. Joe's Pasty Shop was the town's most famous purveyor, but when we wheeled into the parking lot at dinnertime, we discovered that, after 74 years in business, they had closed for good. I think one of us cried.

Thankfully, you can still find the real thing in and around Butte. Town Talk Bakery currently puts out some of the best pasties in town, and Wind's Pasties in nearby Anaconda are authentic, and can also be found in area grocery stores. In Great Falls, Mrs. Wright's Pastys would make the Irish proud with their version. Nothing lasts forever, even Joe's (*sniff*), so when you're pasty-bound, it's wise to call before you go.

Flathead Cherries

When you think cherries, you probably think Washington—either the state that's known to produce the fruit, or the spring bloom of cherry blossoms in DC. Here in Montana, some of the best cherries in the world are grown in orchards along the shore of Flathead Lake, the largest freshwater body in the West. Between the relatively mild microclimate created by the huge lake and the rich, volcanic soil in the valley, cherries love this region. Orchards also grow peaches, apples, plums, and pears, but it's the cherries that get the spotlight, and deservedly so.

"Flathead cherries" is a bit of a misnomer. There is no one species with that name, but a collection of strains including Lapins, Sweetheart, Rainier, Van, Stella, Lambert, and Skeena cherries. When you're traveling between Missoula and Glacier, the shortest route skirts the east edge of the lake on MT 35, where you'll pass the orchards and dozens of roadside cherry stands. There are stands along both sides of the lake, though, as well as in Polson, Columbia Falls, and other towns along the way. Stop at a stand and snag a sack of these plump, sweet, firm fruits. Pass 'em around while you take in some of Montana's most beautiful vistas along Flathead Lake, and you'll probably empty the bag before you get to the next stand.

One note: Cherries you find at stores (and even some stands) before mid-July, when Flathead cherries ripen, are probably from elsewhere. Don't worry, they'll let you know if you're buying the real thing.

Huckleberry Everything

One of the sweet bonuses of hiking the alpine trails of Glacier Park and western Montana is plucking ripe huckleberries off the vine. These purple, pea-sized fruits look like small blueberries, and grow in thick thatches of vines in the shadier areas of the mountains, especially in places that have recently burned. Once they come ripe in midsummer, the chase is on. You might encounter some commercial pickers out there with the plastic buckets, but they won't be the only other huckleberry enthusiasts you're apt to see. Huckleberries are a main food source for black bears and grizzlies.

If you'd rather not be competing with bears while harvesting huckleberries, you'll find them at most western Montana farmers' markets and fruit stands, where a pound of the prized berries will fetch $12 to $15.

When driving to Glacier Park, you'll know you're getting close when you start seeing signs that advertise all things huckleberry, like huckleberry jam, syrup, vinaigrette, barbecue sauce, salsa, candy, and more. At seasonal shops everywhere from Bozeman to Whitefish, you can get huckleberry ice cream, huckleberry milkshakes, and huckleberry chai mix. I recommend treating yourself and your traveling companions to a huckleberry pie, which, to me, is the reason these berries exist. It will haunt your dreams.

Also quite popular are huckleberry-infused goods like candles, lip balm, and lotion. Please think twice, though, before you coat yourself in a layer of huckleberry lotion and set off on a hike through the woods because, you know, bears.

8

A Forgotten Hero in Glacier Park

JAMES "JIMMY" CONWAY FLICKED HIS EYES BETWEEN THE HORIZON AND the control panel as he piloted a single-engine Piper Cherokee south from Calgary, Alberta, on a Thursday morning in September 1985. Directly behind him in the four-seat aircraft sat his mother, Judith. His father, Leo, was strapped into the seat next to her, and Jimmy's 31-year-old wife, Shirley, a nurse, rode in the copilot position. Jimmy's parents had traveled from their home in Beaconsville, Quebec, to join the young Edmonton couple for a week-long vacation in Reno, Nevada. Jimmy and Shirley had placed their children, Shawnna, 6, and Ryan, 2, in the care of a sitter. They were no doubt excited for a few days of adult R-and-R and a welcome break from the rigors and pressures that fill the lives of working parents.

As the aircraft climbed to cruising altitude, its passengers could look through the small starboard windows and see the mountains of Banff National Park in the Canadian Rockies starting to glow in the rising sun, giving them a preview of the scenery they'd be flying over in Glacier Park on their way to Kalispell, Montana, the terminus on their first leg of the flight. Although wind and engine noise made conversation difficult, they may have been chatting about hockey legend Wayne Gretzky, who had just led their hometown Oilers to their second Stanley Cup in only five games over the Philadelphia Flyers. Or the topic may have been their upcoming entertainment choices in Reno, which included big-name singers like Lee Greenwood and Vic Damone, and comedian Norm Crosby. Not exactly the Rat Pack, but this was Reno, not Las Vegas. Still, there would be plenty to keep them occupied in the so-called Biggest Little City in the World. The two couples may even have planned a short hop to Lake Tahoe to catch the Everly Brothers, who were headlining at Harrah's. First, though, they would have to navigate their way through the ominous clouds moving in over Glacier.

Visibility was degrading as the jagged mountains of Glacier-Waterton Peace Park loomed ahead, and wind and rain began hammering the light plane as it flew past the Canadian border. Conway had received a weather update that reported a low ceiling ahead, and obscuration of the peaks. He absorbed the information but was confident at the controls. He'd accumulated 4,000 hours of flight time in various aircraft while working as an operations manager at Aero Aviation Centre in Edmonton, many of them in small air taxis like this Cherokee he'd leased for the trip. He was fully rated on instruments, so he likely shifted his focus in the worsening visibility to his directional gyro, altimeter, airspeed and attitude indicators, and other panel gauges. Seeking some relief from the increasing turbulence, he dropped the plane to an altitude well below that of many of Glacier's peaks. Trying to climb above the cloud cover was out of the question—the plane just wasn't designed to operate at that altitude. The Cherokee had a nonpressurized cabin, and the thin air would be dangerous to the passengers and starve the engine of oxygen. Their only option was to try and stay under the clouds. They were still about 30 miles northeast of the park's southern border, but if Jimmy could thread his way between the mountains in the driving rain and swirling wind, he could set safely down in Kalispell where the foursome could wait the storm out before continuing to Reno.

As many seasoned visitors to Glacier will attest, the park and its weather system sometimes have other plans. It's not unusual to see snow-storms in Glacier Park during every month of the year, and this storm cell had slid in from the west just after Labor Day, carrying plenty of moisture and effectively slamming the door on the park's summer season. With the temperature dropping quickly, crosswinds buffeted the Piper while Conway wrestled with the control yoke and rudder pedals, swooping over Siyeh Bend, a hairpin turn in Going-to-the-Sun Road between Piegan Mountain and the road's namesake peak.

Ranger Jerry Ryder was on duty that day, and conjectured that Conway may have been following the road. "We figured he was flying low for the weather conditions. He was flying just off the deck near the road and when the road made the hard turn at Siyeh Bend, he may not have been prepared to make the turn. He possibly tried to make a turn up the valley, but we don't know what brought him down."

Visibility had dropped to zero. The Piper veered east and plunged into the thick forest on a slope about 3 miles east of Logan Pass, in a box canyon along the south face of Mount Siyeh. One wing was bent backward in the impact while the other sheared off completely. The aircraft came to rest sideways on the hillside among the trees, about a half-mile up from the road.

Dazed and confused, Shirley tried to regain her focus as she looked around the cabin. Jimmy was mortally injured. She looked back at Judith and saw that she'd also perished in the crash. At this point her nurse's training kicked in, and she compartmentalized her grief so she could help Leo, still alive but badly hurt in the seat behind her. As she unbuckled her seatbelt, she noticed that her shoes had somehow come off and were nowhere to be found. Her legs and feet were banged up, and she reeled from the pain in her shoulder, which had been dislocated in the impact. She clambered back to her father-in-law and saw that he had a broken leg and a serious back injury. He could not be moved. Shirley made him as comfortable as she could, and pushed open the plane's single door on the right side and stepped out onto what remained of the wing. Peering through the mist and rain, she searched for any landmark in the unfamiliar terrain. Down the slope, the curve of a road was barely visible in the gloom. Uphill from the plane the firs and lodgepoles gave way to a craggy ridge. A narrow waterfall carried Siyeh Creek over the edge, and she could hear the rush of the water as it flowed past nearby. She likely hadn't dressed for the near-freezing, wet weather, but there was nothing she could do but start walking through the heavy underbrush down to Going-to-the-Sun Road for help. Barefoot, she set off through the woods in the frigid rain, ignoring the pain in her legs and fighting back the shock that was undoubtedly setting in from her shoulder injury. As she struggled through the wet, thick understory between the Ponderosa pines and Douglas firs, prickly vines tore at her clothing. Some inner force kept her moving as she scrambled over fallen trees, tripping over sprawling roots and losing her footing on the slick moss. She may have splashed through the icy waters of Siyeh Creek more than once as she stumbled downhill toward the road. At last she reached the asphalt, and she flagged down a passing motorist who gave her a ride to the St. Mary's ranger station where she reported the crash. She must have been a shocking sight to the rangers at that station, limping in, soaking wet, exhausted and barefoot.

The poor weather precluded a helicopter rescue. A team drove to Siyeh Bend and hiked up to the crash site, where they strapped Leo onto a litter and carried him back down the steep hillside to the road, rolling him along when the terrain flattened out. He was suffering from hypothermia and had shattered his ankle. He'd also received a compression spinal fracture, making the journey down the hill even more delicate as they tried to minimize jostling him on the treacherous terrain. The rescue team loaded him into an ambulance that had arrived from Babb and he was taken to the ranger station, where he was picked up by a helicopter and whisked to Columbus Hospital in Great Falls.

"I'm sure she saved him," said Karene Foreman, a spokesperson from Glacier's assistant superintendent's office, crediting Shirley for her bravery. Ranger Ryder agreed, adding that the Edmonton nurse was "a very tough lady." Shirley was taken to the Great Falls hospital by car, where she was treated for her dislocated shoulder and multiple contusions and lacerations on her legs and feet.

The following morning there was nearly a foot of snow on the crash site, and Going-to-the-Sun Road was closed to traffic. The clouds had lifted enough to allow a helicopter to fly to the scene, though, and a team was able to recover the bodies of Jimmy and Judith. Later that day investigators from the Canadian Aviation Safety Board and the US Federal Aviation Administration arrived at the site to begin their investigations into the cause of the crash.

Back in Edmonton, employees at Aero Aviation were shocked by the news of Jimmy Conway's death, especially in light of his capabilities as a pilot. One company official lamented the loss of the well-liked aviator, adding that he'd been a solid member of Aero almost since the company's inception 10 years earlier. Upon receiving the news, Aero immediately suspended operations for several hours and flew into action. Literally.

In these forested slopes just north of Siyeh Bend on Going-to-the-Sun Road, a four-seat plane from Edmonton slammed into the trees during a rainstorm in 1985, killing two onboard. One of the survivors hiked barefoot through the dense forest to seek help for the other survivor. AUTHOR PHOTO

Two employees flew a plane south to Great Falls, where they stayed until Leo was stable enough to travel and he and Judith could be flown home to Edmonton.

Ten years after the crash, the National Transportation Safety Board released its findings in a typically terse report, laying much of the blame on pilot error. The report concluded that Conway had, indeed, attempted to follow the route of Going-to-the-Sun Road, a last resort given the low cloud ceiling and limited visibility. It's acknowledged that Conway did receive an updated weather report en route to Kalispell, but the findings indicate that he'd made a poor decision in trying to fly through the weather instead of altering his route. Was he overconfident, this small aircraft expert with thousands of hours at the stick? As Conway didn't survive the crash to provide an answer, we'll never know.

Several factors beyond the weather could have contributed to the tragedy. For instance, the Piper Cherokee is a low-wing aircraft, with the wings positioned at the bottom of the fuselage, as opposed to a high-wing plane like a Cessna, where the wings sit atop the plane. If Conway was trying to follow the serpentine road below him during a rainstorm, a portion of his field of view would have been blocked. That possibility was not mentioned in the report. There was no fire or explosion after impact, and no malfunction was identified among the aircraft's systems and controls. Likely, it was a deadly combination of sudden bad weather, bad luck, and Conway's unfamiliarity with Glacier's topography. Any experienced light aircraft pilot will tell you that mountain flying is unforgiving. Some will flat out refuse to fly in the mountains in bad weather. It's too unpredictable, and even the most seasoned aviator can quickly lose control of the situation. Sudden downdrafts, icing, varying density altitude—there are many elements to mountain flying that require special knowledge and ability for pilots operating over such rugged terrain. It's unknown how much mountain flying experience Jimmy Conway had by that time, but the fact that his flight plan took him directly through Glacier National Park would suggest he was comfortable enough with the complexities to take his wife's and parents' lives into his hands for the flight to Reno.

Today, especially in good weather, it's hard to stand at the trailhead of Piegan Pass on the edge of Siyeh Bend and imagine the dread the four Conways must have felt as their plane flew through the rain, unable to see the oncoming wall of spruce and fir that runs along the face of these steep mountains. Hikers walking along one of Glacier's most beautiful trails can see Jackson Glacier, Blackfoot Glacier, and many of the towering peaks that inspire so much awe and bliss in the park's millions of visitors. Virtually none of them will have heard of the crash, which has mostly faded into the mist of Glacier's history. As tragic as the story of the Conway plane crash is, it could have been worse. Were it not for the heroic efforts of a young woman who fought through her own pain, grief, and shock to strike out in search of help—barefoot, no less—the headlines from that terrible event in 1985 could have announced three or four dead in a Glacier plane crash, not two.

9

History on Display at Marias Pass Memorial Park

For many Glacier Park visitors, especially first-timers, it would seem that a trip to the park without a drive across Going-to-the-Sun Road isn't worth the trip at all. It is true that only Going-to-the-Sun bisects the park, roughly following the Continental Divide for many of its 50 miles from West Glacier to St. Mary. It would be a mistake, though, to assume that GTSR is the only game in town.

By all means, you should set aside a full day to take in this incredible drive that serves up Glacier's "greatest hits," enjoyable from the comfort of your vehicle or a tour van. But any Glacier veteran who's explored the other areas of the park will tell you it's far from the only worthwhile road. The drive along US 2, which wraps around the southern half of the park between East Glacier and West Glacier, is one of my favorites. Its 58.5 miles are dotted with dozens of interesting natural features, several lodging and dining options, and plenty of historic sites. One of these spots is a curious pullout about 12 miles from East Glacier, where the highway crosses the Continental Divide in the shadow of Little Dog Mountain and Summit Mountain, looming just across the railroad tracks to the north. To the left is the popular Summit Campground, but that's not the thing that catches your eye as you wheel into the generous parking lot. It's hard to miss the Mini-Me Washington Monument standing proudly next to the road, surrounded by several informational kiosks, a few plaques, and a statue of a man in a double-breasted winter coat and watch cap. This is the Marias Pass Memorial Park, a concentrated collection of nods to some of the most important people and events leading to the creation of Glacier National Park.

The 60-foot-tall stone obelisk was erected to honor Theodore Roosevelt, our first conservationist president. We'll get to him in a minute. First, why is this park situated here, rather than a more obvious spot within Glacier Park, or somewhere with more tourist traffic or commercial enterprise? Simple—it is this very place, the summit of Marias Pass on the Continental Divide, that made the tourist traffic possible in the first place. The man who located the pass for the railroad, John F. Stevens, is the subject of the bronze statue with the sporty knit hat and the determined expression on his mustachioed face.

Stevens, an explorer and civil engineer working for the Great Northern Railway, wasn't the very first man to find and traverse Marias Pass any more than Columbus was the first person to set foot on the continent of North America. Indian tribes had used the pass for hundreds of years. Flathead Indians—the Salish and Kootenai—moved across what they called Bear Pass to reach the hunting grounds of the Northern Plains. Later, Blackfeet warriors, led by a female warrior named Running Eagle, traveled over the pass to stage raids on their Flathead counterparts to steal their horses. Eventually the Salish and Kootenai stopped using the pass, their fear of the ruthless Blackfeet forcing them to find other routes to their traditional buffalo hunting grounds.

John F. Stevens had his own reasons to scout Marias Pass, which he did in 1889. The civil engineer was charged with finding the lowest spot in the Northern Rockies to run a rail line that would cross the Divide, enabling the Pacific Extension to connect their northern routes to the West Coast.

Stevens's interest in civil engineering began early, when he was growing up in Maine. After completing his formal education in Farmington, he began moving westward, and worked as an ax wielder and rod-and-instrument man doing surveys for the city of Minneapolis. Over the next several years he worked for a few railroads across western Canada, and gained a reputation as a crack surveyor, specializing in location and construction engineering. While working on the Spokane Falls and Northern Railway in 1889 Stevens caught the eye of Elbridge H. Beckler, chief engineer for the Pacific Extension project of the Great Northern Railway. His experience working in mountainous territory made him a prime candidate to find and report on the Marias Pass, which would be crucial to J. J. Hill's *Empire Builder*, his long-dreamed of Chicago-to-Seattle line.

Reportedly the Marias Pass had been found in the mid-1850s by a trapper, but its location had not been recorded. Stevens set out from Fort Assiniboine with a horse, a driver, and a buckboard loaded with supplies. Simultaneously, another party, led by Charles Frederick Beals Haskell, had set out from Flathead Lake to search for an alternate crossing to the south.

When Stevens reached the Blackfoot Agency near the east border of Glacier Park, he sent this encouraging message to Beckler: "Line from Assiniboine to this point will not exceed 15,000 c.y. [cubic yards of material] per mile. Distance 130 miles, nothing steeper than 1% grade." Smooth sailing, in other words, for the rail line. From that point, the train would have to find a place to cross the crown of the continent, with a minimum of tunnels, trestles, and steep grades. The fabled Marias Pass was the only place they could make it happen.

Snow had already begun falling in the Northern Rockies by the time Stevens left Blackfoot Agency to venture to the Continental Divide. He was accompanied by a Kootenai scout named Koonska. The men made it as far as an area called False Divide, using snowshoes to tramp through several feet of snow. Temperatures were dipping down in the 40-below range, making travel extremely difficult. The Indian guide told Stevens he could go no farther, so they made a small camp at False Summit and got a fire going to keep Koonska warm. Stevens continued in the direction of the purported pass. Once he reached the summit and determined that the course of flowing water was west, he knew he'd found it. He made a fire and tramped around it through the night to keep from freezing to death before he could report the coordinates back to Beckler.

The following spring Beckler visited the site himself, and proclaimed it the ideal place for the railroad to cross the Divide. With an elevation of 5,214 feet, he wrote in his report, it was "lower than any pass I have heard of in the range crossed by the railroad." J. J. Hill considered a few alternate routes, but decided in 1890 that the Marias Pass would be the best and most economical choice, due to its short mileage and low grade. Not a single tunnel would be needed.

After the Marias Pass triumph, Stevens continued west, where he took charge of Great Northern's surveys east of the Cascades. He reported his findings to Beckler, who was now a big fan. "The work is in good hands," Beckler wrote, "and I know of no one more competent than Mr. Stevens." The indefatigable surveyor continued exploring the forests of the Cascades, seeking the prime route for a rail line over that range. His colleague, Charles Haskell, carved "Stevens Pass" into a cedar tree along the proposed route. It's the name that's been used to this day for a pass on Highway 2, and for the popular ski area at the crest. Stevens was present at Marias Pass on July 21, 1925, when his statue was unveiled. The likeness, created by sculptor Gaetano Cecere, looks as comfortable in the wilderness as Stevens was.

The forests that John Stevens spent his career tromping through were considered an inexhaustible resource by early colonial Americans, until the conservation movement came into vogue with Theodore Roosevelt's ascension to the White House. He was a lifelong sportsman who had made numerous hunting trips out west, gaining an appreciation for the vast country and the myriad species it supported. He also saw firsthand the consequences of unchecked exploitation of our natural resources from mining, logging, and agriculture. One memorable trip that had a profound effect on him was a camping trip he joined at the behest of John Muir. The naturalist had invited Roosevelt to camp with him in Yosemite State Park. "It was like lying in a great, solemn cathedral," Roosevelt wrote, "far vaster and more beautiful than any built by the hand of man."

When President William McKinley was assassinated 6 months into his second term in 1901, Vice President Roosevelt, 42, was sworn in as commander-in-chief, the youngest president in US history. The Bull Moose Republican, whose party bosses had held no intentions of supporting a bid for the presidency, wasted little time in promoting his conservationist agenda. "We have become great because of the lavish use of our resources. But the time has come to inquire seriously what will happen when our forests are gone, when the coal, the iron, the oil, and the gas are exhausted, when the soils have still further impoverished and washed into the streams, polluting the rivers, denuding the fields and obstructing navigation," he wrote. "The forest problem is in many ways the most vital internal problem of the United States."

A childhood passion for birds and taxidermy spurred a revulsion to the fashion trend featuring the use of feathers of exotic birds, which resulted in many species being hunted to the edge of extinction. Roosevelt decided to create the first national bird sanctuary. The erstwhile leader of the Rough Riders in the Spanish-American War had little patience for the political wrangling and circuitous process such an achievement would require, so he asked his attorney general, Philander C. Knox, if there were any reason he couldn't use executive privilege to make it happen. Knox couldn't come up with one, and the Pelican Island federal bird reservation was designated along Florida's east coast for the protection of nesting birds. It's now a national wildlife refuge (NWR), part of the Everglades Headwaters National Wildlife Refuge Complex. The National Wildlife Refuge System is now managed by the US Fish and Wildlife Service, and there is at least one NWR in every state.

Roosevelt was just getting warmed up. By the time he finished his second term in 1908, he had established 150 national forests, fifty-one federal bird reserves, and four national game preserves. With the required congressional approval he created five national parks. Using his executive authority, he established eighteen national monuments, including Devil's Tower in Wyoming, Lewis and Clark Caverns in Montana, the Grand Canyon in Arizona, and Lassen Volcanic National Park in California.

It's hard to overstate the impact Roosevelt had during his 7 years in the White House. He received a Nobel Peace Prize for shepherding peace talks in the Russo-Japanese war. He gave away his niece, Eleanor, at her wedding to Franklin Delano Roosevelt (his fifth cousin). When he once declined to shoot a black bear that had been tied up and held for his arrival (a situation that certain Montana public servants find no compunction with), a cartoon depicting the situation gave birth to the teddy bear. He was on hand to lay the cornerstone of the Roosevelt Arch at the original entrance to Yellowstone National Park. He signed into law the Antiquities Act in 1906, giving the president the power to designate national monuments on public lands, protecting the land and any artifacts it may contain. He published thirty-five books and wrote 150,000 letters.

One of his biggest accomplishments has little to do with conservation. Picking up the pieces of earlier failed efforts by the French and others, Roosevelt oversaw the construction of the Panama Canal, which provided a crucial shipping lane between the Atlantic and Pacific Oceans by cutting through a 50-mile bottleneck in a Colombian isthmus. Roosevelt's first choice for chief engineer to head up the project, John Findley Wallace, failed spectacularly. He was unprepared and disorganized, and his go at the Canal ended much like the abandoned French endeavor—workers were stymied by rains, insects, floods, snakes, heat, and disease. Fortunately, a capable replacement engineer was located and persuaded to head up the Panama Canal project.

His name was John F. Stevens.

Stevens left a successful position at a Chicago railway company to become chief engineer for the Panama Canal. As he had shown throughout his railroad career, he knew only one direction: forward. Stevens went to the newly created nation of Panama and cleaned house. Swamps were drained. Roads and towns were built. Plumbing was installed. He built a dam on the Chagres River to create Gatun Lake, which was the main component of a "lake and lock" design that had been effective on the Great Lakes. Stevens left the project in 1907, and it was well on its way to success. The Panama Canal opened for business in 1914.

History has a way of revealing connections as we dig in, and the Marias Pass Memorial Park brings Teddy Roosevelt and James Stevens together again, long after their paths crossed more than 100 years ago. We may have never been moved into finding that connection had this little monument park not existed, and the man partly responsible for that is also commemorated here, with a plaque inset on a large native boulder.

William Morrison came west after the Civil War. A Massachusetts native, he had been working for an engineering firm in Connecticut, making boilers. Somewhere along the line he caught the railroad bug and

The Marias Summit is the lowest pass in the Northern Rockies, the best place the Great Northern could run their line from St. Paul to Seattle. Surveyor John F. Stevens is immortalized (alongside Theodore Roosevelt and "Slippery" Bill Morrison) at the Marias monument park at the summit. AUTHOR PHOTO

worked as a powderman for a Canadian railway, and after that he spent most of his life roaming the mountains of the Northern Rockies, scraping out a living as a trapper and prospector. He'd secured "squatter's rights" on a 160-acre parcel near Summit, and his timing couldn't have been better.

When the Great Northern began work on the Pacific Extension in 1890, an advance man named Eugene McCarthy was sent out to scout the area for lumber used to make railroad ties. In an attack of naked opportunism, McCarthy filed a declaration of occupancy on the small bit of available land, and the town of McCarthyville was established. Situated near Bear Creek, the town sustained as many as 1,000 railroad workers during construction of the railway over Marias Pass. As was the case with many boomtowns, it was a hard little settlement that bristled with violence and sin. "Slippery" Bill Morrison was already well established by then, and his 16-by-20-foot shack was transformed into a saloon and gambling hall. The mountain man had a reputation as a prairie philosopher with a flowery vocabulary and a sharp mind, and would share his musings at length with anyone who would listen, sometimes as he skillfully separated them from their money in a card game. It was after a successful night of gambling when he received his nickname. There are several versions of the story, but they all involve him winning big at the poker table. Fearing that he would get robbed along the dark trail on the way back to his shack, he supposedly hid the bulk of his winnings inside the empty spike keg he'd been seated on all night, returning the next day to retrieve his money.

Slippery Bill became a local legend, and he hung on in the area long after McCarthyville dried up a mere 2 years after it was established. Morrison's saloon was the last business operating in town, and he was the sole member of McCarthyville's Chamber of Commerce. He worked as a conductor for the Great Northern, but after his locomotive collided with a work train in 1902, he disappeared before an investigation into the wreck could be completed.

He did a stint with the Forest Service after the McCarthyville era, patrolling the Middle Fork drainage of his beloved Great Bear Wilderness. In 1931 Morrison donated his parcel of land to the federal government so they could construct the Roosevelt Memorial on the border between the Great Bear Wilderness and the Flathead National Forest. He died the following year, leaving no known family, and was buried in Conrad Memorial Cemetery in Kalispell.

The president, the engineer, and the prairie philosopher are represented here today, along the road that winds around the southern edge of one of America's most popular national parks. It's worth a stop here at the summit of Marias Pass, to soak in a little history and take in some of the natural beauty that made it so important to provide access to this rugged corner of the Northern Rockies.

10

Growing Up Glacier

DESPITE HAVING A RATHER ORDINARY NAME, BOB JONES HAS LED AN extraordinary life. Sitting back in a brown leather armchair in the living room of his 110-year-old house in downtown Missoula, the bespectacled, white-haired ex-newspaperman shares some of his favorite memories as his fluffy dog Bear (who actually looks more like a little red panda) keeps poking his snout into Bob's pant leg. The 15-year-old dog is deaf as a brick and nearly blind, but, dang it, Bob is in his chair.

As a constant stream of trains rumble through the railyard that's literally across the street, Jones talks about his career as a newspaper editor who had to work his way out from beneath the shadow of his father, Deane Sterne Jones, a former *Missoulian* editor who is a legend in these parts. Bob had studied engineering in college, but veered into newspapers "without taking a single class in J-school," he says. He was a good writer, he adds, but was kicked upstairs into management early on. His career took him to Davenport, Iowa, back to his hometown of Butte, then to Astoria, Oregon, where he was managing a family-owned newspaper when he retired in 1990. He moved to Missoula shortly after that, and the lifelong railroad buff realized a dream by buying one of the oldest houses in Missoula—so close to the farmers' market that he can smell the espresso and fresh-baked scones in the summer.

His tidy bachelor pad is decorated with dozens of photos, artifacts, and memorabilia that reflect his various passions, from the black-and-white photo of the Johnson Flying Service DC-3 on his living room wall to the bookshelf in his "Montana Room" lined with titles by Montana authors Ivan Doig and A. B. Guthrie, to the small plaque on an end

In Essex, halfway between East Glacier and West Glacier on US 2, the Izaak Walton Inn is still a popular destination in winter and summer. The annex on the right is the approximate location of the Mercantile, which Bob Jones's grandparents ran for 40 years. AUTHOR PHOTO

table that reads "I am silently correcting your grammar." Also scattered throughout the home are images of the Izaak Walton Inn and logos from the Great Northern Railway, clues to perhaps the most important piece of Jones's story.

As he recalls some choice memories from a lifetime of experience, Jones occasionally reaches a finger up under his glasses to smear away a tear. After a while I realize that the only time he does this is when he's talking about Essex, Montana. For about 15 years of his young life, from grade school on into college, he spent all summer, every summer with his grandparents in the little railroad hamlet along US 2, roughly halfway between East Glacier and West Glacier. "It gets me," he says. "It's where I live. It's truly in my heart—it's a part of me."

The Great Northern Railway was created from the bones of four struggling midwestern railroad companies in 1878 when James J. Hill went in with three other investors to build a mainline that would run from St. Paul,

Minnesota, to Seattle, Washington. When Hill challenged his locating engineer, John F. Stevens, to find the lowest-altitude route through the Rocky Mountains, Stevens chose Marias Pass on the southeast border of what would become Glacier National Park. At 5,215 feet, it is the highest point on the entire rail line. The route drops in a steep grade westward from there, running 14 miles west to Bear Creek where it flattens out to follow the Middle Fork of the Flathead River.

The settlement of Walton was born there when the tracks came through in 1890. A single eastbound steam engine couldn't pull more than a few cars up that grade in the best of times, and the heavy snow and severe winters of northern Montana made it particularly challenging. Helper crews were stationed at Walton to hitch extra locomotives to the line, enabling the freighters to make it up the pass to Summit. An enclosed roundhouse with a turntable was built, along with water tanks, coal chutes, sand houses, a telegraph station—all the necessary facilities to power the steamers up the Great Northern's steepest climb.

The area of Walton was homesteaded by Tom Shields, and by the turn of the 20th century it boasted a post office and a saloon. The workers were housed in ramshackle section houses, and a tiny community began to grow around the station. In 1907 the railroad yard was expanded with a Y-track, a portable depot, and a boardinghouse. Additional coal chutes were added, and another spout was put onto the water tank. The roundhouse was removed, no longer necessary when a double track from Walton to Summit was completed in 1910. One year prior to that, the C.H. Shaver News Company opened a lunchroom and hotel, planting the seeds of what would become the Izaak Walton Inn.

By 1915 the hamlet of Walton boasted a pool hall, a barbershop, and a couple of modest lunch counters known as beaneries. Small enterprises were built, sold, bought, burned down, and rebuilt as the community took root. Somewhere along the line, the community around the railroad yard was renamed Essex. The town's general store was leased from the Kalispell Mercantile Company until 1917, when a young man moved from Kalispell to Essex to buy the store. Ray Withrow would run the Essex Mercantile until 1951, and his wife, Maude, was the postmistress at the post office located inside the store. The couple had a daughter, Elizabeth, who would grow up to marry a man named Deane Jones. The Withrows were an integral part of Essex's early history, instrumental in the town's development, building houses and stores to serve the community and its residents.

"I got to ride in the cab of a steamer from Essex to Marias Pass and back," said Bob, recalling an early adventure from his time with the Withrows. "Those engineers lived across the street from my grandparents, and we Essex kids would go over while they were sitting on the siding waiting for a train to come up. They would let us come up on the cabs of the engine and watch the firemen shoveling coal." He and his buddies were fascinated with the railroad men. He spent a lot of his summertime roaming around town and watching the gandy dancers, track walkers, section men, hog heads, and other railmen working for the Great Northern. His great-grandfather had been a railroad man, and it was already in his blood. Essex set the hook deep.

Bob's family was living in Missoula, and he started making his annual journey to Essex at the age of five, right around the time the Izaak Walton Inn was opened in 1939. By then the rail line had become known as the Empire Builder, the ultimate legacy of Great Northern's president J.J. Hill. Passengers rode the rails from as far east as Chicago to visit Glacier National Park, with stops near the park entrances at East Glacier and West Glacier. The Izaak Walton was built ostensibly to house railroad workers after a fire had destroyed the Red Beanery, depriving the men of an eating establishment and living quarters. The Great Northern Railway didn't just build the Inn, though, they overbuilt it. A subsidiary of their company constructed the grand, three-story hotel which opened in November, offering twenty-nine bedrooms, ten bathrooms, a comfortable lobby, dining room, even a general store on the main floor. It also had a restaurant.

The railroad, which had financed and operated the grand lodges and hotels within the national park and owned many of its concessions, envisioned a southern entrance to Glacier via the Park Creek drainage, making Essex its gateway. The Inn was built with tourism in mind. US involvement in World War II put an abrupt end to the development plans, and interest in this southern entrance to Glacier was never rekindled. What remains is the still-charming Izaak Walton Inn, named after the patron saint of fishermen who authored *The Compleat Angler* in 1653. The Inn is considered by many to be a hidden jewel of the park, just off the beaten path.

Except for the brief but glorious summers in northern Montana, snow was a constant challenge for the Great Northern. A typical winter in the early 20th century would bring more than 20 feet of snow to the area. Some years, there's a bit more. In 1972 Essex received 526 inches, enough to bury your average Marriott. To help protect the tracks, miles of snow sheds were built along several sections that ran along steep banks where avalanches were a regular occurrence. Crews swelled the population of Essex through the winter as the men worked constantly to keep the tracks clear, but now and then a slide would bury the rails and they would have to wait for a steam engine with a rotary snowplow to be sent out to blast its way through. One year, when Jones was in fifth grade, he was able to experience his beloved Essex in the winter, thanks to a post-war coal workers strike.

"Before Christmas my grandmother happened to come to Missoula, and I rode the bus back up there with her," he recalls. "It was 1946. The coal miners couldn't strike during World War II. As soon as the war was over, they went on strike. That's why all the coal burning schools in Missoula were closed. I got to spend the better part of a month up there. I got to go to school in that one room schoolhouse. Got to be in the Christmas play. Played my flute—I only knew one song," he laughs. It was a typically harsh winter, and Jones remembers vividly how much snow there was. "My grandmother's garden fence was 5 feet high, and the snow came up to the top. My friend Buddy Beale and I shoveled from my grandparents' house clear to the store. It was about 125 yards." It took the boys a few days, and the banks of the path were well over their heads, but they knew the Withrows had to get to the General Store and its post office. Essex, as it had for decades, was counting on them.

Nowadays the Izaak Walton Inn is a mecca for cross-country skiers, snowshoers, and other outdoors enthusiasts who think there's no such thing as too much snow. The Inn maintains about 33 kilometers of groomed trails through the Great Bear Wilderness, and they offer rooms, meals, and equipment rentals to the adventurous visitors who arrive by auto or on the Amtrak. They even have an annual snow festival and ski rodeo. As far as Bob Jones is concerned, though, he'll take Essex in the summer, thank you very much.

As he got into high school and even college, he would bring friends, roommates, even the occasional girlfriend up to spend the summer with him, exploring the Great Bear Wilderness or hiking for miles into the park. While he had few encounters with other people on these adventures, he did see a fair amount of wildlife. He found the mountain goats especially intriguing.

"That was our entertainment," he says about watching the sure-footed beasts gather at dusk near the Goat Lick, years before a parking lot and observation deck were installed there. "My grandparents would take us in their '41 Chrysler and go down to the goat lick. They pulled alongside the highway up above, and they'd sit there with their lights off. There was a bank next to the road probably as high as this ceiling on the upside. And you would sit there and watch and the goats would start lining up on that bank, and it was steep coming down to that main road. Some goat would give the signal and off they would come, across the road right in front of the cars. You'd turn your headlights on and spotlight them. And they would go down that bank to the lick, which was a precipice. It was vertical, and they would just go on it like it was flatland! It was unbelievable."

As a teen, he and his friends would take their fishing gear down to the river to catch bull trout. They were still plentiful, a long way from being listed as endangered. To get to their spot, they'd have to walk across a trestle, like the boys in a famous scene from *Stand By Me*. "And that trestle was really high and had no railing," Jones recalls, his eyes growing wide behind his wire-rim specs. "We were walking the ties and hoping to hell a train didn't come. Then we'd get to the other side and we'd go down and fish the river along the goat lick and we'd go all the way around that corner and we'd be among the goats."

It was during one of these fishing jaunts when he wasn't just among the goats, but decided to imitate them. "We went out on the highway up above, fished all the way around the goat lick and then we climbed up the face on the other side of the blue lick. It was hand over hand. That's the only time I've been scared, I think. I looked back down and that river was a long way below me."

Who among us is lucky enough to have gathered a full childhood's worth of memories exploring the unspoiled wilderness at the south end of Glacier National Park? It was a different world then, and it's the rare youngster who can enjoy the same freedom that Bob Jones had every summer in Essex. His grandfather had horses, so Bob learned to ride. He fished and explored all over the park, enjoying moonlight cycling rides to Logan Pass and wading his horse through fast-running glacial streams. He watched Blackfeet Indians from the nearby reservation town of Browning gather at the Inn to perform a tribal dance. He remembers the horror of watching Pauline, the longtime Essex telegrapher, trying desperately to wave down an eastbound track walker as he was riding a hand cart out of sight, pumping away, unaware that a freight was bearing down on him from behind. (Jones learned afterward that the guy had pulled his cart off the track just in time.)

He still gets back to Essex every 2 or 3 years, when his family gathers somewhere in the Flathead Valley. He'll slip away by himself and take a back road he knows of to avoid the traffic on Highway 2, cross the tracks, and drive right into his past. He's had a pilot friend fly him over the area, giving him the bird's-eye view of all the mountain lakes, forested valleys, icy mountain streams, and iron train tracks that he walked as a kid. Bob Jones, grandson of Ray and Maude Withrow, still visits Essex every day in the blissful memories that cause his eyes to glisten.

"Every ounce of me knows where I belong," he says. "I can't think of a single thing I could replace it with."

Yellowstone National Park

11

Welcome to Yellowstone!

CODY, WYOMING

TEDDY ROOSEVELT CALLED THE ROAD FROM CODY, WYOMING, TO YEL-lowstone's East Entrance "the most scenic 50 miles in America." That's hard to argue with, especially in the fall when the leaves are popping with color. Cody itself is a pretty cool little town, not just a tourist-dependent village that's grown up around a park entrance. If you've never been through Cody and are wondering what the town is all about, the answer is only three words: Buffalo. Bill. Cody. The Wild West showman founded the town in 1896, impressed with its rich soil and farming potential, as well as its beautiful rivers and mountains that afforded not just spectacular scenery but plenty of hunting opportunities. Its proximity to Yellowstone, 52 miles away, was a plus. Today its population is right around 10,000, and the town offers a host of attractions from art museums to a nightly rodeo in the summer. Cody also boasts dozens of excellent restaurants and gift shops, as well as a wide variety of accommodations, from mom-and-pop motels to hifalutin guest ranches.

William F. Cody is widely represented throughout the area, from Buf-falo Bill State Park, which surrounds the reservoir created by the Buffalo Bill Dam, to Buffalo Bill's Antler Inn and Buffalo Bill Harley-Davidson, to name just a few. By far the most impressive monument to his legacy is the Buffalo Bill Center of the West, a sprawling, state-of-the-art com-plex of museums and attractions that not only tell the story of the gun-twirling legend, but ambitiously tackle the history of the region, from its aboriginal inhabitants to the history of firearms in the West, the wonders of the area's natural world, and more. Its five separate museums simply

The Irma Hotel, with its ornately carved, cherry wood bar, is one of the many Buffalo Bill–themed attractions in Cody, the gateway to Yellowstone's East Entrance. A visit to the Buffalo Bill Center of the West is highly recommended. AUTHOR PHOTO

can't be taken in in a single day, so the Center's entrance pass is good for 2 days. The Buffalo Bill Museum tells in great detail the story of the soldier and buffalo hunter who became the most famous man in the world. The Cody Firearms Museum is nirvana for gun history buffs, featuring more than 10,000 items neatly organized and beautifully displayed.

One of the most intriguing features of the Center is the Scout Saddle Company, which opened in 2020. It's a working saddle maker tucked into a small shop at the mouth of the firearms museum. Mark Barcus and Lori Barcus are experienced saddlers who ply their craft in full view of the museum's somewhat bemused visitors who wander past their front counter, and their 1920s-style shop also displays some of the history of saddle making. They started with an apprenticeship program from their saddlery in Lusk, and their training methods are an extension of their philosophy. "The main objective is getting people to care about quality," said Mark. "There comes a point when you have to start buying quality or you won't be able to buy anything." They bring their prodigious leatherworking skills not only to saddles, but belts, chaps, pocketknife cases, journal covers, saddlebags, and other items, many of which are for sale in the museum's online store.

Another of Cody's must-see attractions is the Irma Hotel and Restaurant. Opened in 1902, the hotel was built by Buffalo Bill and named for his daughter. The dining room is a visual feast, and you'll be transported back in time to the dusty Wild West as you dine on a thick bison steak while admiring the 14-foot-tall, cherry wood back bar. Its two massive, arched mirrors are surrounded by intricately carved fleur-de-lis, sinewy vines, and a geometric motif. It's all topped off with a foot-high carving of—what else?—a buffalo head.

WEST YELLOWSTONE, MONTANA

With approaches from several directions, West Yellowstone is by far the park's busiest entrance, and its sidewalks are crowded with throngs of people throughout the summer. Its commercial district makes no bones about why the town is there. You'll find a variety of gift shops, souvenir stores, T-shirt shops—the typical enterprises that exist near the main entrances of most national parks. It's all part of the upbeat attitude of West Yellowstone. They know you're there to have fun, and they work hard to facilitate a good time. You'll hear dozens of languages among the chatter and laughter—perhaps more than its other gateway communities, West Yellowstone caters to international visitors.

There's the usual assortment of wildlife art galleries, watering holes, restaurants, coffee shops, gift shops, and a couple of small grocery stores. If you are hankering for a bison burger, I would highly recommend the Slippery Otter Pub. It's also a popular bar that also offers a ton of local beers. Bullwinkle's Saloon is the preferred hangout for locals and park employees, and also features a liquor store.

The existence of a zipline in town might signal "tourist trap" to travelers, but it's become such a ubiquitous feature in many vacation destinations that it's just part of the landscape. But don't write off West Yellowstone as just a place to gas up and snag an "I Touched a Buffalo" T-shirt on your way into the park—you'll be missing out on a couple of major attractions.

First, the Grizzly and Wolf Discovery Center is a world-class, non-profit facility that offers a real-life glimpse into the lives of these amazing animals. The Center provides a home for wolves and grizzlies that aren't suited to make it in the wild, and they've created a habitat for them that allows visitors to watch the animals interact with each other and put on a show just being themselves. The Center also provides some painless education, through demonstrations and presentations, like testing bear-proof garbage cans. The adjacent IMAX theater features videos about the plights of these threatened species, and it's a great way to get yourself (and the kids) into the spirit of roaming the park, hoping to score a sighting of these beautiful and complex beasts.

Another important lead-in to the park is the Museum of the Yellowstone, part of the West Yellowstone Historic Center. It's housed in a sprawling brick building right across the street from the visitor center, just about the last buildings you'll see before turning onto the road to the entrance. Chances are there's a Historic Yellow Bus parked out front—you can't miss it. And you shouldn't! It's a top-notch collection of displays featuring all manner of park memorabilia, from a fully restored, horse-drawn touring coach to the most famous grizzly bear in the park (don't worry, he's stuffed), Ol' Snaggletooth. There's also a fascinating display about the Beanery Queens, adventuresome women who traveled to Yellowstone seeking jobs with the Northern Pacific as servers in the railroad-owned hotels and restaurants. You can even watch a movie about the tragedy of the 1959 earthquake (you can't avoid hearing it mentioned in the park), which caused the top of a hillside in the Madison Canyon to shear off and slide downhill onto a campground, killing twenty-eight people. The landslide plugged the Madison River, creating Earthquake Lake.

GARDINER, MONTANA
The North Entrance at Gardiner is the original gateway to Yellowstone, predating even the bare-fisted little town of Cinnabar, the Northern Pacific terminus where tourists would catch a stagecoach to take them

into the park. Straddling the Yellowstone River, Gardiner is an excellent jumping off spot for the adventure-minded. The tight-knit community has about 900 year-round residents but swells to several thousand during the summer season. Most of the hospitality-oriented businesses close their doors for the winter by mid-October, but the park entrance is open year-round, allowing access across the northern tier of Yellowstone to the northeast entrance.

In the summer the road down the Paradise Valley is crowded with passenger vans, trailers, and brightly painted school buses all stacked high with plump river rafts and colorful kayaks. The main streets in town are lined with storefront businesses where you can arrange a whitewater trip, a guided tour in the park, hunting and fishing expeditions, and any number of climbing and backpacking excursions. As such, seasonal employees tend toward the young, fit, and fearless. "It's easy to get a job here," one 30-ish coffee shop barista told me. "You can make a lot of money in a season." In the tried-and-true ski bum tradition, most seasonal workers cater to the constant mass of humanity churning through Gardiner on their way to the park, and on their off-hours can be found hiking deep in the wilderness, free climbing some of southwest Montana's dazzling cliffs, or shooting the rapids in the river. There is also a zipline, of course, for those who like their thrills a little more contained.

Gardiner (the town is spelled with an "i" but the river is not) is also ground zero for Yellowstone history. The Heritage and Research Center, located a stone's throw from the Gateway Arch, opened in 2005. It's the clearinghouse for all things Yellowstone. Its archives of Yellowstone history are unparalleled, and available for research purposes to the public. This isn't some dusty warehouse of historic photos (although they have more than 13,000 in their collection), but a comprehensive archive of the area's history, including collections of Native American and European-American cultural artifacts. Manuscripts, journals, documents, records, artworks—this is the definitive resource for the history of Yellowstone, both man-made and natural.

Like all the gateway communities, Gardiner is hopping all summer long. Accommodations are plentiful, but most are booked well in advance. Some of the better restaurants are Wonderland Cafe, the rowdy

Iron Horse Bar & Grill perched on the edge of the river in the shadow of the Yellowstone River Bridge, and the Grizzly Grille at the north edge of town. My favorite place in town for breakfast is the Tumbleweed Bookstore and Cafe. It's low-key, funky, and offers excellent food and coffee. Oh, and books!

[*Note:* After this section was written, Yellowstone suffered the worst flood in its history, causing such damage to the road between Gardiner and Mammoth that it will take years to replace and repair. The old Gardiner Road, a single-lane alternate route that had been used only by park staff and employees, was beefed up and expanded in 2022 in time to carry winter traffic between Gardiner and Mammoth Hot Springs. The National Park Service continues to work with the Federal Highway Administration to improve the 4-mile road to a level where it can carry normal summer traffic, hopefully in time for the 2023 summer season. For up-to-the-minute information regarding road closures and construction status, visit nps.gov/yell/planyourvisit/parkroads.htm.]

COOKE CITY/SILVER GATE, MONTANA

While the tiny hamlet of Silver Gate is 1 mile from the check-in booth at the park's Northeast Entrance, Cooke City, 3 miles up the road, is considered the area's gateway community. Some would take that even farther, pinning that designation on Red Lodge, a former mining town 64 miles from Cooke City, with the serpentine Beartooth Scenic Highway in between. Although Red Lodge is a bona fide tourist destination with its own ski hill nearby, it's not really what I'd consider adjacent to Yellowstone, even though its food-gas-lodging opportunities far outstrip those of Cooke City. Let's call it the gateway to the road to the gateway to Yellowstone Park.

Cooke City was established 2 years before Red Lodge in 1882, when the Crow Reservation border was opened to settlement and exploration by prospectors, who had discovered gold there in 1870. It's an amiable, sleepy little town where the locals are friendly and patient with travelers, and it makes for a great pit stop for food, gas, and some sightseeing. Located near Colter Pass, Cooke City sits alongside Soda Butte Creek at an elevation of about 7,580 feet. Makes sense when you learn it's within sight of Granite Peak, at 12,799 feet the highest point in Montana.

Although it's the smallest of Yellowstone's gateway communities, there's a lot to do in Cooke City besides trying to catch your breath. You can also catch trout. There's fly fishing in Slough Creek, the aforementioned Soda Butte Creek, or any of the nearby crystal-clear alpine lakes. Backcountry horseback rides are available through a couple of different outfitters. If you prefer two legs to four, you can enjoy a hike to the nearby Clay Butte Lookout Tower, and see just how the firewatchers did their thing through the 20th century. Snowmobiling is popular in this area, and you will always see the summertime counterparts, motorcycles, parked in long rows on Cooke City's Main Street.

Several lodges, small motels, and Vrbos line the roadways and are scattered through the woods around town. The Yellowstone Trading Post and the Cooke City General Store are great places to stock up on provisions and score some souvenirs or locally made artwork and jewelry. Pilot's Perk is an excellent spot for coffee and pastry in the morning, and the Beartooth Cafe and Miner's Saloon are great choices for dinner and a libation.

History buffs can enjoy a diamond in the rough at the Cooke City Museum. It's a surprising amount of history packed into a stone and wood building on the main road. Along with the highly detailed displays and dioramas inside, the museum offers a "backyard tour" of a collection of vintage cabins, outbuildings, and mining equipment. See for yourself what life was like for a 19th-century miner living without electricity, running water, or reliable Wi-Fi.

JACKSON, WYOMING

First off, let's do a bit of geographical housekeeping. Jackson Hole and Jackson are not synonymous. Jackson Hole is the alpine valley that lies between the Gros Ventre (say "grow von") Range and the Grand Tetons. The town of Jackson is near the center of the valley, tucked into the foothills along Snow King Mountain. It's also a gateway to nearby Teton National Park, so Yellowstone "double dippers" who post up in Jackson can easily access those two parks.

The seat of Teton County and home to about 10,000 full-time residents, Jackson is a resort town with an old western feel and year-round hospitality. It's a busy wintertime destination with three major ski resorts nearby. Four airlines serve its airport, and the runways are frequently clogged with private jets carrying the über-rich. Jackson Hole has long been known as a popular playground and third vacation home spot for the class of travelers who light their foot-long Cohibas with $100 bills and wouldn't know a self-checkout if it bit them in the butt. The sidewalks of Jackson might rival the throngs of Manhattan in the summer, but you won't see much of the glitterati, the 1-percenters whose median home price is $16 million. The wealthy residents live out of town, their compounds hidden in the national forest, away from the prying eyes of the bourgeoisie. As you can imagine, this is a spendy town. Think Vail, Aspen, Santa Fe . . . that's one face of Jackson.

The other Jackson is the gateway to Yellowstone, 57 miles to the north, just beyond Jackson Lake. While it's the most pricey of all the Montana/Wyoming national park–adjacent communities, they offer the highest level of outdoor adventures and tourist amenities. Their world-class restaurants serve gourmet meals, and the Million Dollar Cowboy Bar, with saddles for barstools, is a must-see. Speaking of giggle soup, for those who imbibe there are three great breweries in Jackson, and Wyoming is also home of the drive-through liquor store. Yes, I said drive-through liquor store.

Being situated in the Bridger-Teton National Forest, Jackson Hole's environs are lousy with wildlife. Moose, bears, bison, elk, all the biggies call this valley home. Wildlife fans will have plenty to check out while staying in Jackson. Before you head out on an adventure, though, make sure to stop at the town square and get some photos of you and your people standing beneath the elk antler arches. There are four of them, one at each corner of the square, and they are impressive. Crafted of hundreds of tightly entangled elk antlers, the arches are big enough that five people can stand abreast under them. The sheds are gathered from the nearby National Elk Refuge, which supports and protects the largest herd of elk in North America. Handily located on the way between Jackson and Grand Teton National Park, it's adjacent to another fabulous feature, the

National Museum of Wildlife Art. The museum offers a different take—it's a collection of art that features animals, arranged to represent the various movements and artists through the history of art. Check out the Georgia O'Keeffe and a couple of Andy Warhols while you're there.

Another bonus to entering Yellowstone from the south is access to the remote, southwest corner of the park. You can get on Grassy Lake Road at Flagg Ranch, a couple miles from the park's South Entrance, and it will take you to Ashton, Idaho. From there take Cave Falls Road to the ranger station, where you can park and explore the Bechler Meadows area, which is loaded with eye-popping waterfalls and excellent trails, including one that leads all the way to Old Faithful. More than anywhere in the park, Bechler is where you will be thankful for bug spray.

Grand Loop Road: Yellowstone's Asphalt Heart

It could be said that the construction of Yellowstone's Grand Loop Road began during the Paleo-Indian period some 13,000 years ago, when an Indigenous hunter tracked a deer along a game trail through the dense forests of the upper Yellowstone River. Maybe that's a stretch, although the recent discovery of an Anzick boy's burial site on the Shields River near Livingston shows that the area was inhabited by members of a Clovis culture at that time. Still, it's no secret that many human pathways originated along the game trails worn by animals who, like the humans who hunted them, moved frequently through the Yellowstone plateau after the last ice age, following the seasons to find the areas that offered the most available food, shelter, and resources. Pathways become trails, trails sometimes become roads. Roads connect to form a system, making it easier and quicker for travelers to get from point A to point B, whether they're moving their families out of the mountains to their tribal hunting grounds, or trying to get to Canyon Village before the showers close.

Thanks to the pragmatic design of the Grand Loop Road, Yellowstone Park is able to connect most of its biggest attractions and important wildlife corridors from the Grand Canyon to Old Faithful, from the bison herds in Lamar Valley to the stately travertine terraces of Mammoth Hot Springs. It is indeed a grand road, and it has seen myriad improvements and changes to its 142 miles, across 120 years of existence.

Generally, Hiram H. Chittenden is credited with the overall design and construction of much of the modern version of the Grand Loop

Road, and the prolific engineer certainly deserves the recognition. But much like the unseen trusses that support many of the beautiful bridges that cross Yellowstone's rivers and creeks, a handful of visionary leaders provided the foundation for Chittenden to put his lasting stamp on the road that makes it all possible.

Nathaniel P. Langford, Yellowstone's first superintendent, saw the need right away for a network of connecting roads. Eager to get the lay of the land, he joined the US Geological Survey led by Ferdinand Hayden in 1872, Yellowstone National Park's inaugural year. The expedition was tasked with exploring and surveying not only the environs of the Upper Yellowstone, but also the Teton Range to the south. Langford had already been through much of Yellowstone in 1870 with the Washburn-Langford-Doane expedition, and the Hayden party returned with an astonishing amount of images and data. They had trekked, measured, sketched, and mapped 9,000 square miles of Yellowstone, by far the most extensive survey of the Upper Yellowstone yet.

For the next 5 years Langford would lobby Congress to appropriate the funds to improve and maintain the park, which would include designing and building a system of roads capable of conveying the wagon loads of tourists that were sure to arrive. The Northern Pacific Railroad (NPRR) was counting on it. The railroad was heavily invested in running spurs off its main line to deliver passengers from the east who couldn't wait to explore the incredible landscape they'd been reading about. [And sometimes not reading about. When expeditioner Charles Cook sent his description of the Upper Yellowstone to *Lippincott's Magazine* in 1869, they purportedly responded with a curt, "Thank you but we do not print fiction."] Up to that point the park hadn't seen more than 500 visitors in a year, mostly because the rail bound hordes failed to materialize. The NPRR, which was heavily tied up in securing leases within Yellowstone for early tourism concessions such as hotels, transportation, and tours, was taking a financial beating and its terminus remained at Bismarck, North Dakota, for several years.

At that time there were only two entrances. The towns of Cody and Jackson didn't even exist yet, and the miners' camp of Cooke City was at the end of a there-and-back road; it wouldn't be connected to Red Lodge and beyond until the 1930s.

In 1873 two roads were built that provided access to the park from the Montana and Idaho territories. A toll road was hacked out of the hillsides and riverbanks between Bozeman and Gardiner, a rutted, narrow track full of hairpin turns that routinely sent wagons tumbling into the Yellowstone River. The Virginia City and National Park Free Road, built by Gilman Sawtell, a hotelier from Henry's Lake, Idaho, connected to the West Entrance and ran 93 miles all the way to the Lower Geyser Basin via the Madison River Canyon. These roads were crucial in giving tourists access to the park, but they were also vital in completing the route between Mammoth and Virginia City that would also allow better access for Army cavalry units moving into the area from Bozeman and Helena to help protect settlers and tourists from Indian aggression.

Now, how to get people to the major points of interest once they were in the park? Langford's successor Philetus W. Norris finally secured $10,000 from Congress in 1878 (that is, when he wasn't busy running around naming things after himself) and the following year he and his team of twenty men set about repairing and improving the existing road between Mammoth and the Lower Geyser Basin, sometimes cutting a new route that would provide less of a grade. The original wagon trails were sometimes built straight up one side of a hill and down the other, with no regard to the effort of the horse teams that pulled the wagons, or the calamity the steep roads would cause. Occasionally the tailboard would fall off a wagon rattling up a steep, badly rutted road, emptying all the contents—including the passengers—onto the dusty hardpan.

The crews successfully negotiated Snow Pass and Kingman Pass, made it through the Golden Gate Canyon, and churned along past Bunsen Peak into the flatter terrain around Swan Lake. Then the steam-spewing flanks of Roaring Mountain came into sight, and beyond that, Obsidian Cliff. The road builders were flummoxed by the "glass mountain," but Norris eventually prevailed by having them build fires to heat up the cliff walls and then dousing them with cold water from a nearby stream, causing the obsidian to crack. The men would then set upon it with picks and axes. Most of them suffered cuts on their faces and arms, as the edge of flaked obsidian is sharper than a steel razor. Remember, this was pre-OSHA. The glittering, black rubble was mixed into aggregate years later when the road was paved.

Within 30 days, the 60 miles of Norris's road was complete. Amazingly, he had done so with only twenty men. Granted, it was little more than a crude wagon track full of boulders and stumps, but with little in the way of funding or time—the Indians were coming!—it was quite a feat.

Yellowstone is laced with rivers and streams and nearly 300 waterfalls. These would require dozens of bridges to facilitate the roads and protect the riparian areas from the damage of repeated fording. Several rudimentary bridges had been cobbled together to complete the Norris road, and it would fall to later engineers to improve them.

One of the first bridges to receive an upgrade was Baronett's Bridge, believed to be the first bridge constructed in Yellowstone. It was built over the Yellowstone River near Tower Junction in 1871 by Collins "Yellowstone Jack" Baronett, on the road between Mammoth and Cooke City. In 1877 much of the log and plank structure was burned by the Nez Perce as they fled the pursuing US Army, and Norris joined Baronett in rebuilding it the following year, adding iron trusses so it would hold up to wagon traffic. It was a lucrative bridge for Yellowstone Jack, as he exacted tolls from the miners, freighters, and hunters traveling to and from Cooke City. In 1903 a steel deck truss bridge was built upstream from Baronett's moneymaker, and the old bridge was torn down in 1911.

Norris continued his explorations through the park, cutting roads along the paths he saw fit to connect the park's major sights. By the end of 1878 there were 103 miles of roads and trails through the park. When park visitors leave Mammoth and head east toward Tower Junction, they cross the spectacular Sheepeater Canyon Bridge over the Gardner River. The span was built to supersede one of Norris's last bridge projects before the end of his tenure in Yellowstone. He'd built a short log bridge around 1880, on a road that started in Fort Sheridan, crossed the Gardner, and snaked up the steep incline of Bunsen Peak. After passing Osprey Falls it met up with the Grand Loop Road above Rustic Falls. That original road is still used today as a scenic hiking and biking trail.

This informational kiosk on the Grand Loop Road near Obsidian Cliff is believed to be the first interpretive pullout in any national park, constructed using architect Robert Reamer's National Park Rustic style. AUTHOR PHOTO

Building roads and bridges requires, of course, a tremendous amount of construction and maintenance equipment. The Yellowstone philosophy from the get-go was to source as many materials as they could from the area. Also, they wanted to build these roads with a minimum of disruption to the natural landscape. The isolated location of the Upper Yellowstone required Norris to bring in all the gear, which he did from his home village of Norris, Michigan, some 1,700 miles away. Upon returning home after his third season as superintendent, Norris ordered all the equipment and machinery, and scheduled it to be shipped up the Missouri River to Bismarck, North Dakota Territory. In a lucky twist of fate, the load missed the connection to its steamship, *Yellowstone*, and that craft was smashed to bits on the Buffalo Rapids. Eventually the cargo arrived at Fort Benton, and trucked overland to Bozeman and brought into Mammoth over the shorter, vastly improved road Norris had built for just this purpose.

By the time Norris finished his tenure in 1881, the park now had 153 miles of passable wagon roads, and 204 miles of trails. Norris had managed to create most of the upper half of what would eventually become the Grand Loop Road, leaving the section from Tower Fall to the Grand Canyon to be built by a successor.

One of the most breathtaking but dangerous additions to the Norris road was the section that runs along the cliff face where Glen Creek flows through the Golden Gate Canyon a couple miles south of Mammoth. The pass bedeviled Yellowstone's road engineers for decades. In 1883, engineer Lt. Dan Kingman built a 228-foot wood trestle that hugged the sheer walls of the cliff, allowing the road to bypass the original path through Snow Pass. It was a much-improved route, providing the additional bonus of an unbelievable view back up the canyon. By the turn of the 20th century, Lieutenant Chittenden was on the scene, and the park's chief engineer embarked on his second stint in Yellowstone by replacing the rickety wooden contraption with a sleek, concrete viaduct that was supported by concrete arches. After the 1932 season, work began on a tunnel through the section of cliff, but in May of 1933 the nearly completed tunnel collapsed. The idea was scrapped, and a new bridge was built to replace Chittenden's, widening the road from 16 to 24 feet, and designed to be free-standing. That bridge lasted until 1976, when an even bigger, better version was built. It is still in use today.

Lieutenant Kingman was an important figure in the advancement of road-building in Yellowstone, as he was the first to propose standards for the roads, including a width of 18 feet with a crowned centerline, ditches on both sides, culverts to carry water underneath, and walls uphill to direct snowmelt around the roads. He also built several bridges during his tenure, and was quite popular with the superintendents. His attitude, which he expressed to the secretary of war (then in charge of the park) that, while these quality roads were needed to carry tourists safely throughout the park, he was mindful that they not bring too much civilization into the park:

"[I]f its forests are stripped to rear mammoth hotels, if the race course, the drinking saloon and gambling table invade it; if its vallies [*sic*] are scarred by rail-roads, and its hills pierced by tunnels, if its purity and quiet are destroyed and broken by the noise and smoke of the locomotive, if in short a sort of Coney Island is established there, then it will cease to belong to the whole people and will be unworthy of the care and protection of the national government." Lieutenant Kingman's prescient awareness of the park's delicate ecosystem and the attendant respect to its exploitation was eventually adopted by the NPS and defines its protective role today.

When Lieutenant Chittenden first arrived in the park, in 1891, he immediately set upon improving the existing roads and building new ones. He completed the road from the Grand Canyon to the Upper Geyser Basin via Yellowstone Lake by the fall, and Chittenden, fueled by unused funds from the previous years in addition to that year's appropriations, kept right on chooglin'. By all accounts he was an indefatigable and efficient road builder, and the completion of the Grand Loop Road shifted into high gear. Butting heads occasionally with acting superintendent Capt. George Anderson, Chittenden insisted on rebuilding the Norris road, which was (and continues to be) one of the roughest sections in the Loop. The ambitious engineer, who had by then earned the admiration and respect of Captain Anderson, was transferred from Yellowstone in 1893. In the ensuing years, road work was done by Army soldiers and civilian transportation workers. Small sections of roads were built or improved and a few bridges were built, including an arch bridge over the Upper Falls of the Grand Canyon and a bridge over the Firehole River south of Excelsior Geyser. New roads included a route between Gardiner and Mammoth Hot Springs, a road from Lake Hotel to the Natural Bridge, and a road from the brink of the Grand Canyon to Inspiration Point. These efforts continued to fill in the gaps in the Grand Loop Road.

In 1899 Hiram Chittenden returned to Yellowstone, and he would provide that final push needed to close the circuit on one of the most brightly shining road systems in the National Park System. Captain Anderson was long gone, and acting superintendent Capt. James B. Erwin was left with exactly $66.01 to work with after the 1897 season. The Army had been in charge of the park for over a decade, and the lion's share of government funding went to the maintenance of the ever-growing Fort Yellowstone, not so much to the maintenance of the park itself. Chittenden was about to change that. Wise in the ways of congressional appropriations and the timing of requests for same, he proposed a one-time allotment of $300,000 to build a consistent, solid, and reliable 300-mile road system within the park. The Belt Line, as it was known then, would follow the existing network of roads and bridges, creating once and for all the roadway Chittenden had envisioned since he first set foot in the park. His proposal also included approach roads, offices, a construction plant, and various related facilities.

Sounds good, said Congress. Here's $89,465 for the next 2 years. It wasn't close to what he needed, but Chittenden started work on the Golden Gate viaduct and worked on planning and building a road from Yellowstone Lake over the Sylvan Pass to the East Entrance in the Shoshone Valley. Two years later Congress came across with $113,000, enough to fund a quality road from Tower Junction to Cooke City, providing access from the park's Northeast Entrance.

A big part of Chittenden's influence during this era was establishing road maintenance as a distinct funding need, separate from construction. Also, after witnessing years of dust and road wear and trying different processes elsewhere, he developed the practice of covering the dirt roads with crushed rock or some aggregate material, then sprinkling the surface with oil. This not only reduced the dust, but helped slow the degradation of the roads from the increasing wagon, pack horse, and carriage traffic.

At the time, a number of visitors thought they had the answer to all the rough roads: railways in the park. Chittenden, as many of his predecessors also had opined, knew this would ruin the world's first national park just when it was really getting started. Once he finished construction of the Belt Line and the related entrance and connecting roads, he figured, people would forget about the trains. His plans included clearing trees near the road to open up the vistas, planting grasses that would attract wildlife, and the use of attractive stone retaining walls and guard walls to pump up the aesthetics of the Belt Line. "In these and other ways the roads will themselves be made one of the interesting features of this most interesting region," he told the International Good Roads Congress in 1901.

In 1902 Chittenden felt that the popular northern entrance in Gardiner could use a suitable structure to serve as a symbolic entrance to the park, and stand as an architectural companion to the elegant train station that had been designed by celebrated architect Robert Reamer, who had instituted the National Park Rustic style with impressive structures like the Old Faithful Inn. The cornerstone of the Gardiner Arch was laid by President Theodore Roosevelt on April 24, 1903, and carriages and stages started rolling through the 50-foot-tall structure in September.

The Grand Loop Road was finished in 1905, and Chittenden was transferred in 1906 to Yosemite National Park, where he brought his prodigious design and work ethics to bear on another national treasure. Yellowstone's most prolific and influential engineer is memorialized in, among other features, the Chittenden Bridge, a gorgeous concrete and steel arch that spans the Yellowstone River just upstream from the Upper Falls.

In 1915 the first automobiles were allowed into Yellowstone, and within 2 years the only horses to be seen in the park would be the ones carrying mounted park rangers, or pack animals on the trails into the backcountry. The Beartooth Highway, a spectacular scenic drive that connects Red Lodge to Cooke City, opened in 1935, and a park check-in hut was built that year. Park visitors from Billings and Miles City in Montana no longer had to make the long jaunt to Bozeman to gain access. By 1939 almost half the roads in the park had a bituminous, or chip seal, surface. That year a 45 mph speed limit was set for most of the Grand Loop Road. By 1966 the entire road was paved with asphalt.

Weather, traffic, earthquakes, and the plateau's unique atmospheric environment all continue to wreak havoc on the park's 251 miles of roadways, requiring constant maintenance. Not a summer goes by when you don't see a road crew somewhere in the park, working to repair some of the historic roadway that allows us to easily access all that America's first national park has to offer. Yellowstone Park celebrated its 150th anniversary in 2022, and there's no reason to think this well-designed, highly functional figure eight—a wonderful attraction in its own right—won't be carrying visitors throughout the park for another 150 years.

Playlists for the Road

Here are a few musical suggestions that can enhance your road trip between Glacier and Yellowstone.

Memory is a curious thing, especially when it comes to music. The ability of music to cut through the cerebral war zone of a degenerative neurological disease such as dementia and make solid connections with life memories from half a century ago (or longer) is well documented. It's said that, among those afflicted with a brain disease like Alzheimer's, typically the last cognitive function to fail is the understanding and appreciation of music. Researchers have found that, unlike other sensory stimuli, music involves several areas of the brain working in concert to process it. The ability of the brain to rearrange its functions to different areas is called neuroplasty. Your gray matter might be riddled with Huntington's disease or amyotrophic lateral sclerosis, but thanks to neuroplasty, you might still be able to tap your foot along with the rhythm of a Bo Diddley song.

Memory is a two-way street. Music helps recall memories, but it also solidifies memories that are tied to visual information. It's how the score or a soundtrack works with a movie. For example, anyone who's seen *Reservoir Dogs* knows that the song "Stuck in the Middle with You" conjures up one of the movie's most disturbing scenes. The song and footage are permanently connected, unlike that poor hostage and his ear.

Driving the spectacular territory between Glacier and Yellowstone National Parks in western and central Montana provides limitless opportunity to create a "soundtrack" moment that will stay with you forever, waiting to be called up whenever you hear the song that first got paired with a stunning piece of scenery you've encountered on the road. The purpose of this list is to share some of those times I've had, when I was caught by surprise as a section of music or a song came on the car stereo that matched the scenery so well it created one of those perfect clips. Occasionally the emotional gut punch has been powerful enough to bring me to tears. Sometimes it's a whole album, sometimes it's just a moment within a song that gives you those chills, a reminder that your big ol' brain is always working with your nervous system to make sure you get the maximum sensory experience. In a state as visually appealing as Montana, almost any music makes for a great soundtrack to the windshield candy you'll experience on your trip.

～

Two things: Obviously, we don't all enjoy the same type of music. Some travelers eschew music altogether, preferring the sound of relative silence while the mountains and rivers and valleys do all the talking. Big grain of salt on these recommendations.

Second, I am of the opinion that once you enter a national park, the stereo gets turned off. There are clearly people out there who seem to think the rest of us cannot wait to hear Bob Seger wailing from their motorcycle speakers as they wheel slowly through a campground, looking for a spot to pitch their tent and ruin everybody's day. Don't be this person. These parks belong to all of us, and it's selfish, boorish, and just downright rude to play loud music while visiting them. Why on earth would you want to drown out the existing soundtrack? The roar and hiss of thermal features in Yellowstone, the whooshing of the wind through the canopy of cedars in Glacier. The shriek of a bald eagle. The thundering grunt of a bison bull or the resounding bugle of an elk. If you still would prefer recorded music to nature's soundtrack, please take a moment to consider your fellow humans, and use some earbuds.

～

Whether you're driving into Montana or flying in and renting a car to visit both national parks, chances are you'll be coming into Billings. To get from there to Yellowstone, the nearest park entrance is the Northeast Entrance near Cooke City by way of the Beartooth All-American Highway. Considered by many to be the most beautiful scenic drive in America, the 68-mile Beartooth is thrilling and picturesque, with views of up to five mountain ranges. For some, listening to music while you make your way up and over this spectacular pass may be sacrilege. For the rest of us, it begs for the perfect soundtrack. One album I've found to be a great fit is *Pet Sounds* by the Beach Boys. The gentle harmonies and delicate melodies of Brian Wilson's mid-60s masterpiece seem a good match for the sweeping vistas and endless views from the top of the world. It's gentle but powerful.

—✦—

There are dozens of potential routes between Billings and Glacier Park. Unless you make it a point to stick to the two-lane state highways, you'll probably be spending a few hours on one of Montana's three interstates. The main east-west thoroughfare is I-90, bisecting the state from Idaho to North Dakota. Driving from east to west you'll pass through the three Bs: Billings, Bozeman, and Butte. That stretch is about 3 1/2 hours, and once you hit Butte the routing possibilities open up. The interstate is kind of meant to be boring, but here in Montana even the interstate isn't all bad. There are mountains everywhere, but mostly far away. On the interstate, cruise control can be forgiven. Here's a set of albums that will help keep you awake, keep your ears interested, and gradually pull you into a Montana state of mind, no matter which direction you're headed:

Faster by Samantha Fish. The latest album from this Kansas City guitarist/singer/songwriter is a powerhouse. Her fiery lead guitar lands somewhere in the blues-rock territory between Susan Tedeschi and Billy Gibbons, and her songs are instantly memorable—edgy, propulsive rock with plenty of modern pop touches. I predict this will spur some family singalongs at 70 per.

Plastic Seat Sweat by Southern Culture on the Skids. This southern-fried trio is hilarious and quirky, and they have the rock chops to back up the laughs. Rockabilly, blues, and surf guitar leg wrestle with some good old hillbilly music here and there. You won't hear them on any Top 40 radio station, but songs like "Banana Puddin'" will have you dancing in your own sweaty seat.

Mudcrutch. Tom Petty's first band had a reunion and even recorded an album in 2008. If you're a Petty fan, it's fun to stretch out and give these Heartbreakers precursors a listen and hear the seeds of one of America's greatest rock bands being sown.

Graveyard Whistling by the Old 97s. These Dallas-based rockers have been doing the alt-country thing since the mid-90s, and no one does it better. Brilliant songwriting, killer harmonies, and great guitar interplay will keep you stroking down the freeway with the energy level high.

Let It Bleed by the Rolling Stones. This is probably the Stones' most country-influenced album, thanks to Gram Parsons's influence on Keith Richards during their brief but intense friendship. Something about a band of snotty Brits doing their take on American country music is a fitting soundtrack for Montana. We're not a sleepy, rural land populated entirely by cowboys and ranchers, although we do have plenty of both. Montana is a state full of variety, contradictions, and surprises. And we rock.

Here's a perfect moment you can arrange: As you're driving past Butte on I-90 (doesn't matter which direction) cue up "My City Was Gone" by the Pretenders. The slightly menacing riff dovetails with the view of the mined-out hillside overlooking the town, and if you've brushed up on the history of Butte, it'll make sense.

For many of us, traveling the endless roads in one of America's most visually stunning states is deeply enhanced by a suitable soundtrack. Moments of musical serendipity can live in your Montana memories for the rest of your life.
AUTHOR PHOTO

If you leave I-90 at Anaconda or Drummond and take the Pintler Veterans Memorial Scenic Highway (MT 1) between the two, you'll pass a couple of ghost towns and the restored mining town of Philipsburg. It's a beautiful drive through the Flint Creek Valley with some breathtaking views from the short, serpentine mountain pass that climbs up to Georgetown Lake. The pastoral mixed with the mountainous calls for some sweet, pretty, sometimes-rocking songs like the tunes on *Barricades and Brickwalls* by Australian country-rocker Kasey Chambers. Minor-key reflections mix with dramatic broad strokes, just like the landscape.

If you're driving from Missoula to Great Falls to get to East Glacier by way of US 2, it makes sense to go up the Blackfoot River canyon toward Lincoln on MT 200. In just a few miles you've left Missoula's urban landscape behind, and you're winding along the picturesque trout stream you may have seen in *A River Runs Through It*. Joni Mitchell's classic *Blue* provides a pure and powerful soundtrack that's equal to the striking beauty of this drive.

I had a moving musical moment one summer on this road as I was heading northeast out of Lincoln toward Great Falls. As I emerged from the dense forests north of Lincoln into the broad valley along the Blackfoot River, the beauty of Montana seemed to unfold before me. My sound system was on shuffle mode, and a gorgeous piece of classical music came streaming out of the speakers at the right moment. Honest to god, a bald eagle flew directly overhead as the song started. Clouds were casting ever-changing shadows on the foothills, and the striking beauty of the landscape was made even more powerful by the emotional swells of the music. The orchestration was stately and lush, and the tune was somehow familiar. It fit the scenery the way a perfect frame complements a wonderful painting. The song was almost over when it came to me: this was "Black Diamond" by KISS, an orchestral version arranged by Yoshiki and performed by the American Symphony Orchestra. Go figure.

Okay, here's something fun—I'm going to show you how to create a couple of musical moments, both on the same drive from Missoula to Polson on US 93 north. Traveling toward Flathead Lake, you'll get into the mountains almost right away as you turn north off I-90 at a truck stop village called the Wye. You'll climb up the four lanes of Evaro Hill, then find yourself rolling through the beautiful pine forests of the Flathead Indian Reservation. Some bluegrass would be good along here, if that's your thing. From Evaro, you'll drive through some agricultural lands and the highway will bend northwest just before you pass through Arlee, a little res town. Here comes the "audience participation" part of this section.

About 7 miles past the Jocko River, the road takes a big right turn, with a steep hillside on the right, and the river down below to the left. As you take the next left bend and approach the little town of Ravali, drop the needle on "In the Air Tonight" by Phil Collins. At the north end of town, MT 200 splits off to the west at the traffic light, and you'll stay on US 93 as it climbs up to the right. If you're not new to this particular drive, you know exactly what you're going to see at the top of the hill. If it's your first time up this road, I won't spoil it.

Clearly, there are other songs that can pack the same emotional wallop as the (perhaps overplayed) Phil Collins classic. Pay attention, though, because another golden soundtrack opportunity is coming up.

As you round the corner past St. Ignatius you'll climb up the Mission Valley straight northward to Ronan, and just beyond that, Pablo, home of the Confederated Salish-Kootenai tribal headquarters. The song you'll be playing next is "St. Cajetan" by Cracker. It's on their debut album. Just a couple of miles north of Pablo there's a traffic light at N. Reservoir Road/Minesinger Road. Start the song as you pass that traffic light, and try to keep it at 55. You'll be rewarded as you crest Polson Hill just past the scenic turnoff. You're welcome.

If your path between the parks takes you south of Great Falls through Helena, there's a gorgeous drive along I-15 between those two cities. You'll be winding along the Missouri River toward the Big Belt Mountains. Roughly halfway between the cities is Tower Rock State Park, a great place to stop for a picnic and maybe a climb up the titular rock itself. I've found an evocative soundtrack for this stretch of Montana highway is *Upland Stories* by Robbie Fulks. He's a brilliant songwriter who engages the brain as well as the heart, and this is one of his more introspective albums that's just right for providing a moving accompaniment to one of the prettiest drives in western Montana that doesn't see a lot of traffic.

Up near Glacier there's a road that practically begs for "Forty Miles of Bad Road" by Duane Eddy. It's MT 49 between Kiowa and East Glacier. This is a two-lane blacktop that would be a hair-raising, second-gear roller coaster even if the surface were in good shape. The road is closed except during the height of the summer season, so the nearly year-round snow covering doesn't give road crews much time for maintenance, I guess.

For those who prefer a less challenging drive between St. Mary and East Glacier, Route 464 between Babb and Browning is the only alternative. It's A bucolic stretch of blacktop that runs through mostly Blackfeet agricultural land through the northernmost reservation in the state. Although adjacent to Glacier Park, it's light years away from tourist-based commerce. Driving this route, somehow Los Lobos's *The Neighborhood* always seemed fitting to me.

Driving into Browning, tribal headquarters for the Blackfeet Nation just 13 miles from East Glacier, one song that seems to pack all the energy and attitude of res life is "Hit a Wall," by Goddammitboyhowdy, a Blackfeet punk band from the 2010s. It wails with the pain, frustration, pride, and even hope of a marginalized people who have spent generations just trying to survive here, in what's left of their homeland. The musicians were in their teens and early 20s when they recorded it, but this pipe bomb of a song holds a lifetime of passion that's as raw as it is fierce. It's the soul of Browning in under 3 minutes.

From Browning you can drive east on US 2 to pick up I-15 at Shelby, or you can head southeast on US 89 (the Ivan Doig Memorial Highway) toward Choteau, where it turns south. Soon you'll be skirting the Northern Front, a great wall of mountain range along the eastern edge of two wilderness areas, the Bob Marshall and the Scapegoat. The power and beauty of these distant mountains meeting the plains is enhanced beautifully with some early Jayhawks, albums like *Hollywood Town Hall* or *Tomorrow the Green Grass*.

Soundtracks for the road are not a staple of most travel guides, and the diversity of people from around the world who visit Montana's national parks makes this far from a universally appealing list. With something as subjective as music, it's a futile task to find songs or albums that will work for everyone. I get it. Sometimes sights and sounds combine in a spectacular happy accident, and sometimes they can be married before-hand by creating playlists. However it happens, I encourage you to try out these suggestions, and definitely find your own style for music that can enhance the visual feast that is all that Montana between the parks.

13

The Pack Is Back

Snow still blanketed Yellowstone Park's Lamar Valley on March 21, 1995, the first day of spring. On a rise near Crystal Creek, eight gray wolves moved restlessly among the aspens and sagebrush on a hillside just north of the main road. They had spent the last 6 weeks penned on an acre of land, giving them time to acclimate to their new environment after being captured and collared near Petite Lake in the forested foothills of Alberta, Canada's Jasper National Park. On this frigid morning, Park Service employees unlatched the broad steel gate and swung it open. The wolves, which included a breeding pair, bolted through the gap and sprinted for the treeline. Almost 70 years after the last known wolf den in Yellowstone had been destroyed just a couple of miles from this very spot, *Canis lupus* was back.

Wolf reintroduction began to take hold, and over the next 3 years 51 wolves from Canada and northwest Montana would be released into the Lamar, a broad plain across northeast Yellowstone commonly known as the American Serengeti. In April of 1996, five wolves were turned loose from a second pen near Druid Peak, giving biologists and wolf supporters an easy nickname for the nascent family: the Druid Pack. By 2001 the Druids would grow into what is believed to be the largest recorded wolfpack in the world, becoming rock stars in the process. As biologists followed, filmed, studied, and recorded the pack's behavior over the next several years, stories multiplied in the media, putting the Druids and the plight of the North American gray wolf squarely into the spotlight.

Their reintroduction to Yellowstone was more than 20 years in the making, although the seeds of the story were planted in the late 1800s, when the natural balance of the West was changed forever. The history of America's western settlement includes the endless conflict of protecting nature while exploiting its resources, but when it comes to the battle over the fate of the gray wolf, it's beyond complicated. Let's just say it might be easier to figure out a solution to something a little more straightforward, like peace in the Middle East.

The near extinction of the American buffalo after the railroads opened up the West in the 1870s is a sobering and well-known story, but it did not happen in a vacuum. It wasn't just the buffalo that were being wiped out. Elk, antelope, deer, moose, bighorn sheep—all game was fair game.

We as a nation may finally be starting to acknowledge our own violent and bloody history, but the short-sighted ignorance of western expansion did far more damage to a complex biological network than any non-native could have foreseen. As the buffalo disappeared from the plains, they were quickly replaced by cattle. The livestock industry exploded in the 1880s and '90s, with vast herds of open range cattle stretching across the West. Unlike bison, cattle are an invasive species to this ecosystem, not a symbiotic part of it. Grazing plains buffalo improve the habitat in ways that help support many other species, from prairie dogs and grassland birds to the native grasses on which they feed. Bison also were an important food source for the gray wolf. When this crucial prey was taken away in just a few years and replaced with cattle and sheep, well, wolves just kept doing what wolves do.

The livestock industry, as you can imagine, was outraged. How dare these predators feed on their privately owned lambs, calves, and slow-moving adult stock? Somebody had to do something. Wolves became the focus of a relentless negative campaign by cattlemen, who portrayed them not just as carnivores, but as cruel, evil beasts that kill just for kicks. Never mind that the environment wolves had enjoyed for thousands of years was suddenly carved up, denuded of its forests, crisscrossed with fences, and filled with millions and millions of dull-witted, stream-eroding, cud-gulping grazing machines. The livestock industry worked hard at swaying public opinion against the wolf. They wanted people to think "Little Red Riding Hood" was a documentary.

It worked. By the early 20th century, wolves were generally seen as vicious, cold-hearted murderers that killed just for sport. One lie that was propagated is that wolves attack people. It's just not true. In the last 120 years, there have been exactly two people killed by wolves in North America. Still, they were treated as an impediment to the white man's dominance of the land, nothing more than vermin that needed to be eradicated. Hunters, as well, branded wolves as the enemy when they saw a steep decline in populations of big game. They didn't like the competition. Even in Yellowstone Park, where Congress had expressly prohibited the "wanton destruction of fish and game," Army soldiers who'd been sent there in 1886 to protect the park's resources and wildlife shot every wolf they could find. Once the new National Park Service took over in 1918, their rangers continued the war on wolves, finding dens and killing all adults and pups within, until they could find no more. After the park's last known den was discovered and destroyed in 1923, there were a few random sightings for a couple of years, many of them misidentified coyotes. Between 1914 and 1926, 136 wolves were killed in Yellowstone. For the next 50 years, although the occasional lone wolf was spotted within park boundaries, biologists could find no evidence that wolves were reproducing in the park. Their eradication was complete.

By the early 1960s Yellowstone's elk populations had grown beyond the park's capacity to sustain them. With the apex predator wiped off the map, grizzlies and the occasional overachieving coyote pack weren't enough to keep elk numbers in check. Out came the guns. Rangers began killing large numbers of elk to bring the population down to a number they thought was appropriate for the available forage, which the animals had seriously reduced with their grazing and browsing. After four thousand elk were killed in a single year, public outrage forced Congress to act. In 1968 Yellowstone adopted a policy of "natural regulation," the idea being that the park's vast and complex ecosystem could seek its own level, like water. The missing link in the equation was Yellowstone's most vital predator—the wolf. The policy was partly a cop-out, as no one in the body politic could offer any answers.

Science could. Even before the wolf's extirpation from the park, biologists were gaining an understanding of the crucial role of predators in Yellowstone. They also discovered that the predator-prey relationship is far from the only influential factor in a successful ecosystem. Aldo Leopold, an author and forester-turned-environmentalist who initially had joined the chorus for eradication of all wolves, came to understand the existence of complex, interconnected relationships among species, and the value of bringing that knowledge to wildlife management. He pioneered the very concept of protecting wilderness and its biota, and he captured in this passage from *A Sand County Almanac* the moment he felt his own change of heart:

"We reached the old wolf in time to watch a fierce green fire dying in her eyes. I realized then, and have known ever since, that there was something new to me in those eyes—something known only to her and to the mountain. I was young then, and full of trigger-itch; I thought that because fewer wolves meant more deer, that no wolves would mean hunters' paradise. But after seeing the green fire die, I sensed that neither the wolf nor the mountain agreed with such a view. . . ."

Thanks to the writings and efforts of Leopold and other naturalists, a consensus began to emerge that wolves are, indeed, a critical piece of the natural puzzle that biologists were working to understand. People like Purdue wildlife biologist Durward Allen, wolf authority L. David Mech, and wolf science pioneer Adolph Murie continued to extol the value of wolves and their importance to the food chain. Public opinion began to turn away from the Big Bad Wolf characterization. By 1970 people were enjoying footage of the exploits of wolves on TV shows like *Mutual of Omaha's Wild Kingdom*.

As environmental consciousness began to expand in the United States, two important events would eventually lead to the idea of reintroducing wolves to Yellowstone. In 1972 President Richard Nixon announced a ban on the poisoning of predators on public lands. As the area surrounding Yellowstone had been ringed with poisoned bait for decades to kill coyotes and wolves, this single act made it possible for the canids to safely move back into the park on their own. But it would take much more than that. In 1973 Congress voted overwhelmingly to pass the Endangered

Species Act, the linchpin that would provide environmentalists and conservationists an avenue by which to advance their plans to bring wolves back to the park.

Pro-wolf groups like Defenders of Wildlife, University of Montana's Wolf Ecology Project, and the Montana Cooperative Wildlife Research Unit entered the fray, and began the long, twisted journey toward wolf reintroduction. They would be fought every step of the way by a most formidable opponent—the livestock industry. Hank Fischer, a field representative for Defenders of Wildlife for more than 20 years, chronicles the intense, protracted political battle in his book, *Wolf Wars: The Remarkable Inside Story of the Restoration of Wolves to Yellowstone.* Sprawled across the terms of seven presidents, the wolf wars were rampant with political posturing, backstabbing, broken promises, befuddling flip-flops, and crippling setbacks. "Although historians may view Yellowstone Park wolf restoration as an important conservation milestone," he writes, "it's not

Gray wolves, extirpated from Yellowstone Park 100 years ago, were reintroduced in 1995, and they have successfully reclaimed their crucial position as apex predators in the park's ecosystem. PUBLIC DOMAIN, PHOTOGRAPHER UNKNOWN

a particularly good model for endangered species recovery. The process took too long, was unnecessarily divisive, and cost too much. The United States has hundreds of imperiled wildlife species in need of help. Unless we adopt new tactics, our nation's efforts to conserve endangered species will fail."

——— ———

The Druids, fortunately, were considered by most to be a success story from the moment they set foot in the park. Within the first year, they had added several pups to their family, and quickly displaced the Crystal Creek pack. Doug Smith, the biologist currently in charge of Yellowstone's wolf program, wasn't even sure the wolves would stay in the park once released. The Druids did wander out of the park in 1996, and the alpha male was shot. The alpha female, FW40, took over the pack, which included her sisters, #41 and #42. After they returned to the Lamar, Smith captured an unprecedented amount of footage of the pack, and his studies of their behavior revealed a complex society that was almost Shakespearean in its pecking orders and sibling rivalries. Videos went into circulation and the story of the Druids became a worldwide sensation. Wolf buffs swarmed into Yellowstone and lined the eastern section of Lamar Road every day, aiming their telephoto lenses and spotting scopes across the valley where the Druids were easily visible near their den along the treeline.

A wolfpack usually has only one breeding pair, and after the death of the Druids' alpha male, a new contender, #21, left the Rose Creek Pack and began to court #40, ultimately becoming the new alpha. His mate squabbled frequently with her younger sisters, in particular #42, a black individual who became known among wolf watchers as Cinderella.

Wolves are innately social, and some interesting and subtle pack dynamics were revealed in a variety of situations. In Smith's documentary, *Wolves of Yellowstone*, a hunting squad of Druids, directed by #21, shadows an elk herd to identify the easiest target for a kill. They're smart. They don't kill healthy elk, it's too much work. Once they decide on their prey, they fan out for the attack. Although the younger wolves clearly show their deference to #21, the alpha allows the strongest, fastest individuals to perform the attack, and watches while they overtake a struggling doe. Unlike grizzly bears, wolves lack the jaw strength to kill their prey with a bite, so several will attack at once, chewing and mashing the flesh of their victim until it succumbs. An elk, one of North America's largest ungulates, is certainly not going to go down without a fight—it can strike out with a sharp hoof and kill a wolf with a blow to the skull, so the risk factor is high for the predators. In the film, the Druids successfully take down the doomed elk, and the pack gathers to feed. Although the hegemony gets a little blurry when they're feeding, #40 is seen still demanding submission from her sisters.

Cinderella, evidently, had had enough subservience and was ready to claim her prince. One night shortly after #40 had given birth to a litter of pups, Cinderella (possibly accompanied by other females) entered the den and killed her sister. She claimed the pups for her own, and #21 became her mate. She had two litters during their first year together, for a total of twenty-one new wolves. All but one survived, making the Druid Pack the largest ever recorded. The massive pack began to expand its territory, engaging in turf wars with other packs. Cinderella ruled the Druids with an iron paw, with a disposition as dark as her glossy coat. Even Lamar Valley's coyotes, whose diet of rodents and occasional carcass scavenging provided little competition for the wolves, were threatened by the Druids. The wolves extended no professional courtesy to their canine cousins— they'd routinely dig out a coyote den and kill everything in it. The valley's population of coyotes dropped by half within the first few years of Yellowstone's wolf program.

Other than humans, whom they avoid scrupulously, wolves don't have much in the way of competition for their prey. A grizzly will occasionally steal a wolf kill, hovering over it and guarding it for days, sometimes covering the carcass with dirt to return to it later. Once in a while the wolves are able to team up and chase off the grizzly, but usually they'll know when they're outmatched, and forfeit their prize to go find more prey.

The original plan for reintroduction had called for 5 years of wolf releases, but the animals were so successful at reestablishing themselves that releases were halted after the second year. Among the Druids, the drama continued, enthralling wolf watchers around the world. Rival packs had formed in the Lamar, and at one point a large male, #113, came calling, looking for a mate. Not on my watch, said #21. The alpha chased off the interloper, but not before #113 had caught the attention of a couple of young females. By now, the alpha pair were 7 years old, graying, and had outlived most of the wolves of their generation. They were losing some of their grip on the pack. As the Druids multiplied, they eventually hit a tipping point where there wasn't enough food to go around. At this stage, lone wolves will strike out on their own, frequently traveling to another region to hook up with other singles and start a new pack. In typical Druid style, however, most of the trouble took place within the pack. Unable to take a hint, #113 returned, and this time he was able to lure away a young female, and then another. Then a young male joined the little pack, although they remained on Druid territory. Ultimately six wolves, led by Mr. and Mrs. #113, split off from the Druids and headed south to claim their own turf. As the Druid pack continued to dwindle, new packs were formed in Slough Creek, Agate Creek, and other Lamar Valley drainages. A white female, #540, paired up with a pale gray mate and ventured south into the Hayden Valley to establish a pack there. In Pelican Valley, east of Yellowstone Lake, Molly's Pack took up residence. The wolves were reclaiming their ancestral lands.

For 14 years, the Druids dominated the territory of the eastern Lamar Valley. In later years the pack would be decimated by mange, only to bounce back when a "helper" male named Casanova joined the pack and began mating with Cinderella while still demonstrating submission to #21, the alpha. The Druids' bloodline produced hundreds of descendants, most of whom left the nuclear family over the years to propagate new packs throughout the park. In 2010, Cinderella was found dead, having likely been chased and taken down by wolves from a rival pack. After her death, wolf watchers reported seeing her mate, #21, howling for 2 days straight. He was left with his daughters, with whom he could not mate. Eventually he stopped fighting off rival males and abandoned the pack.

In 2016, wolf #778, the grandson of #21, wandered out of the park and was shot and killed—legally—by a Montana hunter. He was the last of the Druids.

Although the reintroduction of wolves to Yellowstone is a huge stride toward returning the park to its natural state, the saga is far from over. The ongoing controversy shifts with the direction of the political winds, as ranchers, hunters, and environmentalists still lock horns over dealing with wolves that wander out of the park, where the states have dominion over their management. Gray wolves are removed from the endangered species list, relisted, and then delisted again when population numbers are deemed great enough to support a hunt. During the 2021 Montana hunting season, 184 wolves were killed statewide. Twenty-three of those wolves had come out of Yellowstone Park.

As of summer 2022, there are about eighty-five wolves living in Yellowstone, a number Doug Smith feels is within the acceptable range of population to maintain the balance among the park's ecosystem. "Predation is one of the most potent and important forces in all of nature," he said. "Wolves do not belong in all places. But the places they do belong, we have to vigorously defend and protect. Yellowstone holds the most promise to unlocking the wolves' secrets that are so far unknown."

14

Yellowstone Is an Active Volcano: But How Active, Exactly?

Virtually everyone who has spent time in Yellowstone knows that a large part of the park sits atop a caldera, the dome of a collapsed volcano. This is a thin spot in the Earth's crust where a miles-deep vault of molten magma reached close enough to the surface that it melted rock and sediment, causing an explosion—three, actually—that filled the skies for hundreds of miles with dust clouds, and scattered choking ash several feet thick across the landscape as far east as the Mississippi River. In recent years, panics occasionally flood social media with breathless stories and conspiracy theories about how the Yellowstone supervolcano is "due" for another eruption. A spate of such stories appeared in early 2014 when some seismographic data gathered at West Thumb on Yellowstone Lake indicated some wild earthquake activity, which surely was a signal that a volcanic eruption was imminent. Turns out the data came from a seismometer that was on the fritz. But how likely is it that the Big One will happen any time soon, and most importantly, if it does, will the National Park System issue refunds for those annual passes?

⌐ ⌐

Seriously, once you get a basic understanding of how this particular volcano works, you'll see that the chance of it erupting in our lifetimes is about as likely as pro wrestling being real. The idea that any geological event of that magnitude operating with any sort of regularity just doesn't pencil out. First, let's stop calling it a "supervolcano." This pointless hyperbole just amplifies the speculation and puts a Yellowstone eruption into the range of an extinction-level event. Michael Poland, scientist-in-charge of the Yellowstone Volcano Observatory, said, "I wish the word 'supervolcano' could be banished from the record as it enforces the myth that Yellowstone only produces supereruptions." Also, the popular conception of Yellowstone's next volcanic eruption, with billions of tons of lava, ash, steam, and liquified rock blasting out of a cone in a spectacular plume like a thousand Old Faithfuls, is not an accurate image. "People tend to picture a giant pool of molten magma down there just waiting to erupt, but that's just not the case," he added.

Well, not anymore. A little over 2 million years ago, that's exactly what happened. In the area of the southwest corner of the park, the first and biggest of three supereruptions that would help create the Yellowstone caldera threw about 600 cubic miles of material into the atmosphere, enough to cover the entire continental United States more than a foot deep. It was one of the largest eruptions on the geologic record. When the chamber of magma emptied, the dome it created collapsed, forming a caldera. A second eruption happened 1.3 million years ago, and the third to blow, the Lava Creek Eruption, was 630,000 years ago. The caldera we see on today's Yellowstone map is actually the last of three overlapping calderas.

Let's backtrack a bit. All this volcanic action began about 16 million years ago in the northwest corner of Nevada when a plume of magma deep in the Earth's mantle forced its way up and created a hot spot under the crust. Over the next several million years, volcanic activity burst to the surface like zits on the day of the senior prom, while the North American tectonic plates slowly moved westward across the Earth's surface, changing the location of the hot spot along the Snake River Plain through Nevada, Idaho, and Wyoming to its current place in the northwest corner of Wyoming.

And there it sits, teasing the imaginations and scaring the bejesus out of visitors to the park who wonder if today is going to be the day. After all, there are hundreds of geysers, fissures, and vents literally blowing off steam all over the place. Doesn't that signify an eruption that could come at any time?

Yellowstone Park sits on top of a caldera, a collapsed volcano that blew its top 630,000 years ago. While the magma plume miles below the Earth's crust continues to heat the water and steam emitted by its thermal features like Pink Cone Geyser, the odds of another supereruption anytime soon are extremely low.
AUTHOR PHOTO

Well, no. Not a volcanic one, anyway. While it's true that the hydrothermal action in Yellowstone gets its energy from the superheated rock
and the molten magma in chambers beneath it, fluctuations in hydrothermal activity are more tied to earthquakes, hydraulic activity, and litho-
spheric shifts than signaling any imminent volcanic eruptions. While a
catastrophic earthquake is far more likely to occur in our lifetimes than a
supereruption, it's still not a reason for concern. In fact, you can count on
a few earthquakes happening while you're in the park.

The University of Utah Seismograph Stations (UUSS) operates the
Yellowstone Volcano Observatory, which collects data from the park's
hundreds of monitors, many located on the highest mountain peaks.
They keep a close eye on volcanic and seismic activity. The Yellowstone
area is fairly trembling with seismic action, and the UUSS records 1,000
to 3,000 earthquakes a year. About half the earthquakes occur in swarms,
bunched up in time and locations, typically ten to twenty a day, sometimes several hundred over 3–4 days. But the chances that you'll feel
them are miniscule—99 percent of those quakes are magnitude 2 or
below, which can't be detected by humans.

There are exceptions. The most infamous is the 1959 quake that was
centered near Hebgen Lake. The magnitude 7.5 temblor was the largest
ever recorded in Montana and the Intermountain West, and was felt as
far away as Seattle, Canada, North Dakota, and Utah. The epicenter was
about 15 miles north of West Yellowstone. It triggered an 85-million-
ton landslide on a hillside above a Madison River campground about 5
miles west of the lake, and an entire hilltop came roaring down the slope,
burying a campground full of people. The quake also caused the bed of
Hebgen Lake to rise up at one end, creating a 20-foot wave that poured
over Hebgen Dam into the Madison River. Witnesses saw camp trailers
tumbling down the river along with trees and other debris. Entire sections of roadway crumbled into the lake, hampering rescue efforts. In all,
twenty-eight people died in the quake. The landslide blocked off the river
where it flowed into a narrow canyon, forming Quake Lake. There's a
top-notch interpretive center there that tells the whole sensational story.

So, shouldn't we be more worried about earthquakes in this unstable
area than some sci-fi movie version of a supervolcano eruption? Again, not

really. While earthquakes are notoriously difficult to predict, the UUSS keeps close track of activity that might suggest bigger events, using seismometers and GPS-positioning data to give them a heads-up. They also collect info gathered by other scientific organizations that study the area's geology, including the shifting of tectonic plates, which move slower than the line for restrooms at Old Faithful.

If you do need something to worry about, let's talk about a blast that's more likely to occur sooner than later—hydrothermal explosions. In simple terms, a hydrothermal explosion is the result of pressure being released from an underground chamber filled with the superheated, salty water that circulates throughout the fractured rock of Yellowstone's geologic plumbing system. If there's not a vent or tube to act as a release valve, all that pressure has to go somewhere. The rock reaches a point where it can no longer contain the stress, and the chamber explodes, sending steam, water, and pulverized rock into the air. Since scientists and surveyors started paying attention to Yellowstone in the 1870s, there have been twenty minor hydrothermal explosions. Most of these blasts didn't cause much damage, and many were in the backcountry. One notable exception happened in Norris Basin in 1989 when Pork Chop Geyser became clogged. It blew from the pressure, pelting tourists some 200 yards away with debris.

There have been, of course, some big hydrothermal explosions that left their mark. If you have a detailed, topographic map of the park, take a look at Yellowstone Lake. There it is, shaped like the hand of a 14-year-old who just had the worst day ever in wood shop. At the north end, near Mary Bay, you can plainly see Elliott's Crater, a mile-wide depression on the lake bottom just off Steamboat Point. It was left by a massive hydrothermal blast 8,000 years ago, well within the recorded existence of humans in the area. The explosion that created that crater would have thrown deadly debris a thousand feet into the air to rain down on the surrounding area.

Recent explorations have shown the lake bottom to be an active hydrothermal area, with lava flows moving beneath a thin crust of glacial matter, creating a pretty much constant state of hydrothermal activity. Underwater craft recently captured images of towering silica spires on the lake bottom, several bubbling heat vents, and other formations left behind by the collision of glacial ice and molten lava. Other large hydrothermal explosions in Yellowstone left behind craters at Pocket Basin in the Lower Geyser Basin, Evil Twin at West Thumb, Turbid Lake, and just 2,400 years ago, Indian Pond. Most of the bowl-shaped depressions filled up with water and have low, raised edges around their rims.

West Thumb itself was created by an explosion 173,000 years ago, a volcanic eruption similar in size to the one that created Oregon's Crater Lake. The resulting collapsed dome filled with water and formed the large extension of Yellowstone Lake we know today looking like a thumb that was hit by a hammer (oh, that poor kid). Yellowstone's most recent significant volcanic activity was a nonexplosive rhyolite lava flow on Pitchstone Plateau about 70,000 years ago. Before that nearly all the eruptions in or around the caldera after the last big blast of 630,000 years ago have been nonexplosive basalt and rhyolite lava flows.

As you move through the park, you're surrounded by evidence of the volcanic activity that helped form Yellowstone. If you've picnicked at Sheepeater Cliffs just south of Mammoth Hot Springs, or walked beyond the picnic area along the beautiful trail that follows the Gardner River, you have seen the vertical rows of rocks that form the cliffs called columnar basalt. The oddly uniform formations are the result of a basalt lava flow from an eruption north of Yellowstone about 500,000 years ago. As lava flows cool, they shrink and take on different appearances, depending on the rate of cooling and whether the lava is flowing in a horizontal or vertical direction. When it cools more quickly, as when encountering water or ice, it becomes solid and cracks apart in random segments. When it cools more slowly, the basalt forms into hexagonal columns like pencils stood on end, as the stress is spread out and the cracks form more uniformly. This columnar jointing can be seen in several other places in the park. When overlooking Tower Fall, right across the river you'll see a long stretch of columnar basalt looking like a picket fence near the top of the cliff. It's also evident near Obsidian Cliff, and you may recognize the appearance if you've been to Devil's Tower in Wyoming. That distinctive monolith is composed of phonolite porphyry, a different igneous rock but formed by the same columnar jointing.

Most people drive right past Obsidian Cliff, which juts out of a corner just north of Roaring Mountain between Mammoth and Madison Junction. It's another volcanic leftover, a giant outcropping of mostly black glass, formed when a lava flow cooled quickly, giving little time for crystal formations to appear. Obsidian usually is formed from the upper level of a rhyolite lava flow, the first part of the flow to meet air or water. It's high in silica content, and its relative purity added to its value as a raw material used for tool-making in Native American cultures. Chips of obsidian could be flaked away in fairly uniform pieces and the razor sharp edges—sharper than surgical steel—made it an ideal material for knives, spear tips, and arrow points. The material was highly prized by North American tribes, and was a hot commodity among traders. The composition of Yellowstone obsidian is as unique as a fingerprint, and using X-ray fluorescence to ascertain its source, archaeologists have found Yellowstone obsidian artifacts as far away as Maine.

Tuff Cliff, a tiny picnic turnout a couple miles north of Madison Junction, didn't get its name from the difficulty of scaling its 200-foot rock face. It's composed of tuff, ash-flow that was compacted into rock after the last supereruption. Ash from the Lava Creek Eruption that wasn't carried off in the atmosphere flowed over the Yellowstone plateau like water, propelled by the rapidly expanding gasses trapped within it. This flow of magma, pumice, and ash settled into the valleys and canyons, and eventually cooled and cemented together into vast horizontal layers. This compacted rock is called welded tuff, and it once covered most of the area in and around the caldera. Subsequent lava flows, erosion, and other geological events have covered or collapsed much of it, but some tuff remains, such as the impressive cliff at the three-table picnic area. You can see more tuff cliffs near Osprey Falls, accessible on a trail just east of Bunsen Peak, and drive right by part of the striking Huckleberry Tuff ridge at Golden Gate.

Yellowstone is considered an active volcano, but the chances of it blowing its top any time soon are virtually nil, especially to the level that would be considered a supereruption. The source of the volcanic heat is there, but the heavy heat is deeper now. The upper crustal magma chamber, about 3–9 miles underneath the caldera, is only 5–15 percent liquid, the rest having hardened into rock. Beneath that is a lower crustal magma reservoir 12–28 miles under the surface, and below that is the Yellowstone magma plume, which brings up hot, spongy rock from more than 40 miles beneath the Earth's surface.

Yellowstone's origin story really helps put a lot of the geologic features you see in the park today into perspective. The park has seen some dramatic changes and crazy history since Teddy Roosevelt christened the Yellowstone Arch (which is constructed, by the way, of columnar basalt) in 1903, more than 30 years after its inception. Still, 150 years of Yellowstone? That's a geological blink of an eye compared to the initial creation of this bizarre and beautiful place, which began more than 2 million years ago.

The Devil in Yellowstone

Perhaps more than any other national park, Yellowstone boasts a number of areas that are named after the devil. Considering the hellish environment suggested by many of the park's geothermal wonders, it's not hard to imagine why the early white explorers frequently looked downward for inspiration. Author Wallace Stegner perhaps said it best: "The Devil had a good deal to do with the making of the West, if we may believe the West's place names." Here are a few of their origin stories.

Devil's Cut

As you drive past Floating Island Lake on the north segment of the Grand Loop Road, you can look to the southwest and gaze right into the Devil's Cut. It's believed that the small canyon between Blacktail Deer Plateau and Crescent Hill was named by Superintendent P. W. Norris, although he later claimed a distaste for the name and changed it to Dry Canyon, a typically bland moniker. Park engineer Hiram Chittenden later gave it a slight upgrade to Crescent Hill Canyon, but the original name stuck until geologist Arnold Hague included the canyon in his early-20th-century campaign to rid the park of any and all names that contained "Devil" or "Hell." It's now mostly known as simply the Cut, and it's here where an emaciated, near-dead Truman C. Everts was found after being lost in Yellowstone for 37 days in 1870.

Devil's Hoof

Just a few miles southeast of the Cut, Tower Fall stands at the north end of Yellowstone's Grand Canyon. The jagged shale boulders that rise dramatically out of the river at the base of the waterfall inspired Norris's predecessor, N. P. Langford, during his 1870 expedition with Gustavus Doane and Henry Washburn. Langford, who loved telling people that his initials stood for "National Park," thought one of the rocks resembled what he imagined was the devil's foot, or hoof, proclaiming in his journal that the "huge mass sixty feet in height, which from its supposed resemblance to the proverbial foot of his Satanic Majesty, we call the 'Devil's Hoof.'"

Devil's Laundry

Even the devil likes his colors to be their brightest, his whites their whitest. At least that was the thinking that went into naming this hot tub–sized hot pool in Black Sand Basin, just west of Old Faithful. One of the most popular attractions of the park in its early years, the small, deep pool, also known as Handkerchief Pool, was used to clean handkerchiefs and other small cloth items. The superheated pool reportedly whitened squares of linen, so visitors (or even, incredibly, rangers) would drop a handkerchief into the pool and watch it get sucked down into the inlet as the water drained after an eruption cycle. The item would then shoot back up through the water, supposedly boiled clean. It was later discovered that the thermophilic microbes that lived in the heated water created an enzyme that worked like bleach on the fabric. Eventually all the foreign objects that were tossed into the little pool, including coins, bottles, pins, and other junk, plugged up the hydrothermal plumbing, and the pool went dormant by 1928. The Devil's Laundry was permanently out of order.

Devil's Den

This striking stretch of rugged canyon along Tower Creek above Tower Fall looks like just the place for the Prince of Darkness to fire up a stogie, kick back in a red leather armchair with a *Wall Street Journal*, and enjoy a couple of fingers of Devil's River Bourbon from Texas. That might have been the thinking of surveyor Ferdinand Hayden in 1871 when he applied the name to this chasm that's striped near the top of its steep walls with a uniform layer of columnar basalt. These formations can be found throughout the park, at places like Sheepeater Falls. They were formed when thin, fast-flowing lava cooled quickly, segmenting into uniform columns that are usually hexagonal in shape. Here they're topped with mounds of glacial till where trees and ground cover have grown, setting off the basalt columns like the corrugated rim of a bottle cap.

Devil's Kitchen

What sounds like the perfect name for a hot sauce testing facility was once a popular attraction in the Upper Terrace area of Mammoth Hot Springs. It's believed that the Devil's Kitchen was named by Charles Millard while visiting from Fort Ellis, near present-day Bozeman. A long, narrow fissure in the earth opens up into a large underground cavern that was formed by a hot spring, now dormant. In 1884 a tour operator, G. L. Henderson, built a rickety, 50-foot wooden ladder that allowed visitors to descend into the dank, smelly vault. The floor of the cavern was littered with the bones of deer and other animals that had wandered too close to the opening and fallen to their deaths. The Devil's Kitchen generated so much traffic that the enterprising Trischman sisters, Elizabeth and Anna, built a log cabin snack bar nearby. Visitors would enjoy a cold drink or ice cream at the Devil's Kitchenette after climbing up out of the steamy hell hole. That might not have been a brain freeze from the ice cream they were feeling, though. It could have been the onset of hypercapnia, a condition caused by high concentrations of carbon dioxide that were detected in the cave. Park officials closed the cave to the public in 1939.

Devil's Slide

Although not located inside the park, the Devil's Slide is worth noting. This geologic oddity dominates the ridgeline on Cinnabar Mountain across the Yellowstone River just a few miles northwest of Gardiner on US 89. The broad, rust-colored stripe of rock does indeed resemble a playground slide, with what looks like a guardrail running along its side. Mesozoic and Paleozoic quartz sandstone, shale, and other sedimentary rock formed horizontal layers in the formation, then later tilted on its side to create the vertical, fence-like wall next to the slide after the softer rock eroded away. The distinctive swoop of reddish-brown comes from the Amsden, Chugwater, and Morrison formations. Early settlers had named it Red Streak Mountain, but members of the 1870 Washburn Expedition gave it the more Satanic moniker, and it stuck.

One of the Yellowstone area's most striking geological features bearing a devilish name looms up across the Yellowstone River just north of Gardiner. The Devil's Slide, on Cinnabar Mountain, was named by members of the 1870 Langford-Washburn-Doane expedition. AUTHOR PHOTO

Devil's Stairway

Mary Mountain Trail is one of the park's most popular hikes, starting at the head of the Nez Perce Creek, winding through the wildflower-filled meadows and climbing up to its namesake lake. The Devil's Stairway is a steep stretch of the trail that started as a wagon road in the 1880s. During that time it was the only road between Yellowstone Lake and Upper Geyser Basin. Uphill-bound travelers frequently got out of their wagons and tackled the incline on foot to help lighten the burden on their horses. During a visit to the park in 1890, former New York congressman Guy R. Pelton was asked by his coach driver to walk up the hill. Pelton suffered a fatal heart attack while on the Stairway, resulting in the loss of the coach driver's concessionaire contract. We can assume talks of installing a Devil's Escalator went nowhere.

Demon's Cave

Not far from the Devil's Laundry in Black Sand Basin you'll find Demon's Cave, supposedly named by the celebrated tour guide W. W. Wylie in 1881. This bubbling hot spring cavern just southeast of Black Sand Pool stirred the imagination of many an early explorer, invoking yet another devilish name for a hellish environment in the new Wonderland. One guidebook writer, Herman Haupt, described it in the 1880s as "a deep pit in the geyserite which has been washed out, leaving a crust suspended over a boiling cauldron from which steam is constantly arising, filling the cave with a cloud of mist, which at times obscures the surface of the water below." It's just one of the thousands of entertaining ways in which the superheated waters from below this giant, active volcano find their way to the surface, sometimes inspiring a demonic name in the process.

Dante's Inferno

Standing anywhere in the Yellowstone caldera, close your eyes and point a finger. When you open your eyes, you're probably pointing at an area or geothermal feature that could rightly be called Dante's Inferno. Hell, the whole park could easily have been named for the first part of Alighieri's 14th-century classic, *Divine Comedy*, an idea which surely must have crossed the mind of many European-American explorers. Several writers did use the name to describe any number of hot springs in the park since its 1872 inception, but only one spring has the distinction of claiming the name for good. Park naturalist Al Mebane bestowed the handle on this hot spring in the Gibbon Geyser Basin. The largest pool in the Sylvan Springs group, Dante's Inferno is always roiling, pulsing with rising jets of steam and water. The long, thin forms of dead trees poke up out of the water, old lodgepoles whose skinny trunks still leach water up out of the hot pool. The calcified white bases of these barren snags have prompted rangers and guides to call them "bobby soxers."

Devil's Frying Pan

Nowadays it's listed on the map as Frying Pan Springs, but this little hot spring along the Grand Loop Road just 3 miles north of the Norris Geyser Basin was recognized early on as deserving of a descriptive name for those who could stand the heat and stayed in the kitchen. The bottom of this shallow, olive green hot pool, which is vaguely frying pan–shaped, is riddled with steam vents. The result is a surface that's always popping and sizzling, bringing to mind the deep-fried diet we all ascribe to the Prince of Darkness. Look, we're not saying that the devil eats a lot of fried foods, but he's on his third splatter screen since New Year's.

The Devil's Frying Pan is at the end of a short, accessible boardwalk, and always worth a stop, even just for the hell of it.

15

Fort Yellowstone to the Rescue

A LOW FOG WEAVES THROUGH THE TREES AS YOU LOOK EASTWARD across the canyon from the foot of Mammoth Hot Springs Terrace. Every couple of minutes, the plaintive bugle of an elk echoes through the valley. It's rutting season. The big bulls of Mammoth are seeking a mate, or shepherding their harems of does through the grass. Occasionally you can hear the clack of antlers as two bucks tangle. It's a gorgeous day in early October, and it's one of those years when autumn unfolds in its own sweet time. The cottonwood trees along the river bottoms are the color of a freshly painted double yellow line on the blacktop, but up here it's still mostly green, the air sharp with the tang of juniper and sagebrush.

Uphill, to the west, cars whiz by on Grand Loop Road, where Minerva Terrace comes into view. Most eyes are on the gleaming white walls of the upper terrace and no one seems to know that just a hundred yards down the hill from the road is a half-acre of ground surrounded by a green-painted steel pole fence. The old, decorative gate at the entrance is narrow, barely wide enough to accommodate a team of pallbearers and a coffin. There is no sign or interpretive kiosk, but the scattered white headstones and evenly spaced mounds are a dead giveaway. This is the original Fort Yellowstone cemetery, a long-forgotten remnant of a time when the US Army took control of Yellowstone National Park.

Yellowstone Park had barely been in existence for 10 years when things started going sideways. Vandals, looters, and other thoughtless knuckleheads were leaving destruction in their wake. People were breaking off pieces of geyserite spires and petrified trees, carving their names into travertine plateaus, and throwing all manner of junk into the colorful hot pools. Hunters and trappers were freely poaching the park's bears, mountain sheep, buffalo, wolves, deer, and elk with little thought to laws and regulations, and shiftless concessionaires were bilking tourists out of their money from the moment they stepped off the train in Cinnabar. There had even been a few stagecoach robberies along the park's road, and a couple groups of tourists had been attacked by bands of Indians. Far from the idyllic vacation paradise the park's promoters had envisioned, Yellowstone was becoming a sketchy free-for-all.

The problem was oversight. There was virtually none. By 1885 one superintendent and only ten assistants were administering the park. Poaching, while against park regulations, wasn't technically illegal and punishment, at worst, was a stern finger-shaking and expulsion from the park. Congress had become frustrated with the conditions in Yellowstone, but rather than allocating money to the Department of Interior to hire more people or create infrastructure, they cut funding from its already paltry budget. Only Superintendent David Wear stayed on (unpaid). Meanwhile, Yellowstone's world-famous geysers and hot pools were being systematically destroyed, and its animals were being slaughtered. The buffalo in particular was on its way to extinction. How was the government supposed to provide protection for 2.2 million acres of wilderness? It would take an army.

In the summer of 1886, General William Sheridan instructed the secretary of war to send a regiment of soldiers to Yellowstone to "prevent trespassers or intruders from entering the park for the purpose of destroying game or objects of curiosity therein, or for any purpose prohibited by law, and to remove such persons from the park if found therein." On August 17, 1886, Capt. Moses Harris led Company M of the 1st US Cavalry, about forty men strong, into the tiny village of Mammoth Hot Springs from Fort Custer. Three days later the US Army was officially in charge of Yellowstone.

Camp Sheridan, comprising a handful of tents, was quickly established at the foot of Mammoth's travertine terraces near Liberty Cap, not far from the new National Hotel. Harris, now serving as acting superintendent, dispatched six men to frontier cabins around the park, and oversaw the construction of eight frame buildings at Mammoth, just in time to provide shelter for the troops and their horses from the horrendous winter of 1886-87.

The men of Company M must have wondered what they did to deserve this post as record-setting blizzards started pounding the Northern Rockies in November. Relentless cycles of thaw-and-freeze gripped Montana, the Dakotas, and Wyoming well into the spring of 1887. Ranchers and farmers were marooned in their cabins, and across the prairie cattle froze to the ground and died where they stood. Losses to sheep and free-range cattle were so bad—up to 90 percent of the herd in some cases—that Montana's cattle industry was nearly wiped out. In the Upper Yellowstone, which averages 150 inches of snow in a normal winter, Mammoth Hot Springs was an icebox. Still, soldiers managed to patrol the park, getting around on snowshoes and 10-foot-long wooden skis. Slowly, they began to turn things around. Poachers were caught and escorted out of the park. Vandals were tracked and, in some cases, brought to the features they'd defaced and ordered to scrub away their carvings. Yellowstone's slide into chaos began to slow.

The soldiers of Camp Sheridan continued their mission for the next 5 years, adding buildings to their post and establishing some order in the park. They fought wildfires. They educated tourists. They ran off poachers and kept concessionaires on a tight leash. Soon it became clear that a larger, permanent fort would be needed. The secretary of war proposed a new installation in 1890. The following year, thanks to a $50,000 appropriation from Congress, construction began on what would become known as Fort Yellowstone. The site for the new fort had been selected by acting park superintendent Frazier Boutelle. First to be built was a guardhouse that could hold ten guards and fifteen prisoners, located at the north end of the site where the original road from Gardiner entered Mammoth Hot Springs. Eleven more buildings followed, including officers' quarters, enlisted barracks, a large stable, a commissary, a bakery, and other essential structures. The years 1893-94 saw three more large buildings, including a ten-bed hospital. As the number of men stationed at Fort Yellowstone began to approach one hundred, another troop barracks, another stable, and more officers' quarters were added in 1897.

In 1898 the little cemetery saw its first burial. Over the years it became the final resting place for dozens of soldiers, civilian employees, and their families—there is a surprising number of tiny headstone markers that read, simply, "Infant" or "Baby." The fence was added in 1915, and by 1916 some fifty-four people had been laid to rest in the cemetery. Many had succumbed to infectious disease or some other affliction, but a fair number of the cemetery's inhabitants fell victim to one of the unique hazards that came with living in Yellowstone Park—drowning, hypothermia, avalanche, a fall, and in at least one case, a grizzly bear. In 1917, the remains of nineteen military personnel were disinterred and moved to the Custer National Cemetery in the Little Bighorn National Monument. There are still about forty graves in the tiny cemetery, mostly children, women, and civilian employees of the park. The unused half of the fenced area has seen the forest grow back.

Just a few yards downhill from the cemetery sits a small cabin and a few outbuildings, including a stable and corral where horses are rented in the summer. Although the original cabin is long gone, this area was the domain of C. J. Jones, better known as Buffalo Jones, the park's first official game warden. He arrived in Mammoth in 1902 and got to work building a fenced enclosure designed to contain the fourteen buffalo cows that were brought in from the Allard herd in Montana and the three bulls from the Goodnight herd in Texas. As only two dozen of Yellowstone's original herd remained at that point, Buffalo Jones's mission was nothing less than the rescuing of the species from extirpation. Other enclosures were built in the Lamar Valley and Pelican Valley, and the newcomers interbred with the original herd to maintain what is now a pure strain of wild Yellowstone buffalo.

The Army continued to patrol the park on horseback in the summer and skis in the winter. By 1905 two more troops had been added to Company M, and buildings were added to house them. By 1910, 324 soldiers were stationed at Fort Yellowstone. With their families and civilian employees adding to the population, Mammoth Hot Springs had become a bustling community. As you can imagine, this was an unusual assignment for most soldiers, living in this remote, exotic location and serving both the Department of War and the Department of the Interior. Part enforcers and part promoters, the officers and enlisted men of Fort Yellowstone enjoyed a unique lifestyle. While the enlisted men had fewer opportunities for recreation, there were some perks provided by the Army. For instance, the post gymnasium was occasionally rejiggered into a skating rink in the winter when there wasn't a lot to do during their down time. The Fort also featured a bowling alley, and many of the men occupied themselves with card games. Despite these efforts, Fort Yellowstone suffered one of the highest desertion rates in the Army. Soldiers were rotated out yearly, which really didn't give them the time and opportunity to get to know the area. The married officers were afforded a cushier lifestyle, with larger quarters and domestic help provided by the Army. A robust social life, especially among the officers, has always been an important component of military culture and Fort Yellowstone was no exception. Visiting dignitaries, politicians, and celebrities were feted with sumptuous meals and extravagant parties, and awards ceremonies were common enough that the infantry practiced them on the parade grounds.

Hiram Chittenden was one of Yellowstone's most influential historical figures. The engineer who worked on improvements to the Grand Loop Road had this stone Engineer Office built at Fort Yellowstone in Mammoth, just a few steps from his well-appointed residence to the left. AUTHOR PHOTO

Every evening a squad would fire a cannon atop Capitol Hill at sundown, a welcome tradition that helped signify the passage of time in this isolated wilderness post.

The distinctive look of Fort Yellowstone's red-roofed, white frame buildings began to change in 1902 when Capt. Hiram Chittenden of the US Army Corps of Engineers was granted his request for a two-story, stone office building to serve as his department headquarters. He'd already been allowed a stately, well-appointed residence that had been completed that year, and he probably deserved it. The Roosevelt Arch at Gardiner was reportedly Captain Chittenden's idea, and the talented West Point graduate would be instrumental in the design and construction of Yellowstone's Grand Loop Road. Later he would go on to design the Ballard Locks in Seattle that bear his name. Not exactly a lightweight.

Scottish stonemasons were brought in to build several massive buildings, using sandstone sourced from a quarry between Mammoth and Gardiner. Built in the Colonial Revival style, they included a double officers' quarters, a three-story, double cavalry barracks the size of a typical Hampton Inn, and an elegant Bachelor Officers' Quarters, or BOQ. Today the BOQ contains the NPS's Albright Visitors Center, the Yellowstone Forever bookstore, and a small museum that focuses on the early exploration of Yellowstone.

In 1909 an extravagant stone residence was built for the post commander—who also served as park superintendent—with an eye toward the frequent guests he would presumably be entertaining. The eight-bedroom home featured four bathrooms and four small rooms in the attic. The main floor has a kitchen, pantry, dining room, living room, and parlor. It's the only building out of the sixty-five structures erected for the Fort that still serves its original purpose. While many of the remaining buildings are available for exploration, the superintendent's house is a private residence, and is not open to the public any more than your house is.

Every military installation has a hospital, of course. Fort Yellowstone's original ten-bed facility was replaced by a large stone hospital in 1911 that served military and civilian patients. It stood until 1965, when it was bulldozed after receiving significant structural damage in the Hebgen Lake earthquake of 1959.

Judge John W. Meldrum was a Mammoth resident whose name pops up frequently in the park's history. A longtime fixture in Yellowstone, Judge Meldrum was appointed the park's first US commissioner in 1884 after passage of the Lacey Act. For some reason the judge didn't travel to the park to begin his term until 10 years later, but once he arrived, he settled into the Mammoth Hotel and began supervising the design and construction of a proper commissioner's residence, which included an office and jail on the ground floor. The structure, funded by the Lacey Act, was built using a design drawn up by a soldier. One of Judge Meldrum's most notable criminal cases involved a pair of road agents who held up a caravan of four stagecoaches in 1897 between Canyon and Mammoth, liberating the passengers of $630. With the help of Ed Howell, the infamous poacher whose capture inspired the passage of the Lacey Act, the robbers were caught, bound over for trial, and eventually convicted in Cheyenne, Wyoming, and sentenced to 3 years in prison. Meldrum, the so-called "Grand Old Man of Yellowstone," resigned in poor health in 1935 and died the following year.

As for religious services and rituals, military personnel, civilians, and their families would gather in the mess hall, practicing the tenets of their faith among the faint odors of fried onions and stale coffee. Finally, in 1913 a proper church was built at the Fort. The stone chapel was the last building to be constructed in Fort Yellowstone, and probably its most beautiful. It's built of rough-hewn native stone, with a steeply sloped shale roof. Chunky buttresses add to the building's rustic grandeur, and the interior is replete with elegant woodwork and gracefully curving arched beams overhead. It's the first original building you'll encounter when you enter Mammoth from the east. The chapel is still in use today and hosts several weddings every summer.

When that first company of troops rode into Mammoth in 1886, not a man among them thought the Army would still be running the show three decades later. But as rail travel expanded and brought more commerce and tourism into Yellowstone, the Army's role in its management only strengthened. Ironically, men like Ed Howell, whose unrestricted hunting and trapping on the Yellowstone plateau spurred passage of the Lacey Act, would become essential to the Army's assignment of protecting the park's resources. With a new crop of untested mounted patrols assigned to park duty each year, Howell and other salty mountain men were recruited to join the patrols and share their broad knowledge of the park's wildlife and terrain, occasionally helping to track poachers and other criminals. It's hard to imagine that an untested group of rigid military types could have mastered the vast expanses of the park without the guidance provided by these buckskin-clad backwoodsmen. Ultimately, their intimate knowledge of Yellowstone and its ecology affected the Army's original approach. By the time the Army handed over control of the park to the newly formed National Park Service in 1918, their role had expanded from merely shooing away poachers and vandals to practicing the nascent idea of conservation. Education and protection had become part of the soldiers' mission, making them the precursors of the national park ranger. The modern-day park ranger plays a multifaceted role in the complex system that works to protect the wildlife, plant life, geology, and ecosystem of the park while simultaneously sharing its rich history, both natural and man-made.

Today about thirty of the original buildings of Fort Yellowstone have been fully restored, many still in use by park administration. Some have been converted to private residences for staff, and others are open to the public. Would Yellowstone Park have survived had it not been for the Army's intercession? It's an interesting question, but surely the park would have suffered a lot more damage and abuse as it became more accessible. One thing is certain—the military occupation of our first national park is one of the most interesting and fascinating chapters in Yellowstone's long and curious history.

16

Lost (and Found) in Yellowstone

As THE UNITED STATES RESUMED ITS WESTWARD EXPANSION AFTER the Civil War, the glitter of gold propelled most of the hordes, but some were intrigued by the wild stories that kept coming out of the Northern Rockies about the Upper Yellowstone, a rugged territory filled with shocking and unbelievable natural features. Otherwise credible mountain men like Osborne Russell and John Colter had described a bizarre landscape that featured great columns of steam spouting from the ground, bubbling springs with water hot enough to cook fish that were caught in nearby streams, and stupefying mineral structures that looked like they belonged on another planet. Soldiers, businessmen, scientists, and politicians were drawn to the possibilities of exploring and chronicling the Yellowstone area. Amid the bloody Indian wars being fought across the mountains and plains of the Montana Territories, ambitious expeditions began to penetrate the Yellowstone plateau, seeking to confirm once and for all these incredible reports, and of course to find ways to exploit the resources of said plateau. The expeditions were usually led by Army officers, experienced outdoorsmen with a predilection for violence—men who tended to solve problems with the pull of a trigger. Some were educated in the languages and customs of the Indigenous tribes, and most were adept at survival in the harsh environs and unpredictable weather. They were good with a gun and comfortable in the saddle, these swashbuckling spirits who set out to expose the secrets of Yellowstone.

And then there was Truman C. Everts. A nearsighted, 54-year-old federal tax assessor from Helena, Everts found himself jobless after President Lincoln's assassination shifted the political climate. His friend

Nathaniel Langford, who'd been tapped to become Montana's next governor, also saw his political fortunes go up in smoke among the changes in Washington. Former Civil War general and congressman Henry Washburn was faring better among the political turmoil, having been appointed general surveyor of Montana by President Grant. By the time Washburn arrived in Montana in 1870, he had a plan to explore the Upper Yellowstone region. He joined forces with Langford, who in turn tapped Col. Gustavus Doane, who had already explored and reported on much of the mysterious area. Langford also invited his friend and fellow Vermont native Truman Everts to join them. While it was highly unlikely that there would be any call for the expertise of a tax collector during the survey, Everts had nothing better to do. Besides, he was craving distraction and like the others had been captivated by the amazing stories that were spreading about this curious place. The oldest and unlikeliest member of the cadre, Everts had zero wilderness experience and no military training. Little did he know he was about to embark on a journey that would result in the best "What I Did On My Summer Vacation" essay ever.

The Washburn Expedition, comprising nineteen men, forty horses, and one dog named Booby, set out from Fort Ellis, near Bozeman, on August 22, 1870. After more than 2 weeks of travel through spectacular terrain, including the Grand Canyon of Yellowstone, they reached the southeast end of Yellowstone Lake on September 7. They broke camp on Grouse Creek the next day and turned west. Everts, however, was no longer among them.

Over the next 37 days, what Everts had hoped would be a grand vacation became an extreme test of survival that would push the hapless greenhorn to the brink of death more than once, ultimately making him one of the most famous figures in the history of Yellowstone National Park. In fact, his firsthand account of the ordeal, published the following year in *Scribner's Monthly*, would play a small part in the park's creation.

It wasn't the first time Everts had gotten separated from the group. Several times he'd drifted away from the trail but would eventually rejoin the pack somewhere down the line. This time, in the dense maze of lodgepole and undergrowth south of the lake, he couldn't locate the trail or any sign of the others. Even after the sun had set, he calmly made camp and built a fire, confident he'd catch up to his cohorts before breakfast. He rose at dawn and saddled up, planning to ride up the peninsula between the two southern arms of the lake. "The forest was quite dark, and the trees so thick," he wrote, "that it would only be a slow process that I could get through them at all."

His party, meanwhile, had proceeded northwest along the Continental Divide. Their plan was to camp at Flat Mountain Arm and build a signal fire for their wandering comrade. They expected Everts to emerge onto the shore of Yellowstone Lake, where he surely would have seen the smoke from the fire, or heard the series of shots they fired into the air. Trouble was, he was heading in the opposite direction.

As daybreak bloomed across the forest, Everts picked his way through the endless deadfall and thick underbrush. He found an opening in the trees where he thought he might be able to see far enough to get a fix on his position, so he left his horse and clambered ahead on foot, trying to find a path the animal could squeeze through. The horse had other ideas. Everts had neglected to tie up his mount and it bolted, taking with it all the gear he had fastened to the saddle. This included his bedroll, guns, fishing tackle, and matches. (It also included detailed maps and notes made by Langford on a previous expedition.) He was left with a knife and a small opera glass. After spending half a day searching for the horse, he somehow kept his spirits up, even after discovering that he'd somehow lost the knife. He sat on a log and took stock of his situation, and according to his account, concluded that he'd be reunited with his friends the next day. They'd all have a good laugh, and Everts would go home with a great story to tell. With no coat, no blankets, no food or means of making a fire, he bedded down between some fallen lodgepoles on a carpet of pine needles. Although exhausted from the day's efforts, he couldn't sleep. "The wind sighed mournfully through the pines," he wrote, although it wasn't just the wind giving him the heebie-jeebies. "The forest seemed alive with the screeching of night birds, the angry barking of coyotes, and the prolonged, dismal howl of the gray wolf."

After a sleepless night, Everts made his way back to a spot where he had posted notices for his companions. There was no sign that they had been there. That, Everts wrote, is when he realized he was lost.

Unbeknownst to him, Langford and the others were also posting notices as they traveled, stashing small caches of food and supplies along the way, hoping to sustain their lost friend. Neither Everts nor anyone in the expedition saw each others' notices.

While Everts's exact path through 50 miles of Yellowstone remains largely unknown, he spent several nights in the relative comfort of his little den near the north shore of Heart Lake. Reports from Warren Gillette, Langford, and others reveal some discrepancies in Everts's timeline after he became separated from the expedition. On his fourth day in the wilderness, for example, Everts writes of a snowstorm. Everyone else reported it occurring a day later. Everts probably arrived at the east shore of Heart Lake on September 11, not the 10th as he wrote in his *Scribner's* account. He emerged from the forest on the edge of the lake around midday, and he noted the existence of some hot springs and a single geyser. He could also see the breathtaking form of Mount Sheridan across the lake. Everts had stumbled onto the edge of the Yellowstone caldera. The rest of the party was about 10 miles to the north, rounding West Thumb on Yellowstone Lake.

Historians have little to go on when reconstructing Everts's epic journey through Yellowstone other than his own published account, which was heavily embroidered with the linguistic filigree that seemed a product of the Gilded Age. Despite its flowery prose, "Thirty-Seven Days of Peril" is a compelling read that chronicles a roller coaster ride through confusion, anguish, fear, and triumph, frequently all in a single day.

One of the most important events in the unlikely survival of the lost bureaucrat was his discovery of the elk thistle. After 4 days with no food—and no means by which to capture or kill any—he was struck by the bright green foliage of a bushy thistle growing in the shadowy gloom of the forest. He pulled the plant from the ground and inspected its long, tapering root. He took a bite. Not bad! In the parsnip-like elk thistle—now known as Everts' Thistle—he'd discovered a plentiful food source that grows in much of Yellowstone. This lifted his spirits immensely, and after munching on his fill of thistle roots he found a sheltered spot between two trees to bed down for the night. His hope for survival renewed, he was finally able to sleep.

For 37 days in 1870, Truman C. Everts wandered through Yellowstone after becoming separated from his expedition and losing his horse and all his gear. This is the view he faced as he attempted to hike from Heart Lake to the Madison Range. He eventually was found on a hillside in the Tower/Roosevelt area, but his exact route remains largely unknown. AUTHOR PHOTO

He was jolted awake by the piercing cry of an animal, "a loud, shrill scream like that of a human being in distress. . . ." He recognized the shriek immediately—it was a mountain lion. He quickly scrambled up a tree in the darkness, and spent the next several hours in a terrifying stand-off, the big cat prowling around the base of the tree as Everts screamed and tossed branches down, hoping to chase the beast away. Finally, the mountain lion gave one last cry and bounded off into the brush, per-haps to find more willing prey. Terrified the lion might return, but too exhausted to stay in his perch, Everts climbed down and reclaimed his bed. He slept for a few hours, and just after daybreak awoke with a relent-less train of fears rumbling through his head. Would he be attacked and eaten by some creature like a mountain lion or bear? Would he be scalped by the Indians who were known to roam through Yellowstone on their way to their hunting grounds? Would he fall into a canyon or freeze to death in an early season snowstorm like the one moving in just then? There were a hundred things to worry about, and his optimism took a nosedive when he began to entertain the idea that his expected reunion with his friends might not happen. It became clear that his survival would depend on his own efforts, cunning, and more than a little good luck. As the temperature dropped and snow began to blow in, he gathered his tattered clothing around him and laid down on his bed of pine boughs to ride out the storm.

He wound up staying in that spot for 7 days. He'd found a small hot spring nearby where he could parboil the thistle roots for sustenance. With no fishing gear and no knife, he had no way of killing any of the abundant wildlife. He had a bit of luck during a lull in the storm when a small bird landed within reach of his flimsy lair. He snatched it, plucked it, and ate it raw. Things got worse a few days later when he broke through the crust surrounding a thermal pool, badly burning his hip. His feet and hands were already blackening with frostbite, and this new pain heaped more misery on the myopic explorer. During this time he had one small but important moment of inspiration. It occurred to him that he could use his small opera glass to concentrate the sunlight and perhaps make a fire. When he was able to direct a sunbeam into a small handful of dry wood to produce a swirl of smoke, then a flame, he was overjoyed. In typically poetic terms, he recalled, "I felt, if the whole world were offered me for it, I would cast it all aside before parting with that little spark."

After 10 days of fighting off starvation, animal attacks, festering frostbite, crippling depression, and the painful burn on his hip that forced him to sleep sitting up, Everts prepared to set off in the direction he believed his party would have last made camp, and where they might still be looking for their lost comrade. He headed out for West Thumb. He reached the lakeshore and was able to get a fire going and make camp that night, but the sounds of the dark forest, which surely included the mountain lions and wolves that were closing in on him, kept Everts awake until he was finally overtaken by exhaustion and fell asleep. While unconscious, he pitched forward and fell into the fire, severely burning his hand.

Back at Heart Lake, meanwhile, two members of his expedition, which had split into three search parties, had just missed Everts. They moved on to the southern end of the lake, but found no sign of their lost friend.

The following morning Everts moved north up the shore of Yellowstone Lake, carrying a firebrand to help him start another campfire. As he'd hoped, he discovered his party's previous campsite. His joy was tempered by the disappointment of finding that no supplies had been left behind, nor any indication of the direction they'd taken out of camp. He did find a fork and an empty yeast tin, both of which would come in handy later.

At this point he retraced his steps down the beach, trying to ascertain the route the party would have taken toward the Madison Range, his new destination. Exhausted, he pitched camp that night, built a fire, and fell into a deep sleep. He was awakened by the crackle of burning wood, and jumped up to discover that his bed was on fire, as were the trees surrounding his campsite. His good hand had been burned, and the hair on his head "singed closer than a barber would have trimmed it." He'd started a forest fire.

After marveling at the "terrible beauty" of the inferno which now covered an entire hillside, he gave up on the idea of finding any trace of his compatriots' trail, and embarked on the direction he believed to be toward the lowest point in the Madison Range, where he planned to cross and make his way to Virginia City. This is where his account gets a little sketchy, in part because of the hallucinations he was beginning to suffer. He'd fashioned a carry bag from the upper half of his boots, and even though the bag was stuffed with thistle roots, he was gradually starving. Lacking proper nutrition, his body had begun to consume itself and he noticed that he was losing weight. His limbs had become separate entities from his body, he wrote, and he carried on loud arguments with them when they became recalcitrant about traveling. A steady diet of fibrous thistle roots had shut down his digestive system, and at one point, he said, he threatened to leave his seized-up stomach behind. His inability to get a decent amount of sleep no doubt contributed to the deterioration of his mental faculties.

Acting on the advice of an apparition he called "the doctor," Everts turned back from his route toward the Madison range, and retraced his steps for a couple of days before once again turning north toward the spot where the Yellowstone River flows out of its namesake lake. There were no thistles to be found in this area, but he claimed that he no longer suffered hunger pangs. When he did sleep, he had glorious, detailed dreams of sumptuous, multicourse meals served in the fancy restaurants of New York and Washington. His unconscious knew what his body was craving, although his waking mind rejected the same desires. He ate when possible only to provide energy, he wrote, not to feed his appetite. At one point he found part of a gull's wing, which he mashed up and heated with water in his yeast tin. "Delicious broth," he reported.

Somehow he kept moving during the day, crossing the Yellowstone River and encountering both lower and upper falls, which his expedition party had seen on the way in. One day began to blur into the next, and time becomes muddled in his written account, as he shifted his focus from the details of the terrain to his own inner thoughts that veered wildly from "morbid indifference" to "words of encouragement and cheer" he thought he was hearing from his arms and legs. This had become a bad trip in every sense of the term.

He was able to capture some minnows out of a small, mineral-laden stream. His digestive system refused them immediately, and he assumed the water they'd come from was poisoned. As he neared Tower Fall, he came upon a hollow log in the woods. The tracks around the log left no doubt this was a bear's den, but Everts was so exhausted he crawled into the cavity, after lighting a circle of fire around it for protection. He slept well, but woke to discover he'd started another forest fire. What the hell, it kept the bear away.

By now he was aware that he had been working his way north toward the expedition's original route into the park along the Gardner River. He began to find more elk thistle, but still had to endure more snowstorms, sleepless nights, and bouts of despair. He stopped to light a fire and discovered that he'd dropped his lens somewhere. He had no choice but to retrace his steps for 5 miles to find it.

Thirty-seven days after he'd become lost, it was assumed that Everts had frozen to death or met some other terrible end. Meanwhile, he was still alive—barely—and stumbling along in the area just west of

Crescent Hill in the vicinity of Oxbow Creek, south of the Yellowstone River, unaware that a pair of men were tracking him. Jack Baronett, a mountaineer already familiar with Yellowstone, and George Pritchett, a prospector, had been enlisted to go into Yellowstone to search for Everts's remains—for a hefty bounty, of course. The pair spotted Everts across the ravine, crawling along the hillside trail, seeking shelter from the icy wind. According to Everts, the two approached him and asked, "Are you Mr. Everts?" "Yes," he replied, "all that is left of him." He then asked who had sent his saviors, and just before he passed out, proclaimed, "God bless him, and them, and you! I am saved!" He may well have remembered the scene exactly that way, but according to Baronett, once they ascertained the skeletal creature's identity, Everts threw up his hands and garbled a few words and passed out as Baronett took him over his shoulder and carried him down the hillside and made a camp by the creek. Pritchett set off to fetch help—a 75-mile round trip. Baronett estimated that Everts weighed less than 50 pounds. It took several days of constant care until he was able to travel, followed by months of convalescence in Bozeman, but Everts eventually regained his health, recovering fully from his incredible ordeal.

When it came time to choose the first superintendent of Yellowstone National Park in 1872, Everts was offered the job, largely due to the public's Yellowstone frenzy that had been whipped up by his sensational article in *Scribner's*. Everts declined the position, however, when he found out the job came with no staff, no budget, and no pay. He later married and moved to Maryland to work for the US Post Office in Washington, DC. He died of pneumonia in 1901, but his legend lives on as the only person to become lost in the Yellowstone wilderness and be found alive, nearly 6 weeks later, surviving on little more than his wits and determination.

Big Sky Reading Rooms

We love to snuggle up with a book in our hotel bed where we can enjoy the life of the mind uninterrupted. We listen for hours to audiobooks while the miles unspool behind us on the road. We might sneak a chapter on our phone while locked in a stall at an interstate rest stop. Readers can do it just about anywhere. One of life's most delicious pleasures is to find a comfortable, quiet spot in the great outdoors and crack open a book while letting the sights, sounds, and smells of nature wash over you. Glacier, Yellowstone, and the Montana Swath have abundant opportunities to provide the most beautiful reading experience you've ever had. Here are a few that stand out.

GLACIER

- **Back porch of Lake McDonald Inn:** You'll likely be staying here on your first or last days of your Glacier visit, and spending some relatively quiet time on the rustic back porch, looking out over Lake McDonald, and a reading break might be just the thing after long days of driving or miles of trail hiking in the park. Still, you'll have a hard time keeping your eyes on the page. The mirror image of those skyscraping glacial mountains on the glassy surface of the lake is a breathtaking sight that launched a few million keepsake photos. Might be a good spot to leaf through a magazine.

- **Balcony of Sperry Lodge:** As you're kicked back in a chair on the balcony of the rebuilt historic dorm building, it's easy to be lulled into a train of deep, existential ponderance as you take in the glacial cirque that lies spread out before you. It's the very heart of Glacier Park, and you can't help but wonder about its creation, the universe, and your tiny place in all of it. It's probably not the time to dip into *Infinite Jest*, though. That thousand-page doorstop would feel like hauling a cinder block up the 6.7-mile trail. I would recommend rereading a paperback copy of *Zen and the Art of Motorcycle Maintenance*, a counterculture touchstone that leads to plenty of Big Questions.

- **Swimming beach on Two Medicine Lake:** There's a short trail through the woods from the Two Medicine Ranger Station parking lot, and you may encounter a mountain goat or two browsing through the foliage. Once you make it past some colorful wildflower meadows to the little beach, you'll find it's a great spot to plop yourself down on the ancient sands and soak your feet in the icy water. You'll have the beach to yourself much of the time, and it's a good, quiet spot to get away from the crowded trails, and the negative ions rolling off Two Medicine Lake will help recharge your body and soul.

- **In a hammock at Ben Rover cabin in Polebridge:** One of the most popular Forest Service rental cabins, the Ben Rover sleeps eight, and is situated a dry fly's throw from the North Fork of the Flathead River. There's no cell service, and the cabin has no electricity—it's propane-powered. Entertainment is strictly old school, and the cabin is stocked with a few board games and several books. It's a perfect spot to string up a hammock and let the sounds of the river, the raptors, and songbirds and the foraging deer play around

Taking a break from the road to do some reading in a picturesque spot can really help recharge your batteries. This overlook near Georgetown Lake at St. Timothy's Cathedral is one of those spots that make you feel like a summer day in Montana was created just for you. AUTHOR PHOTO

you like a symphony while you let yourself melt into a good novel or maybe peruse an Audubon guide to identify some of the flora and fauna you've seen in the park.

- **Brownie's Hostel in East Glacier Park Village:** For those accustomed to traveling hostel-style, the social aspect of these low-cost accommodations is a given. It's nice to occasionally get some alone time by sitting on the balcony directly above the bakery/deli/general store entrance and getting lost in a book, surrounded by the deep pine forest of East Glacier and a postcard view of the rugged Rocky Mountains. You'll hear conversations in tongues from dozens of countries wafting up from the cafe below, alongside the glorious aromas from the bakery's creative and delicious treats.

- **Deck of a caboose cabin at the Izaak Walton Inn:** The historic hotel on US 2 about halfway between East Glacier and West Glacier is not technically in the park, but it is in the shadow of Glacier's mountain peaks. The property offers a variety of rooms besides the twenty-two vintage, wood-lined rooms in the main hotel. Lined up on a bluff just across the tracks are several brightly colored cabooses that have been converted into guest cabins. Each has a cozy deck where you can relax in a camp chair and look out at the stately peak of Scalplock Mountain in Glacier, and enjoy some light reading that will be punctuated by the roar of the dozen or so trains that rumble through what was once a major railyard.

YELLOWSTONE

- **Balcony of the Old Faithful Snow Lodge:** The Snow Lodge itself houses one of the restaurants that serves the million-plus visitors who gather every year to watch the most famous geyser in the world. If you're staying at one of the affordable Snow Lodge Cabins behind the main lodge, the spacious balcony overlooking the Upper Geyser Basin is a spectacular spot to relax and watch the crowds come and go while, in the distance, dozens of geysers and vents shoot a constant barrage of water and steam into the mountain air. It may be just the perfect place to read *Wonderlandscape*, John Clayton's thoroughly engaging mix of culture and history that unpacks Yellowstone's tale through the stories of ten of its most memorable characters. Every time Old Faithful blows, get up and stretch your legs.

- **On the porte cochère porch of the Old Faithful Inn:** Staying at the world's biggest log cabin is a bucket list item for many. There are myriad nooks and corners inside the massive, open lodge to sit with a book, and it's especially fun to sit in a rocker or camp chair on the "front porch" and enjoy the comings and goings of the Inn's guests. Historic Yellow Buses drop off and pick up groups for their entertaining tours, and sightseers wander around like ants that have had their hill kicked over. Maybe not the best place to pore over some intricate nonfiction, but the wicked absurdity of a Dave Barry novel like *Sick Monkey* might be a good complement to the calmly surreal scene.
- **On the beach near Fishing Bridge:** Take the trail across from the Ranger Station and you'll immediately leave the throng behind. The hustle and bustle of Fishing Bridge and nearby Blue Bay Campground fade quickly as you cut through the woods and make your way down the easy path to the shore of Yellowstone Lake. You'll come out onto a wide expanse of beach, just as the explorers did in 1870 when the famous Washburn Expedition spent 3 weeks examining and chronicling what would become the first national park in 1872. The beach sees very little traffic, and it's a nice spot to throw down a towel and lie back with a book, the view of the Absarokee Mountains across the massive lake providing some visual tranquility.
- **Sunroom at the Lake Hotel:** You'll surely be surrounded by a dozen or more readers in the elegant, old-world study of Yellowstone's oldest hotel, curled up on the leather-clad couches and luxurious armchairs, looking up occasionally to check out the panoramic view down the lake through the two-story bay windows. It's especially crowded in the evenings, when people linger with a beverage while waiting for their reservations to come up in the Hotel's swank restaurant. In the gift shop across the lobby you can find a copy of *Wrecked in Yellowstone* by Mike Stark. It's the remarkable story of E. C. Waters, one of the most reviled hucksters from Yellowstone's early days. Waters spent 20 years as a concessionaire before he was finally banned from the park, but not before scuttling his massive tour steamboat, the partial wreck of which still remains on the far side of Stevenson Island, viewable from the Sunroom.

- **Tiny, two-chair balcony at Absaroka Lodge in Gardiner:** It's a secluded spot smack dab in the middle of the action in Yellowstone's North Entrance town. The Absaroka—two buildings with every room overlooking the Yellowstone River—is right at the north end of the bridge, and just a delightful and convenient place to stay. The tiny balcony of a single room is just big enough for a couple of chairs, and most are partially shielded from bridge traffic by large cottonwoods growing on the riverbank. Views of Electric Mountain and other peaks in the park create a picture of serenity in the distance while Gardiner crawls with visitor activity year-round. After a day of rambling around the park, build yourself a cocktail, listen to the river below, and spend some time with one of Montana's hundreds of excellent writers, from James Lee Burke to Gwen Florio. You'll feel a little more connected to your surroundings.

MONTANA

- **Missouri Headwaters State Park:** Whether you're overnighting at the campground or just stopping for a break from the interstate, the confluence of the Jefferson, Madison, and Missouri Rivers provides a sweet and satisfying experience for those who want to sit near these flowing clear waters at the head of a wide, picturesque valley along I-90. People love to park and explore the area just 3 miles from the freeway, checking out the historic buildings and gathering info from the interpretive signs along the self-guided tour. Perhaps the ultimate reading experience would be to get comfortable in a spot near where a couple of the rivers run together and read Chapter 21 of *Undaunted Courage* by Stephen E. Ambrose, perhaps the best book ever written about the Corps of Discovery. His account of Lewis and Clark's arrival at the Missouri Headwaters on their journey west in 1805 is nothing short of thrilling, and to read about it at the very place where it happened is particularly satisfying.
- **Greycliff Prairie Dog Town State Park:** About halfway between Billings and Livingston on I-90, Prairie Dog Town is no more and no less than the name implies. In the middle of 98 acres of black-tailed prairie dog habitat, there's a small asphalt parking lot with a couple of benches and

a picnic table. There are no restrooms so it's not a heavily used exit. But it is a great opportunity to sit and read, while the curious but jumpy little critters continually scamper around and pop out of their holes to warn each other of your presence, their own presence, and god-knows-what with their constant chirps and whistles and barks. Granted, it's not for everyone, but you may find the natural cacophony somehow soothing.

- **Radersburg Cemetery:** Sure, it's not highly ranked on TripAdvisor or even listed on a map as a lunch spot, but the original cemetery in Radersburg is a well-kept oasis just east of the Elkhorn Range in the forest-and-scrub lands along US 287, between Helena and Three Forks. If you're a student of Yellowstone history, you may know Radersburg as the hometown of Emma and George Cowan, members of the so-called Radersburg Party, a group of tourists who were famously attacked by a band of Nez Perce as the tribe was attempting to elude the US Army battalion that had been chasing them from the Bitterroot Valley. The intertwining stories of the Nez Perce War, the Battle of the Big Hole, and the capture of the Radersburg Party, all in the summer of 1877, are a stellar example of how through-lines tend to intersect as one dives deeper into history. Although the Cowans are not buried at this cemetery, it's a beautiful spot to sit on your tailgate, munch on a sandwich, and read a bit of *Empire of Shadows* by George Black, an exhaustive history of the settling of the West by European Americans leading up to the creation of Yellowstone National Park.

- **Southern Cross:** High in the hills above Georgetown Lake on Iron Mountain between Anaconda and Philipsburg, Southern Cross is a tiny mining settlement that was inhabited from its inception in the 1870s until the end of 2000, when the last handful of tenacious residents were evicted by the Canadian mining company that now owns the land. The road up to Southern Cross—now officially a ghost town—branches off from the road to Discovery Ski Area. At a bend near the top sits St. Timothy's Memorial Chapel, a thriving facility that hosts weddings, funerals, and even the occasional concert. The grounds offer a sweeping view of Georgetown Lake and the Pintler Range beyond. There's a picnic table under a couple of pines next to the beautiful little chapel, and it's a great place to get lost in a book under a particularly lovely corner of the Big Sky.

- **Sacajawea Park, Livingston:** This drinking town with a fly-fishing problem lies along I-90 about an hour north of Yellowstone Park down the Paradise Valley. Livingston was famously chronicled in Jimmy Buffett's "Livingston Saturday Night," and it's still a fun, not-too-big western Montana burg that has plenty to offer for those looking for a place to explore between the national parks. One favorite area is Sacajawea Park, a gorgeous riverfront greenbelt with a nice walkway along the Yellowstone River. The park features a large playground, a skatepark, tennis courts, and an outdoor pool. Best of all, book lovers, there are several shaded benches where you can sit quietly near the river and turn some pages while the kids wear themselves out before the next leg of your journey.

- **Missoula Public Library:** Okay, it's not outdoors, but the new Missoula Public Library, opened in 2021 after years of COVID- and construction-related delays, could be classified as the Great Indoors. You don't have to take my word for it—the new facility was named Public Library of the Year by the International Federation of Library Associations and Institutions in 2022. The library occupies a city block in the heart of downtown and has quickly become the community hub. Forget your old notions of a dim and dusty, brick-walled, low-ceilinged affair—this library is a stunner. And it's all about open space. There are four floors of books and resources that could keep a family busy all day long, maybe the perfect thing if you happen to roll through Missoula on a rainy day. From toddlers to teens, kids of all ages will find a treasure trove of activities that are physical, mentally stimulating, and just plain fun. For readers, the library is full of secluded nooks, comfy armchairs, study rooms, sprawl-able modern art furniture, and a terrific coffee shop just inside the front entrance. The open design means that no matter where you decide to settle in for a reading session, especially on the building's southside balconies, you'll have wide open views of the Rattlesnake Wilderness, the Bitterroot and Sapphire Ranges, and all the Rocky Mountain beauty that frames one of Montana's prettiest and liveliest towns.

17

Danger and Comfort: Seeing Yellowstone "The Wylie Way"

SAY YOU'RE A FINANCIALLY SUCCESSFUL CAPTAIN OF INDUSTRY CIRCA 1885, living the high life in an East Coast urban center. You go to all the right parties, take in the opera from the best box seats, and enjoy the finest luxuries a person of your station should have. But it's all become so, I don't know . . . dullsville. Your wife and daughters have been raving about the vacation experience that's become all the rage. Europe? Not this year, they say. They want to "see America first," like it says in the advertisements for the new Northern Pacific Railway. And the focus of much of this fascination and nationalistic curiosity? It's a bizarre corner of the Wild West called "Wonderland." Yellowstone National Park is its official moniker, and your family wants to go. But everything about this place sounds exactly like things you've been taught all your life to avoid: boiling hot pools; geysers shooting jets of scalding steam; wild animals such as buffalo, bears, and bighorn sheep, all ready to gore you to death or tear you to ribbons with razor sharp claws and huge teeth. It all sounds perfectly ghastly, yet somehow compelling. But to travel across the continent in a luxury train car only to be picked up by a rattle-trap stagecoach and sleep in the dirt and subsist on boiled horsemeat and pemmican, whatever that is? Or, conversely, to be squirreled away in a posh grand lodge, pampered and spoiled, only to miss out on whatever wildlife and fantastic geological wonders that aren't within view of your room's window? Might as well stay home! What's this, then, a colorful brochure for "permanent" campsites in Yellowstone Park? Luxurious, roomy tents with wood floors and real beds? Hmm. This might be worth a second look.

There was great fanfare and a tremendous sense of accomplishment when President Grant signed the Yellowstone National Park Protection Act into law, creating Yellowstone National Park in 1872. What there wasn't was money. The world's first national park would fall under the purview of the Department of the Interior, which provided no budgetary consideration to fund the new park. Yellowstone's first superintendent, Nathaniel P. Langford, toiled for 5 years with no staff, no resources, no budget, and no salary. In its first 5 years of existence, Yellowstone saw fewer than 2,500 visitors. It wasn't until 1883, when the Northern Pacific Railway completed its Yellowstone spur to Cinnabar, 3 miles north of Gardiner, that the tourism floodgates were thrown open. Horse-drawn "tally-ho" stages would pick up groups of tourists and clatter along the dirt road through the Northwest Entrance to Mammoth Hot Springs, where their tours of Yellowstone Park would begin. This period, from 1883 to 1916, after which motor vehicles were allowed into the park, was dominated by the "carriage trade." Tour carriages and stagecoaches delivered well-heeled visitors to the NPRR-built hotels in the park, where their clean, well-appointed lodgings provided a high level of comfort between guided excursions to the park's points of interest. There were also those who explored the park on horseback, camping in the few dedicated sites available and sustaining themselves with whatever food and personal amenities they carried with them. Little opportunity existed between these two extremes until an enterprising young fellow from Bozeman came up with a solution after taking a local jeweler on a tour of the park in 1880.

William Wallace Wylie had moved to Bozeman from Iowa in 1879, having read Truman Everts's account in *Scribner's Monthly* of becoming separated from an 1870 expedition into the Upper Yellowstone and surviving for 37 days. Everts's descriptions of the rugged wilderness and its spectacular wildlife inspired Wylie to see Yellowstone for himself. It was love at first tour. Shortly after his first solo jaunt, Wylie conveyed a wagon of tourists 50 miles from Mammoth Hot Springs all the way down to the geyser basins, reportedly the first wheeled passenger vehicle to make that trip. Wylie was still working his full-time job as a public school superintendent in Bozeman, and he and his wife Mary Ann started running more tours during his summer break, bringing his students and fellow teachers through the park. The young entrepreneur correctly predicted that as the railroads opened up the West, the numbers of visitors to Yellowstone would multiply, and he became one of the first Yellowstone guides to start monetizing his tours. He did his part to promote Wonderland, as it was frequently called, by giving slideshow and lecture tours in the winter, extolling the glorious features to be found in the park while, of course, handing out brochures advertising Wylie-led tours of same.

These early years of the carriage trade were full of hustlers and opportunists of all stripes looking to cash in on the growing Yellowstone craze. The Department of the Interior was doling out permits and leases liberally, which short-sighted hucksters used to open hastily built hotels, souvenir stands, claptrap lunch counters, and any number of parasitic endeavors that they could come up with to try and get some of that East Coast tourist money that was flowing west by the carload. These independents were typically squashed by Yellowstone's own 800-pound gorilla, the Northern Pacific Railroad, which had a major financial stake in much of the national park's infrastructure. While the US Army was responsible for oversight and security in Yellowstone during this era, the railroad ruled the park's commercial enterprises with a firm grasp. They sold package tours that included travel fare on their railways that would deliver tourists to park-adjacent towns, and the railroad-owned stage companies would convey the visitors to their railroad-built hotels, where they ate at railroad-owned restaurants and toured the park in railroad-hired wagons driven by teamsters who worked for—you guessed it—the railroad.

Wylie was no fly-by-night operator, and his passion for the park steeled him for the long haul. He spent 10 years conducting tours as an independent—always using his own horse teams, his own wagon, and his own camping gear. At the end of the day's tour campers would arrive in camp, dinner already being heated over a nice campfire. By the 1890s tourists had begun to demand a higher level of comfort, and Wylie responded by purchasing a pair of retro-fitted, horse-drawn Pullman cars, lush with luxurious amenities and creature comforts. They were so heavy that each car had to be pulled by a team of Clydesdales. Yellowstone's Grand Loop

Road, still in its infancy, couldn't support the gargantuan wagons, which also played hell with other stage traffic carrying people through the park. They were banned the following year.

All the while, Wylie was keeping an eye on the NPRR's progress as they continued to build grand hotels throughout the park. He noted that wherever the railroad was building one of their giant lodges, they would erect large tents that would stay up through the season, housing workers and tourists alike until the structure was ready to open its doors. In 1893 he traveled to Washington, DC, to lobby the powers that be to allow him to install permanent camps in the park. He got the nod, infuriating the hoteliers that were already annoyed with the amount of business he was siphoning away with his camping enterprise.

Soon, the Wylie Camping Company's distinctive green and white candy-striped tents were sprouting up all over the park. He'd set up camps at Yellowstone Lake Outlet, Appolinaris Springs, Upper Geyser Basin, and on Cascade Creek near Canyon. More than a century before the term "glamping" came into vogue, William Wylie successfully conceived of a middle ground between the comfort and luxury of a top-notch hotel room, and your basic camping—sleeping in the dirt, exposed to the elements, the bugs, and the dangerous animals people came to see. The Wylie Way promised "all the comforts and conveniences of life, maintaining at the same time spice and informality of camp life." He shrewdly designed an experience that would marry the public's seemingly dichotomous desires: to be out among the wilderness, and to be comfortably sheltered and protected from the wilderness. In its first few decades, Yellowstone really was attainable mostly by the moneyed upper crust, those who could spring for the $50 round trip rail fare and the $40 or more for several days of touring the park under the wing of a gregarious and knowledgeable guide. This new style of seeing Yellowstone created a pair of inroads. First, it offered an alternative for the tourist of means to be even closer to "nature" but without the filthy, uncomfortable accommodations that came with being out in it. Wylie tents were large, had high roofs and wood floors, each fitted with its own pot-bellied stove. Every tent contained one, two, or four beds, featuring a soft mattress covered with a floral quilt. A wash basin,

Before autos were first allowed into the park, concessionaires provided all the comforts of home for visitors who preferred staying in a tent to the civilized comforts of a hotel room. Thanks to the Wylie Camping Company, there wasn't much difference. COURTESY OF THE MONTANA HISTORICAL SOCIETY ARCHIVES

side furniture, and a Persian-pattern rug completed the interior, which felt as homey and inviting as a decent hotel room.

Second, and perhaps more importantly, the Wylie Way, while still not exactly cheap, was far more affordable than an NPRR package tour, putting it within reach of the bourgeoisie who longed to experience Yellowstone but couldn't afford to lay out a quarter of their annual income to do so.

As his camp packages became more popular, Wylie kept tweaking his setup to jack up the comfort and give his clients the most unforgettable experience possible. Every Wylie campsite featured a cavernous dining tent where campers ate sumptuous meals off real china set on white tablecloths while enjoying fresh cream and milk from the camp's cow herd. There was an office tent, which offered US Mail service and sold postcards, medicines, candy, cigars, straw hats, and other sundries. Daily laundry service was part of the deal, supplying clients with fresh sheets, blankets, towels, and napkins. After supper, campers could foxtrot the night away on a polished wood dance floor while the same employees who earlier had been splitting firewood and setting up tents would pop corn over the fire, sing songs, or put on skits for the night's entertainment. In the morning, while the campers were prying their eyes open over coffee and hot breakfast, the staff would pack up and move their belongings to the next Wylie camp on the itinerary.

Wylie could not guarantee that his clients would be able to lay their eyes on a real, live bear, and that was the animal most of Yellowstone's visitors hoped to see. Bears figured heavily in the park's advertising—posters throughout the passenger cars of the Northern Pacific's Yellowstone Line depicted cartoon bears, some wearing train engineers' caps, spewing hype about the amazing sights and sounds of the national park, especially bears, bears, bears. Everyone wanted to see some bears. Black, brown, purple—it didn't matter. As long as they could go back home and tell their friends all about their harrowing experience being face to face with a terrifying bear. Wylie did his best to accommodate them. His camps were frequently situated near garbage dumps, which attracted the omnivorous bruins. Sometimes, if a hapless black bear wandered into a Wylie camp, employees would surround the poor beast and try to keep it there until the campers could be summoned to come see it. If they were lucky, the bear would tire of their yelling and throwing rocks at it and would just climb a tree, where they would keep it trapped for hours.

This boorish behavior and utter lack of respect for wildlife seems kind of insane when viewed through a modern lens. But we have to remember that this was at the end of the 19th century, a time when the West was still struggling with "the Indian question" and travel was still mostly horse-based. "Nature" and "wilderness" were just vague concepts that encompassed resources that were meant to be exploited, and as such were infinite in their supply. In many ways Yellowstone spurred the earliest efforts toward conservation, and its very designation as a place that would be protected from development, or the harvesting of its natural resources can be seen as a harbinger of a more enlightened attitude toward the natural world. Wylie was probably not thinking about these things when he was caught planting alfalfa on a small hilltop near the park entrance in Gardiner. He knew the sweetgrass would attract elk and bison near the road in full view of the wagon loads of clients coming into the park. He needed the testimonials. This happened years before the establishment of the National Park Service, and the Army tended to look the other way while he set traps and otherwise messed with the habitat to attract animals and enhance his clients' experience.

It was a hinky way to run a camping company, but compared to some of his contemporaries, Wylie had a sterling reputation. Yes, he may have put out feed to attract game along his tour routes, but another concessioner of that period, E. C. Waters, pulled a lot of stunts that were notoriously beyond the pale, including taking barges full of animals to a small island in Yellowstone Lake, where boatloads of tourists would see them feeding as they motored past on the way from West Thumb to the Lake Hotel.

Whatever tactics Wylie employed, and whatever moves he made to keep abreast of the public's ever-changing demands, it worked. There were several copycat businesses, but Wylie's true love of the park, and those obnoxious-but-comforting green-and-white-striped tents made the business one of the most successful independent operations of his time. Twenty percent of the Yellowstone's carriage trade visitors toured the park the Wylie Way. In 1897 Wylie leased the Park Hotel in Gardiner to serve as his tour headquarters, hosting the visitors coming in from Cinnabar at the terminus of the railroad's Livingston spur. When the railroad extended the spur to Gardiner in 1903, Wylie was ready. His Gardiner Wonderland Hotel was up and running by August of that year.

In 1905, perhaps tiring of shouldering the load, Wylie sold his business to a consortium of operators working within the park. They updated the name to the Wylie Permanent Camping Company, and he stayed on for several years as a paid consultant. Coincidentally (maybe), in 1905 Wylie also won a court case against the Northern Pacific, which he had accused of discrimination. The railroad had unfairly offered customers tours only with their affiliated enterprises in a clear attempt to cut into the Wylie Camp Co.'s business. They were ordered to include the Wylie Co. in any future tour ticket sales. Despite the victory, William Wylie was probably becoming weary of constant government intervention and the cutthroat competition.

On July 31, 1915, a Ford Model T drove into Yellowstone Park, signaling the end of the carriage trade era. The following year, by order of the newly formed NPS, the Wylie Permanent Camping Company was absorbed along with all the park's other tent camping companies into a single entity, the Yellowstone Park Camping Company. The year after that, all horse-drawn vehicles were banned from the park.

William and his wife Mary retired to Pasadena, California, but the camping company bug had burrowed deep. In 1917, encouraged by the NPS, they went on to establish camping businesses in Zion National Park and at the North Rim of Grand Canyon National Park, providing ways for tourists to "see America first" and enjoy these newly designated national treasures. Mary passed away in 1928, shortly after these new concerns were placed under the control of the Utah Parks Co. and the Union Pacific, respectively. William died in 1930.

You can still camp in Yellowstone Park, of course, and there is nothing like peeking out of your tent in the morning and seeing an 800-pound bull elk strolling past your campsite. Most of the campsites, though, can accommodate only an 8-foot-square tent, not really big enough to hold a couple of full-size beds and a wood stove. Technology has given us some pretty incredible modern conveniences that help make tent camping a lot more comfortable and enjoyable, and it continues to be one of the most exciting ways to experience any national park. Still, it will never compare to the pre-car era, when the best way to see Yellowstone Park was the Wylie Way.

18

Uncle Tom's Trail ... of Terror

As YELLOWSTONE'S GRAND LOOP ROAD GRADUALLY GREW AND improved, connecting most of the park's major attractions, the areas around these attractions grew into villages. Nowadays places like Grant Village, Old Faithful, and Tower Junction are compact outposts of commerce and civilization where you can hop onto the Wi-Fi and take a peek at your investment portfolio, wander through an interpretive museum to learn some science and history about the park, or swing into one of the many stores that offer important amenities such as ice, bear spray, liquor, and ibuprofen. One essential item you'll need to add to your list of accoutrements is a trail map. Each year more than 4 million visitors see the park from behind a windshield or a tour bus window, perhaps stopping to walk along some of its 15 miles of boardwalk or simply locate a restroom to offload a couple liters of Monster Energy drink. But as many Yellowstone buffs will attest, the wonders of this mysterious land won't truly get under your skin until you get out of your vehicle and spend some time on a trail. The park's 2.2 million acres are veined with 900 miles of hiking trails, and it's up to you to choose the level of challenge. The West Thumb Geyser Basin Trail, which is mostly a gently sloping boardwalk, is a mere ⅜ of a mile through a spectacular nest of geysers, hot pools, and steam vents along Yellowstone Lake's west edge. Across the lake and a bit north, you can pick up Yellowstone's longest trail, the Thorofare. Backpackers can truly be one with nature along the 34.3-mile trail that takes hikers and pack trips through the park's most primitive wilderness from the north end of Yellowstone Lake all the way to the park's southern border.

And then there's Uncle Tom's Trail. Behind Canyon Village, across the massive gorge of the Grand Canyon of Yellowstone, there's a parking lot for people wanting to hike the South Rim Trail. The lot was put there to serve the original Canyon Lodge, which was abandoned in 1956 as it had become structurally unsound. It's also where you'll find the trailhead to one of the park's most challenging, terrifying, and rewarding hikes.

At just a shade over half a mile there and back, Uncle Tom's Trail is among the park's shortest, but also one of the steepest. Also, probably its most notorious. It's ideal for the steely-nerved type who wants to get close enough to the base of the Lower Falls to get damp from the mist and stand among the ever-present rainbows. Starting at the trailhead near the parking lot, 328 steps lead you down along the near-vertical south wall of the canyon, to a tiny viewing platform that offers an up-close-and-personal view near the base of the breathtaking Lower Falls. It is not for the faint of heart, nor the short of breath. It's one of Yellowstone's oldest trails, built in 1898 by a concessionaire with a vision, H. F. "Uncle Tom" Richardson. If you have the legs, the lungs, and the gumption, I'd recommend tackling this trail as soon as you can. It might not be around much longer.

So who was H. F. Richardson? Why was he compelled to build this ridiculous trail, and exactly whose uncle was he? Let's start with the name. "Uncle Tom" Richardson was given the nickname by his friends in Bozeman, where he was a businessman. It's unclear whether the moniker had anything to do with Harriet Beecher Stowe's best-selling novel, *Uncle Tom's Cabin*, and hard info is not readily available. Known as an outdoorsman and adventurer, Richardson was working for the Wylie Camp Co. in the summer of 1896 when he received permission to build a trail down the steep south wall of the Grand Canyon. He had been ferrying Wylie clients across the Yellowstone River above the upper falls, where a small fleet of company rowboats was kept. After building his trail he went into business for himself. He would pick up passengers on the north side of the river, row them across, and then escort them through the forest to the head of his trail, where visitors would lower themselves into the gorge using a series of ropes and wooden ladders he'd installed. It was roughly equivalent to climbing down the side of a twenty-two-story building.

Probably the most hair-raising trail in Yellowstone Park leads brave hikers down a cliff face to the base of the Lower Falls of the Grand Canyon of Yellowstone, where they can feel the mist and see the ever-present rainbow above the spray. The trail is in a constant state of repair and improvement, so check to see if it's currently open before putting it on your itinerary.

After a damp viewing of the roaring falls, guests would clamber back up the trail and be treated to a fireside meal before Uncle Tom ferried them back across the river. For this experience, Tom was paid a dollar a pop.

Business was great, and Richardson was able to renew his concession-aire's permit yearly, and raked in about $1,000 per season, a princely sum at the end of the 19th century. In 1903 his permit application was denied, and the concrete Chittenden Bridge was built in its current location where it comes off Grand Loop Road to connect with South Rim Drive. His business dropped off, but Uncle Tom continued to ferry passengers and escort them up and down his trail. The following year he applied for a full business permit, and it was granted by acting superintendent Major Pitcher, good for the typical one-year term and revocable at any point by the secretary of the interior. That year he reported having guided 1,147 people. He was granted another permit in 1905, but instructed to cap his fee at $1 per patron. This, it would later become apparent, represented the zenith of Uncle Tom's earning power in Yellowstone Park.

In 1906 the Chittenden Bridge was finished, and the engineers had also built a road that led down along the river. Superintendent Major Pitcher ordered a proper trail to be built in place of Uncle Tom's janky system of ladders and ropes, and that it be open to the public, not a toll trail. Richardson responded that he would be hiring a second assistant because he could not keep up with trail maintenance as it was. With the increased foot traffic a new and improved trail would bring, his maintenance work would increase, he said. Still, since his "tour" was no longer a requirement to gain access to the trail, he dropped his price to 50 cents rather than see business evaporate completely. He reported that 2,248 people had used the trail in 1905. Now he was seeing much of his income slip away as people would no longer have to pay to use the trail.

The Engineer Office oversaw the addition of steps along portions of Uncle Tom's Trail in the 1906 season. Richardson continued to butt heads with park administration over public access to the trail, which was being hiked by more people as the new bridge provided easy access to park visitors. During this time a proposal came in from E. C. Waters, one of the park's early concessionaires. Waters ran a small, steam-powered ship on Yellowstone Lake that carried passengers from West Thumb to Lake Hotel, and was probably the most reviled man to do business in the park. He was constantly scheming, making end runs around the regulations, and was even ousted from the park on several occasions because of his shady business dealings and blatantly ripping off many of his customers. He proposed to the superintendent that he should receive a lease for an elevator he would build in the area of Uncle Tom's Trail. This elevator would take visitors down to the river, and then back up to the canyon rim. The idea was rejected.

Another proposal submitted to acting superintendent Lieutenant-Colonel Brett suggested that Uncle Tom's Trail be carved out and made into a burro trail. This, the superintendent knew, would require cutting a massive gash into the canyon walls, creating a repulsive eyesore in an otherwise idyllic landscape. Again, the idea was nixed.

Also rejected was Richardson's application for a renewed permit to run his ferry/tour business, some time before 1913. That year he wrote to Chester A. Lindsley, a civilian clerk at the Army headquarters in Mammoth, and offered the man 25 percent interest in his enterprise if he would grease the skids and get a permit approved. In April that year, Herbert F. "Uncle Tom" Richardson died in Bozeman from heart complications. He was 59.

His trail long outlasted him. In 1927 the trail was completely rebuilt by Yellowstone Park's Ranger Department, headed up by Chief Ranger Sam T. Woodering, at a cost of $2,321.63. Four sections of stairway were built and six platforms added, one at the very end for viewing the falls. Cable guardrails were added to the platforms, and rigid handrails attached to the stairs. By 1930, 6,500 people were using the trail each year.

Uncle Tom's Trail was closed after suffering some structural damage in the 1959 earthquake. As the early '60s dragged on, the needed repairs for the trail kept getting put off, and the proposed design would be costly, as it featured iron stairs set into rock. Meanwhile, Thomas C. Vint, chief of design and construction for the NPS, made this declaration of the popular trail: "It is the consensus in this office that this trail would be a conspicuous and intrusive development on one of the most important and impressive natural features in the Park. Mr. [Elvin] Scoyen [associate director of the NPS] requests that consideration be given to the removal of the present trail as well as the deletion of this trail construction project." Had Uncle Tom's Trail finally outlived its usefulness?

No way, wrote Park Superintendent Lemuel A. Garrison to the regional director. "The trip into the Grand Canyon of the Yellowstone using Uncle Tom's Trail affords a delightful opportunity for Park visitors to get out of their cars and venture away from the crowded car stops—a type of visitor use we wish to encourage. As expressed by Assistant Secretary Carver, the visitor not only enjoys being there, he also enjoys getting there. Several spectacular views from vantage points on the trail downward are climaxed by the tremendously impressive and moving experience at the base of the Lower Falls. Here one can feel for himself the power of the great waterfall as it shakes the ground upon which he stands."

Finally, from 1965 to 1967, Uncle Tom's Trail was rebuilt, save for the lowest 50 feet and bottom platform, which were removed. The fact that they could be seen from the north rim was unacceptable. Concrete walkways and steel stairs were installed, bringing the old rope and ladder trail to its last iteration in the modern park. In 2018 the trail was closed as its degradation had made it unsafe to the public. As of this writing the NPS has not yet received the funding it needs to refurbish the trail and bring it up to code. There have been several recommendations in recent years from the powers that be in the Park Service that it should be permanently closed due to safety concerns and the high cost of maintenance, so the future of Uncle Tom's Trail remains in limbo. There's a good chance that this little slice of Yellowstone's history may continue to crumble with each passing year, all that remains of the hustle and grit of one of the park's early entrepreneurs.

19

Some Like It Hot

Tom Brock needed a break from the road. The microbiologist was traveling out west, on vacation from teaching bacteriology at Indiana University in the summer of 1964. Yellowstone National Park seemed like a good diversion. He happened to catch a ranger talking about the colonies of blue-green algae living in one of Yellowstone's colorful thermal pools, and Brock was intrigued. He knew that living organisms could not survive in environments much higher than 70 degrees Celsius, yet here was a steaming pool, green with evidence to the contrary. If a photosynthetic life-form like algae could grow in the high temperatures of these hot pools, could there be some other form of microbes living in these hostile environments? After securing a research grant, he returned with a team and collected samples. They dipped some slides into the runoff streams along Firehole Lake Drive, a one-way, 3-mile loop near the Lower Geyser Basin fed by White Creek. By the time they got the slides back to the lab, they were coated with film. Brock peered at them through a microscope and was flabbergasted by what he found. "Effluent at 82°," he wrote in his journal, dated June 20. "Definitely living." Every slide had evidence of bacteria growing on it that had been happily reproducing at 82 degrees C (180°F) in Yellowstone. "That was a 'eureka' moment," he said later. Up to that point it was thought that no life-forms could live in certain extremes of hot or cold environments.

Brock spent the next 10 years studying the thermophiles he found in various sources in the Firehole Lake watershed as well as expanding his field work to locations in California. He amassed a ton of research into these microscopic organisms that not only tolerated, but thrived

Thermophiles such as blue-green algae are the heat-loving microbes that give the hot pools and streams their color. Chains of bacteria create flowing, fern-like clusters that can be seen in places like this inlet stream to Firehole Lake.
AUTHOR PHOTO

in temperatures previously thought much too high to support life. In a paper published in 1967, he wrote, "It is thus impossible to conclude that there is any 'upper temperature of life.'" In the field of biology, this was a game changer. Brock even discovered a new species in samples they collected from Yellowstone's Mushroom Pool. He and his assistant, a graduate student named Hudson Freeze, named the new bacterium *Thermus aquaticus*. Samples were duly submitted to the American Type Culture Collection of the American Microbiology Society (AMS), which stores such samples for research and study. It was these samples that would provide the springboard for unlocking the potential of this previously unknown life form.

So, what does this all have to do with the spectrum of brilliant colors that give Yellowstone's hot pools and streams their kaleidoscopic beauty? Well, when science is involved, it's usually complicated. First off, we need to understand a bit of microbiology. What microbes lack in size, they make up for in number. They're everywhere. They exist in every ecosystem, living in plants, animals, air, arctic ice, boiling hot springs—everywhere. They're in your gut, on the skin of your face, in the food you eat. They make up the majority of the earth's biomass, and are the building blocks of many of the biological processes that enable life to exist.

Thermophiles, the heat-loving buggers that make their home in the scalding waters of Yellowstone, comprise thousands of species which are classified as viruses, bacteria, archaea, and eukarya. Viruses can't reproduce on their own—they have to take over the metabolism of a host cell. Like the wolves in Yellowstone do with the elk population, these microbes play an important role in balancing out the ecosystem—whether they're beneficial, pathogenic, or neutral.

Of the remaining three domains, archaea are the most extreme of the thermophiles. These single-cell organisms have no nucleus, and are found in the hottest of thermal features, but they tolerate other extremes as well. Some are halophilic (living in very salty water) and some are methanogenic (living in environments with no oxygen, like your intestinal tract). Some of the first places thermophilic archaea were identified were Yellowstone's Obsidian Pool and Octopus Spring.

Bacteria are also single-celled microbes lacking a nucleus, but they also help maintain a healthy balance among microbial communities—their chemical exchanges are beneficial, even vital to the systems of the plants and animals that they're associated with. Many species are well equipped to live in high-temperature environments. The multihued mats growing on the flat surfaces around hot pools frequently are billions of bacteria intertwined with entrapped minerals and organic materials which supply nutrients. The microbial ecosystem is a delicate, ongoing balancing act, which is why the park doesn't want people tromping around on the community of organisms that make up these large bacterial mats.

There's the danger of punching through the crust and being boiled alive, sure, but the introduction of foreign microbes carried by hiking boots and flip-flops could wreak havoc on the microscopic ecosystem.

The third and largest group of microbes is eukarya. There are millions of species (only about 1.2 million have been identified) of these most complex organisms, which can be single-celled or multicelled. Unlike their microbe brethren, each eukaryotic cell contains a nucleus, a type of organelle that carries most of its genetic material. Eukaryotes like algae are able to produce their own chemical energy using photosynthesis. These organisms tend to prefer the relatively cooler water near the outer edges of Emerald Pool, Grand Prismatic Spring, or the hot tub back at your hotel. That's right, I'm talking about you. You are a eukaryote.

—~—

Yes, yes, but what about the colors? Simply put, any color you see in or around a geothermal feature in Yellowstone is a direct indicator of the environment currently being enjoyed by the thermophiles living there. But there's more to it than just the temperature of the water—they also choose environments according to the chemistry and pH of the water, which is in turn affected by nutrients and dissolved minerals. The archaea, for example, tend to inhabit the very hottest water, like in the deep center of hot pools such as Grand Prismatic Spring or Octopus Spring. The hottest water absorbs all light waves except the blue spectrum. If the water contains yellow sulfur deposits (you can usually tell by the rotten egg smell), the water appears more green or turquoise. Some thermal features such as Nymph Creek contain superacidic water. Algae are attracted to their low pH and high heat, and long, bright green tendrils created by a series of attached bacterial colonies can be seen waving along the bed of the creek. Seems that ranger Tom Brock listened to in 1964 didn't quite have his facts right, and it was Brock who figured it out.

One glance at the temperature control knob in your car shows that we tend to think of a thermal scale of color going from blue to red, coldest to hottest. In the hot springs and creeks of Yellowstone, it's the opposite. Blue represents the hottest temps, some approaching the boiling point of water. As it cools, usually in runoff streams or near the edges of the pools, the microbes reflect different light waves, going from green to brown to red, yellow and orange, and dozens of combinations that run alongside each other, providing those crazy Yellowstone swirls of color that have been blowing minds since the first Indigenous peoples happened across the geyser basins more than 12,000 years ago.

Knowing that you're looking at billions of living microbes as you take in the surreal beauty of, say, Beryl Spring and its Coke bottle–tinted water, it might be surprising to learn that thermophiles have been at the center of myriad fields of research, including the search to unlock the secrets of the Earth's creation and the attendant question about the possibility of life on other planets. In 1984 a football-sized rock was found on Allan Hills in the Antarctic. It was a meteorite that had been blasted off the surface of Mars by unknown forces 17 million years ago, and rode around in space until it struck the Earth 13,000 years ago. I believe it was on a Thursday. Debate has been raging ever since about whether organic molecules found in the rock were left by microbes, which would indicate that at some point, there was life on Mars. Before you reach for your protective tinfoil hat, you should know that the general consensus among the intelligentsia has shifted. Recent findings indicate that the molecules in the rock were likely caused by a chemical reaction between minerals and water, not little green men or other life forms.

It's not just extremophiles—microorganisms that live in conditions of extreme temperature, salinity, acidity, alkalinity, or radiation—that have changed how we think about the ability of some organisms to withstand extreme environments. The discovery of a microscopic creature known as the tardigrade, or water bear, has expanded the boundaries of what can be considered the outer limits of possibility to sustain life. The tardigrade, which looks like a teddy bear with a pig's face and eight stubby, claw-tipped appendages, has been found to exist pretty much all over the planet, but also in the most extreme environments, from the depths of ocean trenches to the vacuum of space. Thanks to their ability to expel 95 percent of the water in their bodies, they can curl up like a potato bug into something called a tun and achieve a sort of suspended animation with almost zero metabolism. Once exposed to water, these tuns have sprung back to life after enduring up to 20 years of high pressure, radiation, heat, cold, lack of oxygen, and starvation. Tuns have been sampled in water as hot as 200 degrees C and found encased in glaciers. While tardigrades are not technically classified as extremophiles because they don't reproduce in these extreme environments, the study of these amazing creatures is an important tool for astrobiology in the search for life on planetary bodies, and possible insight into enduring long stretches in the space environment for interstellar travel.

❧

Here on planet Earth, it was one of Yellowstone's thermophiles that became a microbiologic superstar thanks in part to the efforts of Tom Brock and Hudson Freeze. After the pair published their findings on *Thermus aquaticus* in 1969, the freeze-dried samples they'd collected sat in storage at the AMS. One night in 1983 biochemist Kary Mullis was cruising up US 101, heading for a few days in his Northern California cabin. He'd always done his best thinking while avoiding crowds by driving at night, and a complex issue was churning in his head: How could he come up with a method to replicate strands of DNA cheaply and quickly? Heating the sample always destroyed the *E. coli* DNA polymerase used as an agent, so more had to be added after the heating step, making the process slow and expensive. Reportedly with the help of a little mind-expanding substance, he came up with the concept of the polymerase chain reaction (PCR). "Would I have invented PCR if I hadn't taken LSD?" he said later. "I seriously doubt it. I could sit on a DNA molecule and watch the polymers go by." He needed a thermophilic polymerase, an agent that would withstand the heat of the reaction, speeding things up tremendously in the lab by not having to add more DNA polymerase after every cycle. "Beginning with a single molecule of the genetic material DNA," he told *Scientific American*, "the PCR can generate 100 billion similar molecules in an afternoon. The reaction is easy to execute. It requires no more than a test tube, a few simple reagents, and a source of heat."

After cooking up the basic idea of PCR, he procured a sample of *T. aquaticus* from the AMS to try in the process. The enzyme it produced, by then known as taq, had been found to exhibit the exact heat-resistant properties Mullis thought his PCR agent needed. No wonder it was named "molecule of the year" by *Science Magazine* in 1989. It worked. The method was quickly patented by Mullis's employer and the world of DNA amplification was changed forever. Mullis and fellow biochemist Michael Smith, who had developed alternate methods of manipulating DNA, shared the Nobel Prize for Chemistry in 1993. The process was quickly accepted by the criminal forensics community, among other scientific disciplines. DNA fingerprinting was a breakthrough in identifying organic material left behind at crime scenes, which was used both in convicting criminals and in exonerating those who had been wrongly convicted. It also provided a surefire method for paternity testing.

The medical research field, as you can imagine, was revolutionized by the advent of PCR. DNA samples procured from prospective parents can reveal any genetic carriers that might indicate potential mutations or disease in their offspring. Diseases such as lymphoma and leukemia can be caught sooner using PCR assays of genomic DNA. PCR-based testing is being used to replace traditional tissue testing methods in searching for suitable matches in organ transplants. From tuberculosis to HIV, using PCR for genetic analysis can detect as few as one bad organism in 50,000.

This leads to an inescapable question: Is PCR being used in the battle against COVID-19? Well, if you've gotten COVID test results from a lab, they probably used PCR.

Another huge scientific benchmark that has helped us swiftly deal with understanding and identifying COVID-19 is the Human Genome Project, an international scientific endeavor launched in 1990, with the goal of mapping and sequencing the entirety of human DNA. It was completed in January 2022. The human genome has 3.1 billion base pairs. It took a while. This knowledge of human DNA is invaluable in identifying mutations linked to cancer, thus enabling the engineering of effective treatments. Thanks to the genomic methods developed during this project, researchers were able to sequence the genome of the SARS-CoV-2 virus. This information was quickly shared across the globe with researchers who used the data to simultaneously develop several effective COVID-19 vaccines, kind of like open-source coding for microbiologists. Since virologists had already been studying the coronavirus for nearly 10 years, these recent advances and revolutionary methods such as PCR are helping to mitigate what some scientists believe could have been massive levels of global instability had COVID-19 been allowed to spread unchecked. Also, we now possess the tools to more swiftly deal with the inevitable viral outbreaks in the coming years.

Tom Brock and his wife Kathie (they'd met when she was on one of his early Yellowstone research teams) married, then moved to Madison, Wisconsin, in 1971, where he went on to chair the Department of Bacteriology. He continued studying Yellowstone's thermophiles until 1975, at which time he shifted his focus to a more local aquatic ecosystem, Lake Mendota, next to the UW-Madison campus. His 1970 environmental microbiology textbook, *Biology of Microorganisms*, is still widely in use, currently in its sixteenth edition. He published more than 250 papers during his career, and authored twenty books.

Brock passed away in 2021, having lived long enough to see the massive ripple effect his field work had on humanity, with its implications for astrobiology, microbiology, medicine, biotechnology, and all the other scientific fields that benefit from PCR and the study of extremophiles. Brock was a dyed-in-the-wool ecologist and conservationist, and his true love remained the research and discovery that continues at Yellowstone National Park, perhaps the most diverse and well-protected laboratory on earth. Who knows where we'd be if Brock hadn't decided to take a spin through Yellowstone on that summer day in 1964?

20

Yellowstone's Latest 500-Year Flood

LEAVE IT TO YELLOWSTONE PARK TO CELEBRATE ITS 150TH ANNIVER-sary with a 500-year flood. On Monday, June 13, 2022, the northern region of Yellowstone suffered the worst flooding event in the history of the park. Due to heavy snowpack brought by late winter storms followed by a cool spring, a broad area along the Wyoming-Montana border was primed for a massive flood that was triggered by an "atmospheric river" from the west that brought a huge stream of airborne water vapor from the Pacific. Several inches of rain fell over the Beartooth Mountains, and warm temperatures not only kept the precipitation from freezing into snow, but the above-average level of snowpack quickly melted, drenching the northern Yellowstone region with up to 9.5 inches of water in less than a day, more than triple Yellowstone's average rainfall for the entire month of June.

The park's major rivers in the north and several tributaries swelled over their banks, breaking hundred-year-old records and wreaking havoc in the greater Yellowstone area from the Gallatin River drainage all the way to Billings and beyond. The Gardner Canyon Road, which connects the north park entrance to Mammoth Hot Springs, lost several sections of blacktop that crumbled into the Gardner River's muddy, raging waters or were completely buried under rock and mud, cutting off the bustling gateway town of Gardiner from the park's headquarters in Mammoth. Gardiner's other main road, US 89 into Yankee Jim Canyon and north up the Paradise Valley, was blocked by rock- and mudslides and parts of the blacktop were under 3 feet of water. Cars filled with hundreds of tourists jammed the streets of the Gardiner, trapped.

In June of 2022, Yellowstone suffered the worst flooding in its history. Huge sections of road, like this curve in the Gardner River Canyon between Mammoth and Gardiner, were washed out by the surging waters. Repairs, which will involve new routes in some cases, will take years. NPS PHOTO BY DOUG KRAUS, PUBLIC DOMAIN

The rest of the world was watching, though, as footage of the flooding went viral. Sixty-foot trees floated down the rivers. Helicopter and drone footage showed breathtaking panoramas of entire sections of towns deluged. A dormitory where park workers and their families lived in Gardiner slid into the Yellowstone River as its banks collapsed, the two-story building bobbing along in the current for several miles like a leaf in a street gutter. Fortunately, its occupants had plenty of time to get out before the collapse. Bridges were destroyed all over the area. In the northeast corner of the park, Soda Butte Creek washed out sections of the main road near Soda Butte and Sheep Creek, making it impossible to get to the Northeast Gate. So much water swept through Soda Butte Canyon that the river changed its course. The Lamar River's flood gauge hit 16.7 feet early Monday, obliterating the previous record flood height of 12.15 feet, set in 1996.

Park superintendent Cam Sholly described the unfolding disaster as a "thousand-year event, whatever that means these days." In terms of perspective, this was actually termed a "500-year flood," which is not a reference to the frequency of this level of flooding, but alludes to the .02 percent possibility of this level of flooding, which statistically is possible once in 500 years.

The skies over the greater Yellowstone area were buzzing with search and rescue helicopters that were fetching dozens of people who had been trapped by floodwaters. One farmer in Stillwater County was plucked from a tractor that had been sucked into the void when the road he was on collapsed. By Monday night all five entrances to Yellowstone Park had been closed. Several thousand visitors were still in the park, trying to figure out what was next. One of them, Sandy Eckart of Red Bud, Illinois, had driven into the park that morning from the East Entrance. "Since we had just arrived in Cody on Sunday afternoon we were unaware of how much rain there had been in the area, but we noticed the waterways on the sides of the road were so full of water and water was running down the rocks along the sides of the road," she recalled. After checking out the West Thumb Geyser Basin, they drove south to the Upper Geyser Basin to see Old Faithful. At the complex there were already signs that closures were spreading. "The workers at the coffee shop were telling us they could not serve food because their workers and deliveries could not even get into the park and that rangers were trying to evacuate people in the upper loop." They drove back out the East Entrance, noting that road closures and barricades were increasing. "There were quite a lot of other people and we discussed how things were slowly closing down. We ended up leaving since there seemed to be too many things closing up/barricaded off, like they were almost suggesting you leave, or that was our impression."

Some ten thousand visitors were evacuated from the park by the end of Monday. Incredibly, there were no deaths or major injuries. As natural disasters go in Yellowstone National Park, this was one of the worst. But it wasn't the first.

~

Flooding of a different kind swamped an area near Yellowstone in 1959, but it was a 7.5-magnitude earthquake that caused the turmoil. The quake, centered near Hebgen Lake in the Madison Valley, caused the surrounding landscape to drop as much as 20 feet, and part of a mountainside in the Madison River Canyon broke away, burying a campground in 50 million cubic yards of rock and debris. Twenty-eight people died. The material was enough to clog up the Madison River at that narrow point in the canyon, creating Quake Lake. You can still see the drowned trees poking up through the surface of the water. As waves crashed over the Hebgen Dam a few miles upstream, residents of Ennis prepared to evacuate in case the dam failed, which would send a tidal wave of blue-ribbon trout stream directly into their town. Some homes in Bozeman were damaged, as were several roads and bridges in Yellowstone Park. Parts of the massive stone chimney in the Old Faithful Inn crumbled into the lobby, and guests were evacuated from the lodge. The second-most powerful earthquake to hit the continental United States at the time, the '59 quake is one of Yellowstone's most noteworthy natural disasters, the subject of numerous books and documentary films.

More recently, rounding out the Big Three of natural disasters, runaway wildfires hit Yellowstone in 1988. A little more than a decade earlier, park officials had come to understand fire's role in the ongoing regeneration of the landscape and naturally caused fires were allowed to burn, since most of Yellowstone was wilderness. Dry conditions coupled with the absolute lack of expected rain caused the park's administration to change their mind, and after mid-July all fires would be suppressed to save structures, human lives, and as much of Yellowstone's quickly burning forests as they could. By the time the snows finally arrived to end the fire season that fall, more than one-third of Yellowstone had gone up in flames. Two deaths were attributed to the fire. In the ensuing years, Yellowstone's ecosystem has rebounded much more quickly than scientists expected, proving that the forest needs periodic fires to clear out dead or

overcrowded trees and understory and create the heat that releases seroti-
nous seeds, leaving a healthier environment for the animals and plant life
that inhabit the intertwined system. It was the largest wildfire in Yellowstone's history, and it would change the complexion of the park—and the
approach of forest stewarding—for generations.

When the floods of 2022 hit, Yellowstone Park was still making a come-
back from the previous few years, as visitor numbers had dropped due to
a nose-diving economy, skyrocketing gas prices, government shutdowns
and, most recently, the COVID-19 pandemic. The park had closed its
gates during the initial COVID lockdown in March of 2020, and reopened
them 2 months later with a limited-service plan designed to protect its
worldwide visitors from the spread of the virus. Hotels, restaurants, gift
shops, and other park amenities would remain closed. Still, the park saw
3.8 million visitors in 2020, down just 5 percent from the previous year.
September and October of that year were the busiest on record.

Guides, outfitters, concessioners, hotels, and restaurants—all the
components of Yellowstone's economic engine—had been dry-washing
their hands in anticipation of 2022's summer season. Starting with the
major road openings in early May, this would be the year when everything
was fully rocking, all the tours and lodges were booked solid, and Yellowstone's economy could finally rebound after several years of setbacks.

Then, on that horrifying day of June 13, it all got washed away. Two days
later Yellowstone superintendent Cam Sholly announced that the northern
half of the park would probably be closed for the rest of the summer. This
included such popular areas as the Lamar Valley, Tower-Roosevelt, and
Mammoth Hot Springs. As for the rest of the park, they would have to
wait and see. They couldn't just throw open the gates and restrict people to
the southern half of the park without a plan, he said. "Trying to put normal
visitation into one loop in Yellowstone is a disaster waiting to happen."

Power was restored throughout Yellowstone by Tuesday, and those who
had been in the park on Monday had exited into West Yellowstone, Cody,
and Jackson, where hotels, lodges, and campgrounds scrambled to find
accommodations for the wave of displaced tourists. No visitors were allowed

to enter the park, as teams of workers and officials began moving through Yellowstone to assess the damage and make plans for recovery, both short- and long-term. The NPS went to work on fixing up the Old Gardiner Road, a narrow dirt road that had begun as a stage road in 1879. More than 20,000 tons of gravel was used to surface the single-lane roadway, and it was opened to one-way employee traffic on July 1. In a stroke of good luck, HK Contractors, Inc. was already in the park working on the Old-Faithful-to-West-Thumb project. Superintendent Sholly, with the help of a national disaster declaration from President Biden, was able to quickly secure federal funding and hustle the crew up to the northwest corner of the park to start work on expanding the Old Gardiner Road to two lanes.

On June 21 he announced that he had also secured $50 million from the NPS to kickstart recovery work in the park. He added that the priority would be to restore access from Gardiner to Mammoth, which would connect to the north segment of Grand Loop Road and the Northeast Entrance road, the only roads open in Yellowstone through the winter.

On June 22, barely 10 days after the catastrophic flooding, the south loop of the park was opened to the public. Entry would be mitigated using the alternating license plate system, or ALPS, an idea that originated in one of the gateway communities. License plates ending with odd numbers would be admitted on odd number dates, even number plates on even dates. During the first day of reopening, just under 5,000 vehicles were counted entering the park, as opposed to the normal summer average of 10,000 per day. I'm no math genius, but under the ALPS system, that pencils out.

Through the nonstop work of a coalition of more than 1,000 people from the Park Service and Yellowstone's gateway communities, most of the park's flood-damaged roads were repaired ahead of schedule. Even Superintendent Sholly must have been amazed when, on July 2, Federal Highway Administration officials completed their final bridge and roadway safety inspections, and the northern loop of the park was opened to visitors. The ALPS was suspended. "We have attempted to balance major recovery efforts while reopening as much of the park as possible," said Sholly. Ninety-three percent of the park's roadways were now open.

While this was great news for the families and travelers who were able to carry out their summer plans and visit Yellowstone, there were still several areas suffering from major damage left behind by the epic flood. In the northeast corner of the park, three sections of the Northeast Entrance Road were obliterated. Pebble Creek Campground was completely underwater. Initially, officials estimated that it would take anywhere from 3 to 5 years to restore the roads leading out the Northeast Entrance to Silver Gate and Cooke City. Thanks to swift action and hard work, Oftedal Construction, Inc., of Miles City, Montana, was able to perform the repairs in time to open the road to the Northeast Entrance by October 15, 2022, barely five months after the flooding. To facilitate the new roadbeds they rerouted Soda Butte Creek in three places, and Pebble Creek in two places. Work was scheduled to continue through the spring of 2023 to finalize repairs on sections of road in the Lamar River Canyon and the Trout Lake Trailhead.

A major section of the Beartooth Highway was repaired enough to reopen a 23-mile segment to the public by late summer, and road crews completed repairs on the Montana side in time to open the pass up completely for several weeks before its annual weather-related closure on September 30.

At the other end of the Beartooth sits the pretty little town of Red Lodge, which is largely dependent upon tourism for its livelihood. When Rock Creek blew up on the day of the flood, it took out the 19th Street Bridge and inundated the town. Water was pouring through doorways into homes, and residents barely had time to grab a couple of precious items and escape. One man was trapped in his basement apartment, water coming down the stairway like a waterfall. He kicked out a window and escaped just in time. Three hundred residents in 147 homes were evacuated. In nearby Fromberg (population 395), one hundred homes were damaged, many left without power and gas. A photo-op visit from Montana's governor failed to appease the residents. One rancher said they'd voted for the governor, but when all their phone calls to state agencies kept going directly to voicemail, it was "frustrating." While the governor and other high-and-dry politicians were putting out soundbites that Montana was "open for business," many business owners and workers in

Yellowstone's gateway communities were wondering how they were supposed to survive when tourists couldn't even get into the park from their towns and their shops were underwater.

In Red Lodge, where entire houses fell into the raging Rock Creek and cars were swallowed up by collapsing roads, residents were still picking up the pieces in 2023. Or wondering where the pieces went. As many as twenty-five area bridges were washed out by the torrent. With only one main road, US 212, running through town, everyone in Red Lodge was affected. One local restaurant owner who runs five businesses said she was out $100,000 in just 2 weeks from lost tourism revenue.

This is a tight, resilient community. Red Lodge has bounced back from tough years in the past, and its residents are confident that this will be the case again with the restoration of the roadways into Yellowstone.

❧

The Old Gardiner Road, now expanded to at 22-foot-wide two-lane blacktop, was opened to the public on Oct. 30, in time to provide access to Mammoth and the Northeast Entrance Road on the Grand Loop. The wolves, elk, bison, and other wildlife of the Lamar Valley certainly don't need a steady stream of visitors to get on with their lives, but the visitors need the roads, and the NPS has been working with several federal agencies to expedite repairs to provide total access to the park in time for the 2023 summer season. At the time of this writing, most of those goals have been achieved.

Sadly, some businesses in the gateway communities of Gardiner and Cooke City did not survive the crippling financial blow of the truncated 2022 summer season. Most managed to hang on, though, and the promise of a "normal" 2023 season was enough to get them through a tough winter.

When video of the crumbling Gardner Canyon Road flashed around the world on that stormy summer day in 2022, it exposed the flawed location of a riverside roadway that began as a stage route more than a century ago, carrying the likes of Teddy Roosevelt and President Chester Arthur into the northern segment of Yellowstone. A permanent replacement road will likely take years to plan and build along a less vulnerable route, with minimal environmental impact. It's a huge undertaking, but park officials don't want to have to go through all this again when the next 500-year flood hits Yellowstone National Park.

THE MONTANA SWATH

21

See, Rock City!

On the classic rock radio station that's always playing in my head, Paul Stanley belts out the lines from "Detroit Rock City," one of my favorite KISS songs, whenever I think of going to visit Rock City. Detroit is sometimes called Rock City to reflect its contributions to rock 'n' roll history, from Iggy Pop and Bob Seger to Eminem and Aretha Franklin, not to mention its namesake record label, Motown. But here I'm not talking about a 25-hour detour from Montana to Michigan. Nor am I considering driving 2,000 miles to Lookout Mountain in Chattanooga, Tennessee, to "See Rock City," as southerners are commanded to do by hundreds of barn roof signs all over the South. I *have* been to that famous attraction, where I walked the Enchanted Trail through Fairyland and stood on the summit where you can see seven states (I know, it sounds like an afternoon at Burning Man, but it wasn't).

Nope, I'm talking about Montana's own Rock City, one of the most impressive and curious treasures of the Treasure State. It's also one of the best reasons why anyone visiting both of Montana's national parks should try to build some extra time into their inter-park travel. Among Montana's rockhounds, fossil hunters, road warriors, geology buffs, and nature lovers, Rock City is a well-kept secret. (Well, until now.) Located north of Great Falls along I-15, a popular thoroughfare between Glacier and Yellowstone, Rock City is less than 45 minutes off the interstate, and will reward visitors with some of the most jaw-dropping scenery to be found under the Big Sky. You might even lose your mind.

Rock City, located in a bend where Dupuyer Creek flows into the Two Medicine River, is a bizarre playground of geological oddities like spires, hoodoos, caves, and sandstone mushrooms. AUTHOR PHOTO

Fourteen miles south of Shelby, MT 44 runs west off I-15, straight as a ruler for 14 miles into Valier, a sleepy little town of about 500 in Pondera County. Valier sits along the northern end of Lake Frances, a popular spot where water-skiers and Jet Ski aficionados run circles around each other in the summer, while anglers fish for walleye, yellow perch, and northern pike year-round. The locals are hip to Rock City, but oddly, this striking geologic formation seems to be hiding in plain sight from most people in the surrounding area. During a recent stay in Great Falls, I asked several people if they'd been to Rock City. Most, including a few Great Falls natives, had never heard of it. I learned about it from a friend, a local bookstore owner who's a naturally curious individual like myself. He did his best to describe the place, but I was not really prepared for the stunning weirdness and incongruous beauty of it.

From Valier, head north on Montana Street, which becomes MT 358, also known as the Cut Bank Highway. Drive about a mile out of town and instead of following the sharp bend west, keep going straight north on Rock City Road. The gravel surface eventually gives way to dirt as you continue past Bullhead Road, Dean Road, wheat fields, and duck ponds. In about 7 miles the dirt road becomes a two-track. It's pretty slow going after that, and if it's wet or snowy, the trail can degenerate into the sticky mud known locally as gumbo. It's best to have a four-wheel-drive vehicle with good ground clearance. It's also possible, of course, to walk that last half a mile. Once you crest a hump in the last rolling hill of the farmland, the ground slopes away and the Northern Front of the Rockies comes into view, and the Two Medicine River runs along a small canyon directly in front of you. You'll be at the edge of Rock City, overlooking a mile-long section of badlands carved out of the prairie, filled with hundreds of hoodoos—fat, mushroom-shaped sandstone structures that have been eroded over thousands of years by wind, water, heat, and ice. The fantastical shapes create a mesmerizing landscape, reminiscent of the dramatic geology of Utah's Bryce Canyon or Zion National Parks. The scene is otherworldly, with crazy structures towering overhead or squatting at footstool height, many looking like giant, fossilized cow pies. A closer inspection reveals that the shapes are stratified, comprising hundreds of layers of sandstone. This geological freak show is a remnant of a vast inland sea that covered the Northwest through the end of the Cretaceous Period millions of years ago.

But how, exactly, were these layers created? How did erosion leave such specific and unusual shapes? It has to do with the location of Rock City on the inside of a long river bend, and its proximity to the Rocky Mountain Front, just a few miles to the west. This area is part of the Sawtooth overthrust belt, formed between 150 million and 800 million years ago when Pacific tectonic plates slid under North America plates to shove overlapping layers 5,000 feet skyward, creating the East Front of the Northern Rockies. Large humps of volcanic magma surfaced from the superheated earth beneath the crust, raising the landscape and creating the soft rolling hills of north-central Montana. Much of the Northwest was covered with an inland sea—up to 600 feet deep—and the overthrust was like jacking up a bathtub on one end. The water receded, eventually flowing across North America to the southeast and into the Gulf of Mexico, layering the area with sediment. Virgelle sandstone created from the sediment was compacted into layers with every season of flooding and spring runoff that carried more sediment, right up to the last ice age 15,000 years ago. The top layer of sediment, rich with iron and cemented together by hematite, is much harder than the sandstone layers underneath, and the mineral also accounts for its reddish color. As the Two Medicine River flow eroded the soft sandstone down to the layer of capstone, the water created fissures and cracks in the rock, finding ways to seep down into the softer sandstone underneath. Spring runoff and flooding from rainstorms increased the volume and pressure of the water, and as it flowed around sandbars and bends in the river, hydrodynamic instability caused streams of water to flow in the opposite direction in places, a phenomenon known as the teapot effect. This created increased flow under the capstone, causing further erosion as the water continued to chew away at the rock, leaving the larger slabs of capstone on top. As the river carved its way down into the canyon, it left behind the bizarre toadstool structures, which are still being eroded by wind, rain, and water.

Earth sciences aside, Rock City is just flat out cool. As it's not a popular destination, there's not much traffic. It's not a state park, wildlife reserve, or anything official, really. As of this writing there is a barbed wire gate stretched across a cattle guard, and a modest wood post fence delineates the parking area. There's an interpretive sign that explains the area's creation probably better than I have, and it lists a few hazards to watch out for. Rock City sees a few target shooters nearby, and serves as an occasional party spot for the locals—watch out for broken glass in the parking area—but there's a good chance you'll have the place to yourself, making it the perfect spot for some quiet exploration, both interior and exterior. Several well-worn paths weave through the forest of hoodoos and spires, some leading through a tight squeeze between two monoliths, others opening up into house-sized cirques. If your imagination suggests you might be wandering around on an alien planet, you're not the only one. Rock City was considered as a location for the movies *Starship Trooper* and *Galaxy Quest*.

Give yourself at least a couple of hours to explore this incredible rockscape. It deserves more than a quick walk-through, and at this point in your trip you may find yourself needing a vacation from your vacation. At the western end of the rock field you can look over the edge of a cliff and see where Birch Creek flows into the Two Medicine, a couple hundred feet below. Upstream, the cliffs are bristling with more spires and hoodoos for several miles.

There are several trails that run along the cliff faces and over the outcroppings to lead you down to the river that built Rock City. Massive slabs of sandstone have cracked into smaller, refrigerator-sized rocks that lie along the edge of the water. Sandbars indicate areas where sediment built up enough to change the river's path as it flows, working endlessly to return to sea level. Look down as you walk along the riverbank and you may find some fossils. North-central Montana is a hotbed of dinosaur remains, and the earth this far beneath the surrounding grasslands is prime fossil territory.

Like most other unusual geologic sites in the West, Rock City seems to hum with a powerful energy, and its remote location makes it a perfect vision quest backdrop. Tribal members from the Blackfeet Nation, whose reservation starts just across the river, consider this sacred ground.

Look up from the river and the many spires and wild shapes looming over from the cliffs can cause a touch of vertigo in even the most grounded of souls. It would seem an inviting place for rock climbing, but the soft sandstone is just too unstable, and a shelf or outcrop that might appear sturdy could crumble away under minimal pressure. Still, there are numerous plateaus and notches in the cliffs along the trails that are stable enough to explore. Little half-caves and natural benches provide a great spot to take a minute and enjoy the vistas of this gorgeous landscape.

There are a few hazards to watch out for. Rattlesnakes are not uncommon in the summer months. Bears have become an issue in most parts of western Montana, even here in the Golden Triangle. Until recently, no grizzlies had been seen this far east of the Northern Rockies in a hundred years. After several sightings over the past few years near Conrad and Stanford, though, it's clear that these bad boys are expanding their range from the Bob Marshall and Scapegoat Wilderness areas that make up the Northern Continental Divide Ecosystem. Global warming has affected the availability of huckleberries and white pine bark beetles, two of their main food sources, forcing them to seek new territory. One of the harsh realities of the livestock industry in Montana is that ranchers sometimes lose animals to predation from grizzlies and wolves. It's a conflict that's playing out on ranches and in courtrooms across the state as we try to find a balance between environmentalism and agriculture. As bears are famous for their refusal to respect man-made boundaries, it's always good policy to carry a canister of bear spray. You'll also need standard hiking accoutrements like water, bug spray, and good sunglasses. Montana sees a few 100-degree days every summer, and it can be a punishing heat out on the hard-baked badlands. Protect your melon with a good hat. Find shade when you can, and don't forget the sunscreen. The trails down to the river can be a bit tricky, and a hiking pole may add some confidence. The cliffs are popular with raptors, so binoculars are a must for birders. Of course, you'll need a camera because you'll find it's impossible to adequately describe the fantastical shapes and freakish formations of this special place.

If you see any images of "Rock City" in brochures or TV commercials or travel websites, they almost certainly will be photos of Detroit or some dramatic shots of the granite monolith on Lookout Mountain in Tennessee. Maybe that's a good thing. Part of the appeal of Montana's version is its mystique. Once you've seen it, you can't forget it. Even those who have already taken in the dramatic scenery in both of Montana's national parks will scratch their heads in wonderment when they see Rock City.

Yes, But Where Are the Two Dots?

Why choose between Opportunity and Wisdom when you can visit both? A lot of Montana's towns sport some unusual, even confusing names. Some are rarely pronounced correctly. Here are a few of the more colorful ones and their origin stories.

Absarokee

Pronounced "ab-ZOR-kee," this town in Stillwater County was named for the nearby Absaroka Mountains, which got their name from a mush-mouthed version of *Apsaalooke*, a Crow word meaning "children of the large-beaked bird." An early settler with poor penmanship resulted in the discrepancy in spelling. This historical goof happened more often than you might think. (See: Gardner River vs. Gardiner, the town.)

Amsterdam

The Northern Pacific Railroad had a tendency to name Montana towns on its line after foreign cities and countries: Havre, Jordan, Lima, Sumatra, Troy, etc., typically at the whim of some railroad executive. Amsterdam was no exception, although it *was* home to a sizable Dutch community when the nearby Manhattan Malting Company employed many of them at the turn of the 20th century. Safe to say the settlers were more aligned with the Christian Reformed Church than with their European counterpart's red light district.

Belfry

This little town in Carbon County was named for an investor in the Yellowstone Park Railroad. Nothing originally to do with bats, vampires, or anything remotely creepy, although the K-12 school's ball teams are known as the Bats.

Big Sandy

Historians are a little wobbly on this one, although it's generally agreed that the name is derived from Big Sandy Creek in Choteau County. One version of the creek's name origin points to a pioneer muleskinner named "Big Sandy" Lane who cursed the flooded creek so vehemently that it dried up on the spot.

Big Timber

Located near I-90 between Bozeman and Butte, Big Timber is a fine example of the utter lack of imagination employed by the Literal Names school of thought that gave us the towns of Square Butte, Big Mountain, Lakeside, and the Red Delicious apple.

Billings

When you're filthy rich, you get to name things after yourself. Frederick Billings was a lawyer from Vermont who worked his way out to California after the Civil War, where he helped settle land claims and became a millionaire by the age of 30. Along the way he bought a share of the Northern Pacific Railroad and wound up owning much of the land around what is now Montana's largest city. Somehow it seems appropriate that a city named after a lawyer should be called Billings.

Cooke City

Montana history buffs will recognize the name Jay Cooke, who was a financier who poured money into the Union effort of the Civil War, and was also a backer of the Northern Pacific Railroad. He also footed the bill for the storied Washburn-Langford-Doane expedition into Yellowstone, which led to the designation of the world's first national park. Ironically, the isolation of his namesake town kept it from becoming very productive during Montana's mining boom.

Eddies Corner

Almost everyone who writes about this area in the Judith Basin where US 191 t-bones into MT 3 insists on jamming an apostrophe into "Eddies." That's wrong. When W. E. "Ed" McConnell built a cafe-bar-gas station in 1949, he used lumber supplied by the Edwards family. "Eddies" refers to the multiple Eds involved in the creation of the business. It's been owned by the Bauman family for all but the first 2 years of its existence.

Essex

Located about halfway between East and West Glacier on a lovely, 60-mile stretch of US 2, Essex is a little railroad town freighted with history. There's a lot of conflicting info out there about the origins of this area's name, but it's generally agreed that its first name, Walton, was bestowed by James Willard Schultz, a European-American explorer who spent years living among the Blackfeet and writing books about it. When the Great Northern Railway ran their Empire Builder over Marias Pass in 1890, Schultz, a compulsive namer of places, chose the patron saint of fishing, Sir Izaak Walton, as his inspiration. It lasted for a few decades before the GNR changed it to Essex, after a county in England. The original name lives on, however, in the historic Sir Izaak Walton Inn, a large hotel built in 1939 to house the army of rail crew needed to keep the tracks clear in the winter. The Izaak Walton Ranger Station also still stands, and is listed in the National Register of Historic Places.

Geraldine

Welcome to Mrs. Rockefeller, Montana. The Choteau County townsite was built on the Milwaukee Road, and Geraldine was named after the wife of William Rockefeller. The wealthy industrialist had just gained control of the Anaconda Copper Company in 1900 and wanted to expand the railway to capitalize on Asian trade on the North Pacific coast. The exquisite depot was christened in 1914 with a New Year's Eve dance. The Milwaukee Road ended its run in 1980, and the depot was preserved. It's now listed in the National Register. Our secret hope is that Flip Wilson's dress is buried there.

Joliet

This Carbon County town on US 212 just southeast of Billings was named for Joliet, Illinois. As for the original Joliet, 2022 saw the first Blues Brothers Convention there at the town's historic correctional facility from which John Belushi's character, "Joliet" Jake Blues, derived his name. James Belushi filled in for his late brother with Dan Aykroyd (Elwood Blues), in what Aykroyd called an effort to "purge the prison of its bad karma."

Kremlin

Largely populated with Russian immigrants during the homesteading boom of 1910, Kremlin is believed to have been named by farmers who saw mirages in the fields that resembled Moscow's famous citadel. It is not known how much cheap vodka these farmers carried with them into the fields. After thriving for a few years after the Great Northern Railway came through, the little settlement shrank after the Depression and forced many farmers to seek greener pastures. Today the population hovers around one hundred.

Lolo

This small town where Lolo Creek flows into the Bitterroot River sports one of the more curious names in Montana, and the origin of its name is muddier than the river in spring runoff. Lewis and Clark's Corps of Discovery camped there at Traveler's Rest, and one story has the name being derived from "Le Louis," the French spelling of Lewis. Another possibility is that it comes from the Chinook word for "pack" or "carry." My pet theory that it's the answer to the standard limbo question, "How low can you go?", has received no support from any legitimate sources.

Manhattan

This small town of about 2,000 people in Gallatin County near Bozeman went through a couple of name changes in its time, and its lasting moniker did have a thin connection to the Big Apple. It was dubbed Hamilton when it was established in 1865, then a new ranching community named Moreland was established nearby, threatening to swallow up the little burg until the Manhattan Malting Company from New York set up shop in 1891, and Manhattan had a new identity. When Prohibition hit in 1920, the company went out of business. Manhattan remains a strong agricultural community.

Maxville

Robert R. MacLeod, a Philipsburg livery stable owner, must have been quite proud when the residents of Flint, a small station on the railroad spur between Drummond and Philipsburg created around 1888, decided to rename the town Macville in his honor. Its original name had come from the beautiful Flint Creek that meanders through the valley. Paperwork was submitted to establish the new name with its first post office. Either someone filled out the form before they'd had their coffee or some clerk got sloppy when copying the information over—when the approval came through, it was for the little town of Maxville. I don't know, it sounds kind of cool in an '80s-meets-beatnik sort of way.

Opportunity

Between the town of Anaconda and the Clark Fork lies Opportunity, a town with a difficult history. When Dr. Henry Gardiner established the community as part of the Anaconda Company's ranch properties, he wanted to convey the idea that its residents were being given the "opportunity" to raise their families in a rural setting. Indeed, in its early years Opportunity was a picture of American bucolic bliss as mining families planted vegetable gardens and raised livestock on their 10-acre parcels, fulfilling the town's name. Unfortunately, the booming industry that sustained them would inflict the damage that would choke the town. Toxic waste materials from the copper mines upstream were dumped into ponds around Opportunity, poisoning the water and ruining the soil. One hundred years later, ARCO removed millions of tons of toxic material that had washed down the Clark Fork to settle behind the Milltown Dam. What did they do with all that killer sludge? Railroad cars delivered it back to the settling ponds of Opportunity. The legal battle with the residents is ongoing.

People sometimes wait a long time for opportunity to knock. In this case, maybe they should have hidden behind the curtains and pretended that they weren't home.

Power

If you're traveling between the parks on I-90 between Shelby and Great Falls, you'll pass the little town of Power. A stage station was established there in 1886 by Frank and Guy Steele, and Power became a dot on the map in 1910 when Montana businessman and US senator Thomas C. Power bought the land, platted the town, and named it after himself. He'd already established a heavy presence in Helena, building the Power Block, a massive, ornate building downtown. You could say the man wielded a lot of . . . what's the word? Influence.

Pray

Some Montana visitors mistakenly believe the town of Pray is somehow affiliated with the Church Universal and Triumphant, a religious doomsday sect that made headlines in the late 1980s when its leader, Elizabeth Clare Prophet, had her followers building fallout shelters in preparation for a coming nuclear war. Nope, that crew were based elsewhere in Paradise Valley. Nor is the town's name an exhortation to appeal to a higher power. It's named after Montana congressman and federal judge Charles N. Pray.

Rapelje

Pronounced RAP-el-jay, this little wheat farming community northeast of Billings was named after John M. Rapelje, a Northern Pacific Railroad honcho in the early 20th century. Notably, it's the birthplace of Rib Gustafson, a legendary veterinarian who served the ranching communities north of Great Falls for decades. His son, Wylie, is a country musician who yodeled the original "Yahoo!" jingle in 1996.

Ringling

At about one elephant's height above 1 mile in elevation, Ringling is located in Meagher County, surrounded by the Castle, Crazy, and Belt Mountains. I say elephant because, yes, it's that Ringling: John T. Ringling, of the Ringling Brothers Circus, proved up in Old Dorsey in 1910, with the idea of buying a cattle ranch, then building a railway between Yellowstone and the brand new Glacier National Park. The little town was renamed New Dorsey, then Leader, and was moved to a new site before the railroad decided to honor Ringling by naming the new railway station after him. It stuck, and Ringling is still a going concern today, although there has never been a documented sighting there of an elephant or any other circus animal.

Rocker

This music fan was disappointed to learn that Rocker is named not for a hard-driving guitar player, but for the wooden box used by placer miners to separate gold from gravel and rocks in the sluicing process. It would be of some consolation if there were a nearby town named Roller, but no such luck.

Roscoe

Not far from Joliet lies the little town of Roscoe. Originally named Morris in 1901, it was renamed in 1905 to alleviate confusion in the post office with the town of Norris. It's believed that it was named after a local resident's horse, not the sheriff from *The Dukes of Hazzard*, who spelled his name with no "e."

Stanford

Smack dab in the center of Montana, the seat of Judith Basin County is home to about 400 people. And one white wolf. In the Basin Trading Post stands Stanford's top tourist attraction, the mounted figure of the Ghost Wolf. The notorious white wolf terrorized area ranchers for 15 years until it was shot in 1930, after it had killed some $30,000 worth of livestock during its run. No one knows how the wolf escaped trapping and death for so long. Another unanswered question is how the town got its name. The town was established as a trading post by Thomas C. Power in 1875, and there are a few explanations of why it's called Stanford. One version has a postmaster naming it after US senator Leland Stanford of California. Another has Joseph and George Bower establishing the town and truncating the name of Stanfordville, New York. Or possibly it was named to honor Maj. James T. Stanford of Great Falls. If the Ghost Wolf knows the answer, he certainly isn't talking.

Two Dot

The town was named after the esteemed publisher of excellent books about the American West. That's not true of course, I'm just pandering. This one's no big mystery—the name was inspired by the two-dot brand of local rancher H. J. Wilson. When the Montana Railway reached the town in 1900, it enjoyed a brief period of prosperity, supporting

Montana is full of places that sport some pretty curious names. Some have interesting stories, some not so much. Eric "Roscoe" Ambel, famed roots rock guitarist from Brooklyn, might be disappointed to learn that Roscoe, Montana, was not named for him. Sorry, 'Scoe. AUTHOR PHOTO

a bank, a newspaper, hotel, hardware store, and other businesses. Today, the Two Dot Bar is the sole enterprise still operating in a town that could have been named after a single face on a six-sided die.

Virginia City

When gold was discovered on the Ruby Creek near Alder, thousands of prospectors and miners flooded the area. Supporters of the Confederacy named the townsite Varina, in honor of the wife of Jefferson Davis. When Dr. G. G. Bissell filed the official documents to establish the town, he changed the name to Virginia, likely saving the world from a million tasteless limericks. Virginia City would go on to become the territorial capital, and now is a living embodiment of a classic frontier town.

Waterloo

Gold miners populating the Jefferson River in the mid-1800s led to the establishment of a permanent settlement. A brouhaha over the proposed location of the post office created so much turmoil that residents named their town after the Battle of Waterloo, although the ultimate location of the post office had somewhat less impact on the course of world history than its namesake skirmish. The one-horse town is still there, but the post office closed in 1971.

22

The Little Shell Tribe, the "Newest" Nation in Montana

IN BELCOURT, NORTH DAKOTA, ON JUNE 16, 2022, THE TURTLE MOUNtain Band of Chippewa Indians were thrilled by one of the most significant events that can happen in the world of the Plains Indians, the birth of a white buffalo. It happens only once in five million births, and the ivory-colored calf is considered by many natives to be the most sacred of blessings. Tribal Chairman Jamie Azure said, "The white buffalo calf that we were gifted by the Creator is a sure sign that our prayers have been heard. It was told in prophecy, generation after generation that this sacred white buffalo would again return to our people in a time where we would be resilient in our way of life through our teachings and ceremonies." Perhaps the appearance of the white buffalo is symbolic of a recent victory achieved by a Montana tribe whose members share the same ancestors as their Chippewa brothers and sisters living in neighboring North Dakota.

The Little Shell Tribe of Chippewa Indians of Montana finally received federal recognition as a sovereign nation in December 2019, after more than 150 years of trying. They had gained official recognition by the state of Montana in 2000, and federal recognition not only gives the tribe access to federal resources like medical care, education, and health insurance, but it solidifies their very identity in a state where they had no reservation for their entire existence. It was an achievement and a tribute to the long, hard fight sustained by generations of the Métis, one of the most maligned, oppressed, and overlooked peoples in North American history, even though they made significant contributions to that history.

With the stroke of a presidential pen, the long battle for recognition of the Landless Indians of Montana finally reached its end—although other battles had just begun.

~~~

The Turtle Mountain Reservation lies in the heart of the Red River Settlement Zone (RRSZ) in North Dakota, where Ojibwa bands had come south and west from their Anishinaabe homeland near the Great Lakes. As Europeans began exploring and settling across North America in the 1600s, the decline in wild game and usurpation of land began to push the Native peoples west and south into the Dakota Territories. Demand for beaver pelts from Hudson's Bay Company (HBC) and the Northwest Fur Company sent armies of trappers and fur traders into Canada's western environs, mostly French, Scottish, and Irish emigrants. The Ojibwa recognized the benefits of a healthy trade relationship with the newcomers. Native traditions required a familial connection to enable this commerce, so they began to intermarry with the European transplants, an arrangement known as "*a la facon du pays*," or "of the country." Subsequent generations of this ethnogenesis were known as Métis, a French word meaning mixed-blood. The Métis developed their own distinct culture, mostly an amalgam of French and Ojibwa traditions, with their own language, their own style of dress, their own rituals, and their own hegemony within the tribe. They roamed over 10 million acres of territory, moving with the seasons and following the buffalo. Their multicultural heritage, though, would eventually be one of the biggest obstacles the Métis would have to overcome. The other, in part a result of this synthesis of races, was the lack of a tribal land base.

Before a border existed along the 49th Parallel between Canada and the United States, Northern Plains tribes were spread across the Dakota Territories and Rupert's Land (chartered by the HBC), in present-day Manitoba, Saskatchewan, Alberta, North Dakota, Montana, Idaho, and Washington. The Métis formed a confederacy with the Assiniboine, the Chippewa, and the Cree. This Indian version of the League of Nations, known as Nehiyaw Pwat, is believed to have helped them present a united front to settle conflicts with other Northern Plains tribes and coalitions like the Sioux, the Crow, and the Blackfeet Confederacy that included the Piegan, Blood, Siksika, and Gros Ventre tribes. It was a partnership that helped enable the Métis to flourish, and eventually strengthened the Natives' footing when dealing with the trappers and traders of the HBC. The Métis, who would sometimes intermarry with Blackfeet, Chippewa, or Cree, congregated in the areas around the trading posts of southern Manitoba and northern Minnesota, the RRSZ.

Around 1802 the Métis would come up with a revolutionary invention that would give their people a major advantage in transporting goods and game, as well as the piles of buffalo hides that were now in high demand by a Hudson's Bay Company that had shifted from the fine beaver trade to buffalo robes. The Red River cart is thought to have had the biggest impact on the lifestyle and mobility of the Pembina Band. The cart was an ingenious design that was made entirely of native materials and contained no metal, largely unavailable in the Red River area. It was built using two 12-foot oak shafts that formed the side frame of the cart as well as the stems that would yoke the pony that pulled it. A pair of 6-foot-tall spoked wheels rimmed with buffalo hide strips were connected by a wooden axle and attached to cross braces at the rear of the poles to form a frame. A cargo box was positioned on top of the frame to carry the payload, sometimes as much as 800 pounds. The box and floorboards were joined using mortis and tenon—like in a split rail fence—and everything was lashed together with wet strips of buffalo rawhide, which would shrink and tighten as it dried, creating a strong bond. The Red River cart quickly became ubiquitous throughout the Nehiyaw Pwat territory, a symbol of Métis ingenuity. The wooden axles were not greased, and trains of the carts could reportedly be heard from miles away, the screech from the wheels once being described as a thousand fingernails being dragged across a thousand panes of glass.

The Red River band of the Métis were loosely based around the mouth of the Pembina River, which flowed into the Red River. *Pembina* is the Chippewa word for high cranberry, found abundantly in the area and used in their prized pemmican. The RRSZ was the heart of the Nehiyaw Pwat's empire of trade across the western United States and Canada. By then the "Iron Confederacy" had incorporated rifles, metal-tipped arrows, and the horse, introduced from Spain, and they had attained control of all territory around the river systems that flowed into the Hudson Bay. At a time when Lewis and Clark's Corps of Discovery was still just a gleam in Thomas Jefferson's eye, these tribes being pushed down from Canada were an integral part of the biggest economy in the Western Plains.

In the mid-1800s western settlement shifted into high gear, ratcheting up the number and severity of conflicts between the Indians and European Americans. The United States was dead set on expansion, even invading Mexico in a land grab. The Mormons were on the move westward, where they would ultimately establish Deseret in what is now Utah. The discovery of gold in Montana brought a wave of prospectors flooding down the Oregon Trail, hoping to strike it rich in the "new" world. Tribes were being squeezed into smaller areas, with little consideration given to their existing claims of the land. Like other Northern Plains tribes, the Chippewa had continued moving westward into North Dakota and Montana, where they followed the buffalo, sometimes serving as guides for hunters and traders. Their seasonal circuit would take them from their homelands in North Dakota all the way to the Front Range of the Northern Rockies, where game was abundant, and then back home to winter in the Red River area. Bands tended to live in groups of about twenty-five families, about what a given area of land they occupied could support.

As the United States was ramping up toward the Civil War, the government began to enjoin the Natives in a series of treaties that benefited the settlers moving out west by providing access to the land while giving the appearance (to them, at least) of making fair compensation to the Indians, granting them hunting and fishing rights on their own homelands, along with the promise of monetary compensation. Once the tribes were induced into signing these treaties, they were frequently rewritten after the fact or simply ignored when entities like the burgeoning railroad saw fit to force Indians off the land they desired.

In 1863 the Pembina Band and Red Lake Band entered into the Old Crossing Treaty—signed by the second Little Shell—that gave the United States passage through their territory. In exchange the tribes were "given" the aboriginal lands northwest of Devil's Lake, and promised an annuity of $20,000 for 20 years, with the idea that the Natives would shift their culture from hunting to agriculture. The Métis had other ideas. They continued moving west, pulling their noisy carts deeper into Montana, living in their seasonal encampments and occasionally establishing a settlement, like Lewistown. Pembina bands ventured as far west as St. Mary's Mission in the Bitterroot Valley, to where Father DeSmet had been guided by a Métis named Gabriel Prudhomme. There is a replica of a Red River cart at the mission today. Prudhomme also was a part of John Mullan's expedition to map a railroad route in the 1850s, which became known as the Mullan Road.

After the Civil War, other Red River Métis, under the leadership of Louis Riel, staged a rebellion in Assiniboia (now Manitoba), after a newly confederated Canada tried to muscle their way into establishing a province in 1869. While trying to establish a Métis-Chippewa nation, Riel wound up shooting a pro-Canada agent to death and fled to the United States to avoid prosecution, but not before securing some important concessions, including French-speaking schools and preservation of the Catholic church for his tribe.

Riel, perhaps the most famous political figure in Canadian history, had self-exiled in the United States for 15 years, including time at a mission near Great Falls. He petitioned the US government for a reservation in the Lewistown area, but like so many other requests for the United States to live up to its obligations to the displaced Indians, it failed. In 1884 he was once again persuaded to join the fray for the Métis, this time in Saskatchewan. It didn't end well for him. After the British army quelled the uprising, Riel was captured, convicted of treason, and hanged in Regina.

By the 1870s the Pembina Band of Chippewa, led by Ayabe-Way-We-Tung, the third chief to bear the name Little Shell, began pressing the US government for a reservation for the Turtle Mountain Chippewa. As the colonization of Canada continued marching westward, settlers began swallowing up the lands already occupied by the Chippewa, Cree, and Métis. In 1872 Little Shell petitioned the US government to establish a reservation and acknowledge the Turtle Mountain Chippewa as a distinct tribe.

Little Shell was still the tribal leader in 1892 when the Turtle Mountain Indians were subjected to a strong-arm swindle so heinous it holds a significant spot in the history of the American West. A commission of three federal representatives, led by North Dakota senator P. J. McCumber, convened at Turtle Mountain with a committee of Chippewa and Métis who would negotiate for the relegation of their lands and settlements. While Little Shell was away at Fort Peck, a US Indian agent, John Waugh, handpicked the thirty-two-member Native committee, choosing Chippewa and Métis individuals he knew he could manipulate. Previously, Little Shell had proposed to the McCumber Commission that his band would be open to a reservation along the edge of the Fort Peck Reservation at the mouth of the Milk River along the Missouri, in exchange for the Turtle Mountain lands, which offered far fewer resources for the tribe. Also, the government would pay the tribe $10 million for the 9.5-million acre tract of land. The commission responded by first purging some 525 names from the tribal roles as being ineligible to participate in the treaty. This, of course, enraged Little Shell, who was not even allowed to speak as he wasn't on the thirty-two-man tribal committee. He walked out of the negotiation in disgust.

The commission pushed forward. In September they published a list of tribal members they considered to be legitimate and could remain on the reservation, which was now 10 percent of their original homeland. The next month, all the Métis who were not on the list received a letter demanding that they leave the reservation immediately under the threat of arrest. The commission continued their arm-twisting with the malleable tribal committee, and in October announced that they had reached an agreement. The tribe would relinquish control and rights to the 9.5 million acres of Turtle Mountain land, and would be paid the sum of $1 million—a dime an acre. They could live on the Fort Peck Reservation if they wanted to, but they couldn't stay here. Most Métis left the area to find new homelands that hadn't already been claimed by homesteaders. Their people still refer to the infamous McCumber Agreement as the Ten-Cent Treaty, a prime example of how entire Indigenous cultures were hoodwinked and displaced by the US government during the Treaty Era.

The Red River Métis band began to fragment. As the 19th century ended and their main cultural resource, the buffalo, had all but disappeared, the landless Indians scattered to far-flung parts of Montana, North Dakota, and south-central Canada. Small knots of their people settled in Choteau, Dupuyer, Havre, Malta, Glasgow, and other communities across Montana's northern tier, frequently burned out of their own homes and chased off the land. Considered not Indian enough to live on a reservation, yet not white enough to acquire a homestead or receive government assistance, the Métis fought through the 20th century for federal recognition and its attendant benefits, while the displaced tribe's socioeconomic status continued to deteriorate. After the third Little Shell died in 1904, the recognition effort was largely taken up by a tribesman named Joe Dussome. For more than 50 years, Dussome petitioned the government and worked doggedly to try and attain government acknowledgment for his tribe.

There would be several false starts. In the 1930s the government bought 37,000 acres of land near Box Elder, with the idea that all of Montana's landless tribes would be contained on one reservation. This included the Cree, led by Chief Little Bear, and Chief Rocky Boy's Ojibwa, and the dissipated Métis. But the Chippewa-Cree of Chief Rocky Boy's Band, whose origins were the Turtle Mountain Pembina Chippewa, were given the reservation. Montana's Métis, considered too numerous for the state's smallest res, were left out. Forty acres of land near Great Falls was purchased during that time, but (mostly white) locals couldn't accept the idea of even a 40-acre reservation in their backyard. In the early 1940s a farming-based Resettlement Plan was discussed for Phillips County, but the war intervened and the plan died on the vine.

A big step forward came in 1978 when a federal program was established that provided a set of criteria around which a tribe could officially petition the government for recognition. The Little Shell Tribe was officially acknowledged as an entity, and in 2000 the tribe received official

The Little Shell Tribe of the Chippewa Indians of Montana recently achieved official recognition from the US government, after more than 130 years of existence as a homeless tribe. Their headquarters is in Great Falls near Hill 57, one of their traditional areas of residence. AUTHOR PHOTO

recognition from the state of Montana. They still had no homeland and no federal recognition, but at least they had an identity in the eyes of the government.

Finally, the Little Shell Restoration Act of 2013 was folded into the National Defense Authorization Act and signed into law in December 2019. It was a long overdue victory for the 6,400 members of the Little Shell Tribe, who now would be eligible for medical care from Indian Health Services, federal housing programs, education funding, and other resources. The irony of the victory coming as part of a $738 billion bill that provided funding for the very military that spent decades slaughtering thousands of Natives in the 1800s was not lost on many tribal members.

In Great Falls, the Montana Little Shell Tribe of Chippewa Indians headquarters resides on 3 acres of land they bought in an area called Hill

57. It's where many of the Little Shell have congregated for much of the last 50 years, living in crushing poverty, ignored by the federal government and shunned by other tribes who don't consider the landless Métis "real" Indians. The tribe is still scattered around Montana, and their members have married into families on every reservation. At their headquarters they have a tribal chairman, Gerald Gray, and a duly elected Tribal Council to help the Little Shell of Montana steer their people forward. They never doubted their own identity. This is a culturally rich, historically significant tribe that began to establish themselves in the western territory 400 years ago, when they were part of a society that practiced a communal existence with the land, not dominion over it. It was a time in North American history when all the Anishinaabe peoples were considered to live "under one robe." While that era of Native cohesion and cultural freedom may have passed, the Little Shell Tribe of Chippewa in Montana has earned a legitimate place among the other 573 federally recognized Indian tribes in the United States.

23

Remembering Butte's Own Disneyland

To TWIST AN OLD WESTERN IDIOM, BUTTE IS UGLY AS SIN AND TWICE AS interesting. Located at the junction of I-90 and I-15 in a valley atop the Continental Divide, the Mining City is a scarred survivor that proudly wears its big heart on its rolled-up sleeve. Its residents are known to be stalwart and generous—a Butte native might knock you off your barstool to make his point, but then he'll help you up, buy you a pint, and give you the shirt off his back. If he's of a certain age, he may even get a tear in his eye as he regales you with stories of Butte's beloved Columbia Gardens, a pocket Disneyland that for 75 years was a treasured oasis of joy for the families of this storied mining community.

Butte's bare-knuckled reputation and difficult history are well documented. What started as a mining camp when gold was discovered here in 1864 quickly grew into a settlement, and within 20 years Butte was the center of Montana mining. The Anaconda Copper Mining Company, established on a played-out silver mine in 1881, became one of the richest companies in the country. Their focus had pivoted to copper just in time to supply the nascent electrification of the United States.

Copper was king, and the Company, as it was called, honeycombed Butte's hillside with hundreds of miles of tunnels and shafts more than a mile deep. By 1896, 210 million pounds of copper per year were being produced, a quarter of the world's supply. Butte's population grew to nearly 100,000 as workers poured in from around the world, drawn by the promise of steady work and riches pulled from the hard rock below. At its peak of activity around the end of World War I, it was thought to be the largest city between San Francisco and Chicago.

Butte's—or rather, the Company's—success brought with it the inevitable clashes between labor and management. The friction between organized workers and Anaconda was fierce—full of violence, strikes, arson, and even murder. It was far from a typical "company town" where the workers looked up to their employer as a benevolent provider. Butte is still a staunch labor town, one with a deep history of union pride.

It also was the biggest melting pot in the West, rivaling the cosmopolitan nature of San Francisco. The Irish were always the largest group of immigrants, but other ethnicities added to the rich mosaic of cultures, each nationality tending to congregate into distinct neighborhoods. Italians lived in Meaderville, the Irish settled in Corktown and Dublin Gulch, the Cornish and English in Centerville, and the Chinese in (you guessed it) Chinatown. For many immigrants, Butte wasn't just a place in Montana, but represented the United States as a whole, their new land of opportunity. Hence its other nickname, "Butte, America." Butte's unique geological makeup, containing over 130 mineral species, provided yet another moniker: The Richest Hill on Earth. It's estimated that $48 billion worth of precious metals have been produced there in a century of mining. By the dawn of the 20th century, the Anaconda Company had made its two owners, Marcus Daly and F. Augustus Heinze—and William A. Clark, a third magnate—ridiculously wealthy.

The Copper Kings ran their industry with an iron fist but were not blind to their need to produce some goodwill among their employees when they could. As the story goes, William A. Clark was taken aback one day by the sight of a group of grubby children playing games in the dirt. They told the magnate they had nowhere else to play. Money can't buy happiness, he knew, but it could surely build an amusement park big enough to generate it. And it certainly wouldn't hurt his standing among Butte's rank and file as he was eyeballing a run for the US Senate.

Columbia Gardens opened in 1899, situated on 64 rolling acres surrounding a defunct racetrack in Horse Canyon, a wooded ravine just a few miles east of the city. Clark hired J. R. Wharton, the president of the Butte Electric Railway Company, to secure the land and oversee the development of a sprawling wonderland anchored by a magnificent, three-story pavilion with an indoor dance hall that could hold 3,000 foxtrotters. A wide boardwalk led to a massive midway full of pinball machines and carnival games, with vendors offering ice cream, hot dogs, popcorn, snow cones, and more—all the childhood favorites. There was also a sports complex with a grandstand, a petting zoo, and a man-made lake where visitors could paddle around in rented boats or glide down one of the long metal slides into the water. Columbia Gardens was a wonderful gift to the people of Butte. It was J. R. Wharton's baby, but of course Clark, a ruthless opportunist, was happy to take the credit.

At the top of the hill sat an enormous greenhouse where colorful and exotic flowers were cultivated. The Gardens lived up to its horticultural moniker, with numerous manicured flower beds planted throughout the grounds, including carefully tended gardens in the shape of a harp, a butterfly, and the symbol of the Anaconda Company, a golden arrowhead. Many remember the Gardens being the only green place left in Butte.

And then there were the rides. The most popular was a roller coaster, the only one in the state. "I remember getting on that roller coaster in the very front, and I would ride it and just stay on it," said Sue Orr, whose father Joe owned Butte's iconic Finlen Hotel in the mid-1960s. "And being the poor little rich girl that I was," she added with a laugh, "I would just hand the guy a dollar bill and stay on it all day." The coaster, an all-wood structure originally built in 1906 and upgraded through the years, was always full. And it was scary. There were no lap belts. Even though crews would go in and tighten all the nuts and bolts every night, riders could feel the framework shudder and sway as they white-knuckled the iron hand bar, shrieking and holding on for dear life while the metal cars bumped their way around corners on maple runners. The fear that the entire contraption would fly apart at any moment was part of the appeal. "There's no way I would get on a carnival ride now," said Orr. "But when you're 6 or 7 years old, you're fearless."

Other survivors of multiple roller coaster rides agreed. It really slapped you around, recalled one rider, insisting that today it would be classified as a violent ride. The roller coaster induced lots of laughter, screams, a few tears, and definitely the occasional post-ride hurl. It's not hard to imagine a motion-sick youth refunding a bellyful of cotton candy, buttered popcorn, turquoise licorice ice cream, and other midway treats as he staggered away from the ride.

Other rides included a Ferris wheel and a carousel. The Ferris wheel was removed in 1925, but was soon replaced by the Giant Biplane Swing, inspired by Lindbergh's 1927 Atlantic crossing. The ride consisted of a 65-foot-tall steel tower that would spin around, swinging the boxy, kid-sized aircraft replicas at the end of a cable. At the front of each plane, a washing machine motor spun the prop fast enough to blow the hair back on the kid who was lucky enough to nab the pilot seat, as centrifugal force lifted the planes into the air. While not as heart-pounding as the roller coaster, the biplanes were popular with the kids who loved the sensation of being airborne. They would soar up over the carousel and wave to their families and friends milling about below, who were probably busy trying to avoid being strafed by vomit from the roller coaster.

It was the stately carousel, though, that eventually became the flagship attraction of Columbia Gardens. After a couple of lesser versions spun their way into oblivion, the glorious third iteration was built by Chicago's Allan Hirschell Company and installed in 1928. The 16-section platform had three rows of hand-carved, painted horses, and a couple of ornate benches for the adults. "It was a gorgeous carousel," said Chuck Kaparich, a Missoula cabinet maker who supervised the construction of his town's classic merry-go-round, inspired by a childhood spent visiting Butte to ride the painted ponies in Columbia Gardens. Many who whiled away their summer afternoons at the Gardens still remember the carousel's organ music booming out across the park. "That's the ride everyone remembers with such fondness," said Kaparich.

Extended families with food-laden baskets took advantage of a generous picnic area that provided plenty of tables, grills, and shade for people to spread out and enjoy their meals during a mini-family reunion. Kelly Rosenleaf has plenty of fond memories of her family outings when she was a girl growing up in Great Falls. After her parents split up she would frequently visit her father in Anaconda, which meant plenty of trips to the nearby Gardens. "We would often take a picnic because we didn't have money for buying food at the food vendors there for half a dozen kids. That was not happening. It was lovely. There was a flower area with lots of trees. We would spend the day there, probably from late morning to late afternoon, maybe 4 or 5 hours. It was a big adventure." She also remembers "cracking the bars," something kids tried to do while riding the cowboy swing, a unique tandem ride at the playground. It was a cross between a seesaw and a swing, and two kids sitting astride would push and pull until their arc took them high enough where the parallel support bars would connect with a loud bang.

For several generations, Columbia Gardens was the beating heart of the Mining City, always there to provide a breath of fresh air, a happy and safe respite from a dirty, hardscrabble existence. But as the 20th century wore on America's—indeed, the world's—energy needs changed. By the late 1960s Butte had fallen on tough times. Solid state transistors and microchips had arrived, and the demand for copper used in wiring and vacuum tubes plummeted. Mining had moved above ground, as open-pit mining had become more economically viable than hard-rock mining below the surface. Things went from bad to worse in 1973, when political unrest in Chile led to the loss of the Company's Chuquicamata mine, the world's most productive. By then Butte's population had dropped to less than 20,000 as people left the area to find work. It became a town of boarded-up buildings and empty streets. The Anaconda Company was scrambling. All they had left was the pit, and they needed to expand it. Things got even uglier when the insatiable acquisition of property by the Company coincided with a series of suspicious fires in the central and uptown districts, directly west of the pit. Some property owners were believed to be torching their own buildings to collect the insurance, a more profitable move than selling to Anaconda, which was offering less than market value. Many in Butte pointed fingers at the Company itself, accusing them of using arson as a way to remove obstacles to their growth.

As for Columbia Gardens, the extravagant facility had already become a money pit for Anaconda. The shrinking population, coupled with the growing popularity of road tripping, among other factors, caused attendance to drop. Expenses to maintain the white elephant became untenable. To satisfy their creditors, the Company had to trim to the bone. The dreaded announcement came in February 1973: The upcoming summer season would be the last for the historic amusement park. The people of

Butte were stunned, and the outcry was immediate and loud. The local paper was bombarded with letters protesting the demise of Columbia Gardens. Perhaps to reduce the blowback, the Company issued some vague reassurances that they would help finance a relocation effort.

"It was the only thing Butte had that was good," said Company employee Lyle Metz. "It was absolutely heartbreaking." As the Gardens closed for the final time on Labor Day, its devotees allowed themselves a little hope that the park could be reborn elsewhere. Those dreams went up in smoke on the night of November 12, 1973.

"People were devastated when the fire happened," said Kelly Rosenleaf, recalling the blaze that erupted in Columbia Gardens' arcade building, where most of the rides were stored during the offseason. While much of Butte was watching the Chiefs and Bears on *Monday Night Football*, the wail of sirens brought people out of their houses. Fire crews and civilians raced to the Gardens, where the conflagration quickly spread to the rest of the arcade and the adjacent boardwalk. The massive pavilion was completely engulfed, and flames licked at the wooden roller coaster. Hundreds of people watched, horrified and helpless. "Everything went," said Sis Beech, wife of caretaker Ted Beech, in a 1990 interview. "You wouldn't believe it. Everything was gone."

Officially, the cause of the fire was attributed to an overloaded electrical transformer in the arcade building, despite the fact that most of the power to the structure had been shut off 2 months earlier. The recent rash of suspicious fires in town led many to believe that this tragic blaze was just a little bit too convenient for the Anaconda Company. Russell Malahowski, whose senior prom was the last event held in the pavilion, never believed the official explanation of the catastrophe. "There were people who said, look, the only spark that was involved in the origin of that fire was the spark from the cigarette lighter that torched the thing," he said. "Back then the joke was that Butte was the only town with a brand-new fire engine that already had 40,000 miles on it."

After the object of 75 years' worth of priceless childhood memories was reduced to ashes, the Company proceeded to mine the area, but it was a bust. "I think I've got more gold in my mouth from my dentist than they got out of the hills out there," said Butte native Don Orlich. To this day,

A beloved attraction to thousands of kids who grew up in the Mining City, Columbia Gardens burned down in a mysterious fire in the 1970s after entertaining generations of Butte families. This is the original wooden entrance arch that survived the fire and is currently located in the foothills outside Butte.
AUTHOR PHOTO

many in Butte believe the mining effort at the Columbia Gardens site was a sham, as the Company had achieved its true objective of wiping the money-sucking amusement park off the map.

Anaconda was acquired by ARCO, a division of British Petroleum, and in 1983 they ceased all mining operations in the Mining City, leaving a cratered, barren moonscape on the hillside that looms over the town.

Today, a few remnants of Columbia Gardens are scattered throughout Butte. Kids can still enjoy cracking the bars on the cowboy swings, which were moved to a city park. The wooden arch that once greeted visitors to the Gardens somehow escaped the fire and was relocated to a side road west of town. The Spirit of Columbia Gardens Carousel, a replica of the iconic Gardens ride, was opened in July 2018, sporting thirty-two hand-carved horses. A lovingly restored car from the original roller coaster is prominently displayed nearby.

Perhaps the most vivid artifacts of Columbia Gardens are the stories and memories of the people who spent so many sun-drenched summer days of their childhood cavorting in the playground, gorging on treats, feeling the thrill of a roller coaster ride, and just enjoying being a kid in the happiest place in the richest hill on earth.

24

Where the Buffalo (and Others) Roam

AT THE SOUTH END OF THE FLATHEAD VALLEY, THERE'S A HOME WHERE not only the buffalo roam, but the deer and the antelope also play. The Bison Range is far from the only place in Montana where you can see our national mammal on the hoof, though. Whether you're visiting Glacier or Yellowstone or traveling in western Montana between the two national parks, you will almost surely see some bison, even if you're not looking for them. Just south of Missoula, the Oxbow Cattle Co. runs a herd of bison right next to MT 93 in Lolo. Mogul Ted Turner owns more than a dozen bison ranches in southwestern Montana. To the north, between Browning and East Glacier on MT 2, the Blackfeet herd is frequently bunched up alongside the Helen Clarke Memorial Highway, about 7 miles west of town. In the United States, about 500,000 head of bison are being ranched for meat, many of them throughout western Montana.

On the Flathead Indian Reservation, situated among the rolling hills that straddle the border between Sanders and Lake Counties, a wild herd of American bison thrives in a natural habitat much like they have for the last hundred thousand years or so, protected from hunting and ranching. The Bison Range covers 18,766 acres of habitat that supports a population of 300–500 bison, and it's one of the best places in the country to observe this impressive beast in a natural setting. As with so many cultural treasures in the West, the Bison Range has been the focus of a conflict between Indigenous peoples and white descendants of the European-American settlers who swarmed across the West in the 19th century. Struggle over control and ownership of the preserve and its herd raged on for more than a hundred years. This time, though, the Indians won.

The largest mammal roaming the West, the American bison is also one of the most fascinating. You can watch them in their natural element at the Bison Range, north of Missoula in the Mission Valley. AUTHOR PHOTO

Before we get to that, let's address the buffalo in the room. Or is it a bison? As its taxonomy clearly insists, the American bison (*Bison bison*) is not a buffalo. True buffalo include the Asian water buffalo, found mostly in Southeast Asia and India, and the Cape buffalo, found in Africa. But, as with the pronghorn antelope, which is not a member of the antelope family at all, sometimes the sheer weight of common usage can overpower the dictionary. Thus, the terms buffalo and bison have become synonymous.

President Theodore Roosevelt signed legislation on May 23, 1908, setting aside land to create the National Bison Range, one of the first wildlife preserves in the country. The following year the initial herd was donated by a Conrad bison ranch, and in 1910 the first bison calves were born on the Range. That's the travel brochure version. In reality, the foundation for the Bison Range goes back to the 1870s, when it became clear to Salish, Pend Oreille, and Kootenai tribes that the buffalo, so integral to their cultural and spiritual existence, was quickly being wiped out by the settlers coming out west on wagon trains and railways. While many shot the animals for sport, sometimes shooting from train windows and leaving them to rot, there was a deliberate and more sinister reason to extirpate buffalo from the plains: it would deprive Native Americans of their main food source, crushing their way of life and driving them onto the reservations. Indigenous peoples who had lived as part of the land for up to 20,000 years were seen by most involved in western expansion as savages, mere pests to be eradicated from the lands colonizers treated as their "eminent domain."

In the 1870s tribal leaders gave permission for a group of buffalo that had been captured in Blackfeet territory to be brought across the Continental Divide to establish a small herd on the Flathead reservation. Michel Pablo and Charles Allard purchased ten of the buffalo and set upon growing their herd. The Pablo-Allard herd would eventually swell to about 300 by the end of the century, all the while roaming free in the low hills west of the Mission Valley.

It was becoming clear by that point that the tribes had lost the battle for their aboriginal lands, and the iconic herd was gradually being sold as parcels of tribal land were pieced off to white settlers. It was the Pablo-Allard herd that provided several buffalo to Yellowstone National Park in 1903, when the park's original herd was hunted until fewer than two dozen animals were left.

The establishment of the National Bison Range (NBR) was the final indignation. The entire area of tribal lands was fenced off and, in violation of the Hellgate Treaty of 1855, put under the purview of the Department of the Interior. The NBR's creation was lauded as a conservation victory for Teddy Roosevelt and the continued rebound of the bison population, but it was accomplished by ripping out the heart of the tribes' native lands. For this, they were paid $1.56 per acre.

The main thrust of the Hellgate Treaty was to grant the tribes water rights in exchange for 20 million acres of tribal lands. As settlers moved into the fertile Flathead Valley and "proved up" on their allotted 160 acres, Indians began to lose access to the streams, rivers, and groundwater that provided drinking water, irrigation, and fishing. As the 20th century wore on, lawsuits proliferated, pitting white ranchers and farmers against the Confederated Salish and Kootenai Tribes (CSKT) in a fight over use, maintenance, and access to waterways on the reservation. It was a fierce, complicated debate that carried on for generations.

Finally, after nearly a decade of squabbling over its content, a water compact was crafted by Montana's two senators, Jon Tester and Steve Daines, in a rare bipartisan effort. It was included in a massive defense spending bill, signed by the president on December 23, 2020. The compact was ratified by the CSKT tribal council less than a week later. The $2.3 billion compact will have a sweeping impact on the arable portions of the Flathead Reservation. Millions will be invested in the rehabilitation of ranching and farm lands, including the installation of livestock fencing and irrigation canal and ditch screens, as well as efforts to control noxious weeds. The Flathead Indian Irrigation Project, which dates back to 1904, will receive the funding to continue its mission of creating and repairing irrigation infrastructure for tribal and nontribal irrigators on the reservations.

The Compact was a huge turning point for the rights of the sovereign tribes. CSKT Chairwoman Shelly Fyant said, "Now we can avoid decades of acrimonious litigation on streams across much of Montana and protect many streams with sufficient amounts of water to make sure fish can survive."

Oh, and the land and property of the National Bison Range was handed over to the tribes. "Who better to [manage the Bison Range] than the original inhabitants of the land who depended on the buffalo for centuries? That was our mainstay," said Fyant.

On the Bison Range, as it's now known, the wildlife couldn't care less about the political wrestling match over their domain. The preserve's terrain ranges from wetlands to rolling prairie to small mountains, and it's home to herds of elk, pronghorn, white-tail and mule deer, black bear, and the occasional mountain lion. More than 200 species of birds have been identified on the Bison Range, making it a boon to birdwatchers as well as bison buffs. Increasing numbers of visitors from around the world come through the gates to wheel along the gravel ribbon of Red Sleep Mountain Drive as it winds through the refuge into the higher elevations. There are a couple of short nature trails, but this is not a place designed for a lot of hiking. Again, bison. As in Yellowstone Park, approaching a bison is a major no-no. But what magnificent creatures they are, and you can observe them to your heart's delight from the safety of your vehicle.

It's important to remember that this is real wildlife habitat, not a zoo. There's a chance you could drive through the whole loop and not see a single bison. Their movements are unpredictable, and they roam throughout this sprawling area, seeking food and water. If you don't encounter any of them near the road, don't forget to look up. You might see a lone male lying on a hillside like a posted sentry. These crusty old bulls tend to self-isolate from the herd when they're past their breeding prime. They won't be around long enough for their hair to turn gray, though. Bison tend to live only about 20 years, a seemingly short lifespan for such a robust animal.

One buffalo that lived to the ripe old age of 26 was Big Medicine, a rare white buffalo born in 1933 on the Bison Range. An albino bison calf appears about once in five million births, and this one quickly made national news. Some rather unimaginative wag named it "Whitey," but its powerful significance to Native American culture earned its prevailing handle, Big Medicine. He wasn't a true albino, as he had blue eyes, not pink, his hooves were tan, and he sported a distinctive, dark brown thatch of hair between his horns. Big Medicine was indeed a large specimen. He was just a tad smaller than a Jeep Renegade turned on its side. Twelve feet long from nose to tail, he weighed more than 1,900 pounds in his prime and stood 6 feet tall at the top of his hump. He was a prolific breeder, even siring a white buffalo of his own in 1937. The albino calf was born deaf and blind, but lived for 12 years. Big Medicine died in 1959, and he was stuffed by renowned tribal taxidermist Bob Scrivener. His mount resides in the Montana Historical Society museum in Helena.

As the entire Bison Range is fenced in, the bison are truly protected, unlike their counterparts in Yellowstone Park. There, bulls start moving north out of the park in the spring, especially in the Steven's Creek area, seeking fresh forage. To the cattle industry, this is unacceptable. Many ranchers fear brucellosis, an infectious bacterial disease that is frequently carried by bison and elk. Ranchers are apprehensive about wandering bison intermingling with their cattle and passing on the disease, which would be disastrous to their bottom line as it causes cows to abort or produce a stillborn calf. This is why bison that migrate outside of Yellowstone Park in the spring are captured and sent to slaughter (the meat and hides are distributed to the tribes), or allowed to be "hunted" by tribal members and less-than-sporting sportsmen. Never mind that there has not been a single documented case of a bison passing brucellosis to a bovine cow. It's nearly impossible. The bacteria cannot thrive in warm weather, and it is only passed to an animal that consumes birth material from a bison cow's first calving. Bison calf season is brief, from mid-April to late May. Also, nearly all the bison walking out of the park are bulls, which cannot transmit the disease. Elk can. There are many recorded instances of cattle being infected with brucellosis by elk, yet thousands of the animals are left to move freely in and out of Yellowstone. Sure, they are hunted, but not methodically shot or captured the moment they cross an invisible boundary. There are no easy answers to the bison–cattle wars being waged in Montana, a state that has about three times as many cattle as it does people.

Another big difference between the Bison Range and Yellowstone is that there are no wolves on the Bison Range. While Yellowstone's bison live under the constant threat of the apex predator, that may not always be the case, depending on the prevailing politics surrounding wolf recovery efforts in Montana. The hunting and ranching lobbies, employing some successful arm-twisting, persuaded the state to allow a portion of the Yellowstone wolfpacks, which had been carefully reintroduced and managed to a healthy population, to be hunted as they, like the bison, wandered out of the park.

Lewis and Clark wrote in their journals of the massive herds of buffalo they encountered on their journey to the Northwest in 1806. Before the wagon trains, before the railroads, there were 30 to 75 million bison thundering across the Northern Plains. "The moving multitude . . . darkened the whole plains," they wrote in their journals. We nearly wiped them off the face of the earth, only to bring them back from the edge of extinction. We set aside a 2.2-million-acre national park for them to thrive in, only to shoot them when they set foot outside that park. The bison is a proud symbol of the West, and the animal's behavior is the very definition of resolve. Their massive humps are pure muscle, giving them the power to swing their giant heads back and forth through deep snow so they can get down to the grasses that sustain them. When the herd is overtaken by a winter storm, they turn and walk directly into it, knowing it is the most direct path out of it.

Bison are endlessly fascinating animals that can really put on a show, whether it's a couple of bulls knocking heads over the attentions of a female in the fall, or writhing around on their backs in a dirt wallow in the summer, raising clouds of dust while they try to rid themselves of pesky biting flies and winter shag. The opportunity to witness them in their natural habitat on the Bison Range is one of the most exciting bonuses of building a little "Montana" time into your journey between the two national parks.

25

Ladies and Gentlemen, the Virginia City Players

AT LEAST FOUR MONTANA SETTLEMENTS ARE CALLED THE "CRADLE OF Montana history." One of them, Virginia City, is the cradle that's still rocking. Established near the site of the biggest gold strike in the Rocky Mountains, Virginia City and its sister settlement Nevada City are still going strong. A couple hundred or so hardcore Montanans live there year-round, but it's summertime when the erstwhile mining towns explode with activity. Thousands of tourists swarm into these restored western towns, many on their way to or from Yellowstone National Park, about an hour and a half away. They check out the bars and restaurants, maybe pick up some souvenirs at the quaint little shops that line the Wallace Street boardwalk, or pan for real gold at Alder Gulch. Many will catch the Brewery Follies at the historic Gilbert Brewery, a decidedly adult experience featuring comedy raunchy enough to make Dave Chappelle blush. And then there's the Opera House, where the "Illustrious" Virginia City Players perform melodrama and vaudeville in the classic mold. The Players, as they're called here, are the oldest continually running professional theater in Montana, and the company boasts a history that's as dramatic and complex as the story of Virginia City itself.

It all started on a sunny afternoon in May 1863, when Bill Fairweather, Henry Edgar, and four other dusty dudes discovered gold in a burbling tributary of the Ruby River just southeast of present-day Butte. The gold hounds had been on their way to Bannack to resupply after a run-in with a band of Crow Indians, and had camped along a creek lined with alders.

A couple of the men chipped some material off a rock outcrop and caught the sparkle of gold flakes. By the next afternoon the group had pulled 10 ounces of gold from the ground. The news spread quickly through a territory already inflamed with gold fever, and soon thousands of opportunists began pouring into Alder Gulch to stake a claim. As mining camps began to spring up overnight, the township of Virginia City was established, and one of the first structures built was a brewery. Hey, priorities.

They call it a boom because it happens fast. The avarice, greed, and rampant crime that was typical of western boomtowns quickly peaked in Virginia City, with the capture and hanging of a gang of road agents known as the Innocents, by an infamous posse of vigilantes imaginatively named the Vigilantes. How bad was the situation? Well, for starters, Sheriff Henry Plummer was purportedly involved with the road agents. But that's a story for another time.

Most miners were on the square, just working to survive and hopefully come away with their share of the gold that rested beneath their feet in Alder Gulch, which would eventually prove to be the largest surface gold strike in the world. It was a hard, dirty, and frequently disappointing life, so the men were always ready for some diversion to take their minds off the troubles at hand, and help get them through the frigid Montana winters. Sucking down suds at Montana's first brewery wasn't the only form of recreation they enjoyed. Gambling and getting liquored up were ubiquitous, of course, and troubadours drifted from one mining camp to the next, bringing music and stories to a bunch of bored men who were starved for entertainment. Naturally, there were a few brothels scattered along the 14-mile-long settlement, as Alder Gulch came to be known, where ladies of the evening served the miners' biological urges. Many of the men had acquired more sophisticated tastes in entertainment; some were known to carry the works of Shakespeare in their bags. Plays were in demand. On March 13, 1867, the Amateur Dramatic Association gave their first performance, a comedy called *Used Up*, and a long-running tradition of live theater was established in Virginia City. By that time about 7,000 people were living in the newly designated Territorial Capital. In 1875 a devastating fire swept through Virginia City, wiping out most of the town and leaving 10,000 people homeless. The town was rebuilt, but by this time the boom was quickly becoming a bust. Things picked back up in 1899 when the first dredging operation was brought in, and gargantuan machines carved a massive gouge up and down Alder Creek, trying to scrape up every last speck of gold. By 1922 they called it quits, leaving behind a mangled stream lined with huge piles of earth that remain today. The town emptied out, save for a couple hundred hard cases who hunkered down through the Montana winters, eking out an existence while the Chinese moved in to sift through the tailings for any gold they'd missed.

The Depression made life even more challenging in the dwindling town. There were no jobs. People were tearing down buildings to use for firewood. Virginia City was on its way to becoming just another ghost town.

Enter Charlie Bovey and his wife Sue Ford Bovey. Charlie and Sue visited Virginia City from his Great Falls ranch in the mid-1940s, and decided that it would be a great repository for his growing collection of western buildings and memorabilia, then residing at the Great Falls fairgrounds. Charlie, a successful rancher and heir to the General Mills fortune, began restoration work on several of Virginia City's structures, and started having his acquisitions of 19th-century buildings and collections of artifacts around the state moved to Nevada City and Virginia City.

One evening at the H.S. Gilbert Brewery during the Fourth of July weekend in 1948, a handsome young man named Larry Barsness was entertaining patrons by singing some showtunes, accompanied by the old upright piano. Larry, who was visiting Virginia City from Lewistown with his wife Dori and brother Jack, had suffered a broken back in a car accident a few years earlier, making him undraftable for World War II. He'd been doing some acting in regional theater in Oregon. Charlie happened to be at the brewery that night, and when Larry started crooning some Gilbert and Sullivan, Charlie was enthralled. He struck up a conversation with the young actor, and asked the trio if they'd be interested in writing a show to perform at an upcoming miners' convention in Great Falls. Dori and Jack quickly churned out a melodrama, *Clem the Miner's Daughter*. It was a hit. Charlie asked the Barsnesses, how would they like to form a summer theater company right there in Virginia City? In 1949 the Virginia City Players performed their first show, and they're still at it today.

Those first few plays were done in the brewery, but the Players quickly outgrew that cramped venue and Bovey moved the company into an old stone livery that had been converted into a theater and opera house. To accommodate professional theater productions, however, some changes had to be made, starting with knocking out the back wall to make room for a decent stage. The next step was digging out the floor to provide raked seating and to create an orchestra pit for the music that accompanied the 19th-century melodramas that the Players would be performing.

"It wasn't a theater by any means," recalls B. J. Barsness, who was about 5 years old when her mom and dad started the Players. "It was just a flat floor. I think they built a small raised stage, not very tall. No more than a foot. So people sat on folding chairs. And then afterwards they'd have a square dance. The pit was not dug until about 1957, somewhere in there."

Ben Tone had been working in Oregon with Larry and Dori, and Larry brought his friend out to Virginia City to join the troupe. "Actors did everything," said Tone. That included helping dig the pit, which had to be large enough to hold the Cremona M-3 photoplayer, a 16-foot-long Rube Goldberg contraption that allowed one keyboard player to supply piano, pipe organ, drums, flute, violin, cymbals, and percussion. During the early days the cast and crew would walk next door to the Bale of Hay tavern after their show at the Opera House, where they would put on an informal performance and pass the hat to supplement their meager pay. A weekly cabaret show at the Bovey-reconstructed Wells Fargo steakhouse became part of their routine as well. Tone, like most actors of the day, was a renaissance man who not only manned a shovel to help dig the pit, but also helped Barsness build and paint the sets. One thing he couldn't solve was the clatter of the Opera House's tin roof when precipitation hit. "It was impossible to perform if it was raining or hailing," he said. Like many who come to visit Montana, Tone fell in love with the area and eventually made it his permanent home. He moved to Bozeman in the early '60s and taught at Montana State University until his retirement in 1982.

The Virginia City Players, Montana's oldest continually operating theater company, serves up classic melodrama and vaudeville comedy all summer long in their home space, a former livery that was converted into a theater.
WIKI COMMONS PHOTO BY MURRAY FOUBISTER

By 1952 the Players had become an integral part of Virginia City's Old West charm, thanks to quality productions, talented actors, and the Boveys' constant additions of buildings and attractions to Virginia City and Nevada City. "Virginia City was packed," says B.J. "I have photos of cars lined up, parked the entire length of Marshall Street. We have to remember that it was in the 50s, and westerns were all the rage. All of Montana came to Virginia City to see what Charlie had done. And they stayed for the shows. There was a point in the 60s where we had to do two shows a night on Saturday."

Larry and Dori divorced in 1952, and in 1957 he married Pat Perry from Townsend. They had two children, Kris and Eric, who immediately became involved in the family business. Kris Barsness recalls a production of *Rip Van Winkle* when she was seven, playing opposite her older sister B.J. A photo from the *Great Falls Tribune* shows Kris sitting on B.J.'s lap onstage, wearing the very same dress and playing the same part her older sister had when she was 7. That dress, as well as many of the early costumes used by the Players, came from a surprising source. Kris and some of the other actors picked out clothing and shoes from the inventory on display at a dry goods store that had been in town since its inception. Last owned by the McGovern sisters, it closed for good in 1945. "At the beginning of the season we were let into one of the stores and would pick out the dress I wore, we would get shoes that were still in the boxes. Brand new shoes, never been worn," said Kris. "Isn't that crazy?"

B.J. also has vivid memories of raiding the old shop for costumes. "Charlie said go take what you want from this store. They left all the stock. So all the years I was growing up, we had authentic whale bone corsets."

Pat wasn't an actress, but she was happy to run the business side of things. While Larry served as the artistic director and continued to perform onstage, Pat did the books, ran the box office, handled the marketing and advertising, and put her kids to work both onstage and off. Kris and Eric ushered, they sold programs, ran the lights, helped build costumes—whatever was needed. A set of bunk beds was even built into the box office so the two kids could sleep there. As Kris recalls, she and Eric also served as a pint-sized marketing team for the company. "We used to take trips over to Yellowstone and our parents would give Eric and me posters for the Players and have us go into the stores and ask people to hang the posters because they knew they couldn't turn kids down." Onstage, they were treated as a unit. Any time children were needed to fill out a scene, Kris and Eric were on the boards.

As if their upbringing wasn't crazy enough, in the early '60s Larry started taking the family down to Mexico, loading them up in the tour bus to spend the offseason. "They took the seats out and put our cribs in, and diaper pails," says Kris, "and drove to Mexico. I don't know how they did it with two little kids. Can you imagine?"

For the first few years they stayed in a small town outside Mexico City, occasionally bringing the odd cousin or two. "We were there all summer," says Kris. "It was wonderful. We traveled all over the place. Back in those days you could still climb the pyramids. We were able to climb to the top of the pyramids and do all that."

While the kids were scaling pre-Columbian monuments, Larry was busy reading 19th-century plays and scheming for the upcoming season. The family would typically head back to Virginia City in March.

"It was probably an 8-month gig for them in those days, including the touring and stuff like that in the fall," says Eric of those early years for the Players. Part of their agreement was living rent-free in a house in Virginia City owned by the Boveys. It helped them save enough money to winter in Mexico every year. "We went down maybe 4 months every year," says Eric, "then we'd come back and my dad would start building scenery and getting stuff ready for the summer. He spent the winter figuring out what plays he was going to do so by the time we got back he could design the scenery and start building it."

Eric was never bitten by the acting bug like his sisters, so he moved into the construction and tech end of theater, preferring to work behind the scenes. Like B.J. and Kris, though, he never really considered his upbringing to be that unusual. "We didn't think twice about it growing up. It just seemed like it was what everybody did."

Today Eric is eyeing retirement from a long career as a carpenter. He splits his time between Helena and Virginia City, spending much of the year in the very same home his parents did. He also spends a lot of his time working to preserve the cultural heritage of Virginia City, as well as performing the constant upkeep required by a 150-year-old house.

As the Players moved into the late '60s, attitudes toward live theater and Larry's own approach to the material were evolving. Initially, Larry and Dori had wanted to pull away from the broad, cartoonish "meller-drammer" that had become popular by the time they launched the Players. "They came upon this opportunity at a time when melodrama was just being reevaluated," says B.J., who has enjoyed a successful career in theater, moving from acting to directing. "There was a collection of [plays published by] the Princeton Press. It was about 10 volumes and I had several of them until a few years ago, but [Larry was] arguing that there was merit to the old melodramas because in the 20s there was a generational backlash." By the time Larry left the Virginia City Players in 1969, the pendulum had started to swing back toward the Snidely Whiplash, mustache-twirling style of theater that had some fun with the material at its own expense. Judy Ferree took over the company and ran it for the next decade, making a hard turn away from the mellerdrammer back to the more high-minded approach of classic melodrama. By all accounts, she was a brilliant writer and director. She was succeeded by Bruce Hurlbut, another well-regarded figure in regional theater. It was during Hurlbut's era that Missoula-based actress Stacey Kimble first arrived in Virginia City. She would go on to become an important character in the Players' history, spending three separate stints with the company, starting as an actress in 1985. As a kid, Kimble (then Gordon) had developed an interest in acting while spending her summers in Bigfork, on Flathead Lake. "I was 9 to 14," she said. "I lived at the theater. There was another little girl who lived near me and was interested in the theater too. We would go and sit out back of the theater and just wait for the actors to come out. A couple of them once in a while would say, well, you can help me learn lines, and they'd pay us 50 cents. I knew that's what I wanted to be when I grew up, I just didn't know how in the hell you do it." After a trip to Virginia City where she saw the Players, she felt her destiny was set. She'd already acted in a few community theater productions and was working at a Bozeman radio station as an on-air announcer when she got the call from Hurlbut to join the Players. Kimble arrived in Virginia City just when the town was entering a downturn. "In '85 we still had packed houses on the weekends," she said. "But by '89 the crowds had dwindled." She left the Players after that summer. A depressed economy played a part, as hotels struggled and fewer rooms were available for overnight visitors. But it was Charlie's death in 1978, followed by Sue's 10 years later that really put Virginia City into a tailspin.

Bovey Restoration Corp. operations were passed down to their son, Ford, who was unable to continue the rebuilding and restoration. "He didn't have the vision his parents had," says Kimble. Erik Barsness is more blunt in his assessment: "What a waste. He had such a great opportunity there to do something and never did."

B. J. Barsness (now Douglas) was persuaded to return to the fold in 1992, then Kimble stepped in the following year when she and her friend Greg Johnson, artistic director of the Montana Repertory Theater, teamed up to manage the Players. For a couple of seasons they continued at a high level, bringing in playwright Roger Hedden (*Bodies, Rest and Motion*) to direct, working with scripts by the likes of J. M. Barrie and George Bernard Shaw.

Still, it was a difficult time for Virginia City. With visitor numbers tailing off and much of the town falling into disrepair, Ford put the town and its contents up for sale. A few private buyers came sniffing around, but ultimately the town was saved when the state of Montana purchased most of the buildings and the Historic Heritage Commission was created to administer Virginia City and Nevada City and the majority of their buildings as tourist sites.

Now the Virginia City Players are operated as a concession, as are all the other businesses in town. It's still one of the most popular attractions in the area, and most summers are busy enough that reservations are required. After being shut down for 2 years during the pandemic, the theater has come roaring back under the continued direction of Bill and Christina Koch.

❦

A hundred and fifty years ago, after a long and strenuous day of scraping the Alder Gulch for gold, exhausted miners would straggle into Virginia City seeking food, drink, and entertainment. Today, it's not that different. Only instead of a flood of hygiene-challenged prospectors on horseback and wagons, it's throngs of curious tourists piloting RVs and SUVs on the road to Yellowstone, or perhaps locals driving out from Butte or Bozeman, seeking some top-quality melodrama onstage at the stone Opera House. The Players proudly carry on the tradition started in the 1860s by the intrepid Amateur Dramatic Association, whose motto still captures the spirit of this vibrant, fascinating Montana town: "Ours is the land and age of gold, and ours the laughing time. Old Times will end our story, but no time, if we end well, will end our glory."

26

Montana's State Parks:
Like National Parks, Only Smaller

MILLTOWN STATE PARK
JUST EAST OF MISSOULA NEAR THE JUNCTION OF MT 200 AND I-90, Montana's newest state park encompasses the confluence of the Blackfoot River with the Clark Fork, a sacred Indian fishing ground known to the Salish as "the place of the mature bull trout." It's also the spot where the Milltown Dam was removed in 2008–2009. For almost 100 years, the 21-foot-high dam, built to supply hydroelectricity to the lumber mill town of Bonner, held back more than 6 million tons of sediment rife with toxins and heavy metals that flowed down from the Butte mining operations 112 miles upstream. Periodic flooding and ice jams threatened the aging structure, and it was just a matter of time before it would fail, sending a catastrophic tidal wave of poisonous sludge through the middle of Montana's second largest city. The dam's removal was at the center of a white-hot controversy for several years, as locals were divided over what action should be taken—if any—about the eroding structure and the ticking time bomb of toxic waste.

Under the direction of a Superfund cleanup, the area has been rehabilitated and enhanced with walkways, landscaping, picnic areas, and plenty of riverside trails through the beautiful little park, complete with interpretive signs that tell the story of the confluence, where the Blackfoot River once again flows freely into the Clark Fork.

Beavertail Hill State Park

Situated along the Clark Fork 30 miles east of Missoula, Beavertail Hill State Park is a quick, easy opportunity for Missoulians to get in some camping, hiking, fishing, and exploring just a half-hour from home. Its small campground is full of pleasant sites with plenty of shade, and the whole area is a riot of different trees, from pines to cottonwoods to willows and quaking aspens. A self-guided nature trail runs alongside the Clark Fork, where you'll see osprey plucking trout out of the river, kingfishers making kamikaze dives into the water, and graceful great blue herons prancing in the shallows. There's a handy boat ramp for rafts, and an amphitheater near the campground for evening nature talks. It's a state park oasis surrounded by private land, but there are lots of opportunities to explore its riparian areas. There are also two full-size tipis on site, the Beavertail Tipi and the John Mullan Tipi, and they're available for camping for a fee.

Granite State Park

High above Flint Creek Valley in the Beaverhead Deerlodge National Forest, the bones of a little mining town called Granite are available for exploration. Hector Horton is generally considered to be the first to discover silver in the area in 1865, and 10 years later the Granite Mine was in full swing, as the town's population swelled to 3,000. Eventually $40 million worth of the precious metal was extracted from the mountain, but the silver panic of 1893 sounded the death knell for Granite.

Nowadays there are several self-guided ghost town trails winding through the area, a lovely little valley where several building remnants hunker among the dense fir trees and understory. There's enough left of the three-story miners' Union Hall that it doesn't take a lot of imagination to picture its original splendor, which boasted stained glass windows and a cast iron front wall.

A visit to the Ghost Town Hall of Fame in Philipsburg's Granite County Museum is recommended before you tackle the 3-mile dirt road to Granite. This is some steep, narrow, rocky, first-gear, chew-a-hole-in-your-seat-cover, all-wheel-drive stuff. The views of the Pintler Mountains are fabulous, and (unless you're driving) you'll be looking directly across a ravine to the back side of Discovery Ski Area. When the boulders on the road's edge start looking like tombstones, you'll know you're almost there.

ANACONDA SMELTER STACK STATE PARK

One of Montana's tiniest state parks, Anaconda Smelter Stack State Park's main feature is a replica of the 60-foot-diameter opening atop the iconic smoke stack looming directly to the east. At 585 feet, the stack, as locals call it, is the tallest brick structure in the world. If you're within 25 miles of Anaconda on I-90 you can't miss it. At the park, what looks like black sand covers the ground within the 3-foot-tall brick ring. It's slag, a by-product of the smelting process. Coarse and shiny, it is what you see in huge piles all over the hillside around the stack, where it accumulated over the 100 years of the Butte mining smelter operation.

Locals rallied to save the iconic structure from demolition after Anaconda's copper smelter shut down in 1980, and the replica ring is surrounded by hundreds of tiles bearing the names of people who donated time and money to build the park and save the stack. The stories represented in the park are an important part of Butte's copper mining history, and the impact it had on the West. There's a great copper sculpture, created by student volunteers, of three miners near the entrance, which is bracketed by a pair of 10-foot-wide iron smelter buckets. There's not much in the way of shade on a hot summer day, but it's worth a stop if you're passing through Anaconda.

LOST CREEK STATE PARK

As is the case with so many of Montana's state parks, the drive into it is a big part of its appeal. Lost Creek Road branches west off MT 273 just east of Anaconda on the road to Warm Springs, and it passes by some ranches and farms (including a small herd of yaks) before climbing up into the forest between two huge granite mountains striped with color. Lost Creek has some spots big enough to fish, and lots of people take advantage of the many pullouts and picnic areas on the way up to the campground. The spectacular limestone cliffs and granite formations are home to bighorn sheep, pika, golden eagles, and other wildlife. The narrow, graveled road ends near Lost Creek Falls, which come into view less than 100 feet up a blacktop path from the parking lot. The 50-foot falls are graceful and picturesque, tumbling through the shaded forest over boulders and downed trees, providing an idyllic backdrop for a picnic or just some creekside navel gazing.

Lewis and Clark Caverns State Park

The huge limestone caverns about 45 miles west of Bozeman were carved out by the waters of an inland sea, probably during the last ice age more than 15,000 years ago. The caverns were discovered in 1892 by a couple of local ranchers, and around 1900 an opportunist named Dan Morrison filed a mineral rights claim on the area and started leading tours underground. Hundreds of people explored the caverns before the railroad filed suit against Morrison for the rights to the land. You know who had never seen the Lewis and Clark caverns? Lewis and Clark. They did come within a few miles of it when they camped on nearby Antelope Creek, but the name is really just a tribute.

This is Montana's original state park, and it's one of the best. The guided tour of the caverns, offered May through September, is a fascinating, 2-hour journey for those who are comfortable being hundreds of feet underground in some dank limestone chambers looking over their shoulders for Townsend's big-eared bats. Camping, hiking, biking, and exploring the park's 3,000 acres, as well as fishing in the nearby Jefferson River, make for a memorable side trip in your drive between the national parks.

Madison Buffalo Jump State Park

The first Indigenous tribal members who encountered the bluff that would become the Madison Buffalo Jump might have thought, man, we couldn't have designed the more perfect buffalo jump if we tried. The rolling prairie overlooking the Madison Valley ends abruptly at a sharp rock outcrop which drops 20–30 feet straight down to a grassy slope that gradually flattens out, providing easy access to the animals after they'd been driven off the precipice. The semicircular cliff offers plenty of ledges and notches in the rock face where the buffalo runner could crouch after drawing a herd of buffalo along the cliff's edge. Hunters at the top would drive the herd forward, and their momentum would carry them over the edge, where others would be waiting below to process the carcasses. Several tribes shared this jump for around 2,000 years, up until about 200 years ago, when buffalo hunting was transformed by the introduction of the horse.

The state park is about 15 minutes of narrow, winding blacktop from I-90, a half-hour west of Bozeman. Several trails are cut through the area, some leading up to the cliff top offering panoramic views of the Madison River Valley. A roofed interpretive kiosk on a hill facing the cliff offers merciful shade and informational signs, an easy quarter-mile walk up from the parking lot.

MISSOURI HEADWATERS STATE PARK

The confluence of the Jefferson, Madison, and Gallatin Rivers marks the official headwaters of the Missouri River, a significant piece of the picture that was being assembled by Lewis and Clark's Corps of Discovery in their quest to find an inland trade route between St. Louis and the Pacific and Canada.

There's also some major local history centered here. Just across the street from the Headwaters campground there's an old pioneer hotel, one of the last vestiges of Gallatin City. Actually, it's left over from Gallatin City II. The first Gallatin City was established in 1863 near the mouth of the Gallatin River, which was named for Albert Gallatin, secretary of the treasury during Lewis and Clark's journey. Twenty-five pioneers put down roots of a community they thought would be a hub of river commerce, serving the gold camps of Virginia City to the south and Helena to the north. When downstream waterfalls put the kibosh on steamship travel, they moved the settlement 2 miles south, across the river, on a stage line. The new town, Gallatin City II, thrived for a while. They had a flour mill, a racetrack, stores, and a busy stage stop. When the Northern Pacific laid its mainline several miles to the south, the town quickly faded away. A Gallatin III was briefly considered, but the diminishing returns brought in by subsequent sequels shut down that plan.

Gallatin City's rich history includes the story of Fannie Campbell, the 19-year-old daughter of one of the town's founders, who was en route to join her family with her older sister aboard the steamship *Bertrand* when the boat wrecked on the Missouri about 25 miles north of Omaha, Nebraska. The girls managed to reach the riverbank, where they watched the ship sink to the bottom. Their continued efforts to reach Gallatin City were met with more disaster, but they eventually made it, and Fannie ultimately became an important figure in Gallatin City's history. Fannie Campbell's incredible story is told in great detail at the Headwaters Heritage Museum in Three Forks, one of the biggest and best historical museums in the state.

Tower Rock State Park

Here's another great stopping point, right along I-90 between Helena and Great Falls, where you can get in a little hike and check out a significant point along the Lewis and Clark trail. Tower Rock itself is a single peak at the end of a mile-long formation along the Missouri River. While the Corps set up camp at the spot, Meriwether Lewis climbed up the 424-foot Tower Rock to gain a view of the surrounding area. That's so Meriwether. "It may be ascended with some difficulty nearly to its summit," he wrote in his journal, "and from there it is a most pleasing view of the country we are about to leave." The Corps had reached what's known as a habitat edge, the interface between the prairie and the mountains. It's an area where wildlife from both ecosystems gather to seek water, nest, or hunt for prey. A botanical study revealed a unique habitat where over one hundred species of prairie and mountain plants were found to coexist, and only do so at the edge of the mountains. Lewis realized that the expedition was leaving behind the prairie, and with it the buffalo that had sustained them across the Northern Plains for months.

A quarter-mile trail runs along the massive formation, gaining about 200 feet in elevation before culminating at a small, polished granite bench. That marks the end of the official trail, but an unofficial path clearly leads the rest of the way to the top of Tower Rock. Signs exhort hikers to wear sturdy shoes and bring water. They are not kidding.

Sluice Boxes Primitive State Park

Sluice Boxes is a handy spot for Great Falls residents, located about 30 miles south of town between the Electric City and White Sulphur

Springs. It's a gorgeous chunk of west-central Montana situated around Belt Creek, one of the most beautiful waterways in the state. At the northern edge of the Lewis and Clark National Forest, limestone cliffs create a stunning valley that brackets the creek, intruding into the stream here and there to create waterfalls and cascades that give the park its name, suggesting the riffles of water that ran through a sluice box, a device prospectors used to separate gold from the material scooped up from a creekbed.

There's an overlook at the top of the road that provides a sweeping view of the canyon and its dramatic geology, then it's a short drive down the hill to a small parking lot just across a bridge over the creek at the head of the park, which lies partly on land owned by the Haglund family, who are kind enough to provide access for hikers and floaters.

The trail goes more than 9 miles up the Belt Creek canyon, and there is some steep, rocky terrain involved. There is a ton of wildlife as the park isn't normally overrun with visitors. Deer, bighorn sheep, marmots, pikas, and all manner of grassland birds can be seen while hiking along this pretty little stream. Huckleberries pop up along the trail, but please make sure you are confident in identifying your berries before you ingest them. Let's just say I speak from experience and leave it at that.

GIANT SPRINGS STATE PARK

Like most cities on a river, Great Falls makes the most of its local waterway. Their urban riverside park is easily accessible, with broad concrete paths for walking and biking along the "Mighty Mo," and plenty of well-maintained, shaded picnic areas. Just downstream from Black Eagle Falls, the most dramatic and picturesque of several waterfalls along the Missouri, lies perhaps the prettiest spot on the 14 miles of riverside trail, Giant Springs State Park. Located on the east bank, the heart of the park is the eponymous spring, one of the largest freshwater springs in the world. Its crystal clear water, pumping out of the earth at a steady temperature of 54 degrees, comes from the Madison Aquifer, a massive water table underlying five US states and three Canadian provinces. About 150 million gallons a day flow out of the spring and into the adjacent Missouri River. The surrounding walkway and footbridge frame a natural infinity pool, a pond so clear that you can easily see the undulating plant life

Giant Springs State Park in Great Falls is an oasis of trees, trout, and a captivating freshwater spring that pumps about 150 million gallons of water a day into the Missouri River. Pelicans, cormorants, gulls, and other waterbirds congregate on the Mighty Mo, providing great birding opportunities. AUTHOR PHOTO

20 feet beneath the surface. It's so ridiculously colorful that you might wonder if it's a displaced submarine ride from a Disney park. Most of the spring water flows over the edge of the semicircular terrace, cascading over rocks into the Missouri River, the country's longest. There's also a channel that flows for 201 feet from the spring into the Missouri, creating the Roe River, named by Guinness World Records as the world's shortest.

The park surrounding the spring is an inviting greenbelt of well-manicured grass between mature trees providing plenty of shade in the summer for picnics, weddings, family reunions, or travelers taking a break on their drive between the parks. The spring also supplies water for a trout hatchery that features a "show pool" containing hundreds of circling trout. They're mostly rainbows, some as big as your leg, with a few striking golden trout cruising through the water like golden gods. A quarter buys a handful of fish kibble, and when the surface starts to boil as the trout slash back and forth, fighting for the tidbits, it's a sight you won't soon forget.

SPRING MEADOW LAKE STATE PARK

Helena boasts a wonderful little urban state park, and it's quite handy, sitting on the western edge of town. Spring Meadow Lake was created on the site of the Steadman Foundry, a former gravel pit and factory, and the whole project has been designed to provide a safe and comfortable nature experience for Helenans seeking a nearby respite from the concrete and asphalt of the city.

The lake covers most of the park's 61 acres, and it's a popular spot for paddleboarding, kayaking, fishing, swimming, and picnicking. As you stroll along the 0.8-mile nature path that circles the lake, you'll pass by several informational kiosks and displays touting the presence of wildlife such as osprey, painted turtles, bats, and birds. The grassy area near the parking lot slopes down to a small, shallow arm of the lake where kids can splash around in the water (complimentary life jackets are available to borrow) or feed the ducks and Canada geese that hang around the park hoping to cadge a free meal.

It's a great spot for kids to learn to fish, and the lake is stocked with trout, bass, and sunfish. There's even a 50-foot-wide ADA-compliant fishing dock on the southwest bank. A pavilion is available to rent for family parties, and a snack bar offers ice cream and cold drinks in the summer.

The lake can also be accessed from the south end, where the original foundry building is now home to the Montana WILD Education Center, which houses more than one hundred wildlife mounts and aquaria full of native fish and other aquatic species. Outside there's an osprey nest on display (the real one is down by the lake and yes, it's occupied) and a real bear trap the kids can check out.

If you're spending any time in Helena during your visit to Montana, you may find that Spring Meadow Lake State Park is just the kind of nearby outdoors experience your family could use to take a break from the road.

27

Buffalo Soldiers: Winning the West on Two Wheels

CHOOSE YOUR ROUTE FROM MISSOULA TO YELLOWSTONE NATIONAL Park—you can't go wrong. Head south on US 93, take a left on MT 43 near Hamilton, drive over Skalkaho Pass and you'll cut through the Big Hole Valley, some of the most picturesque scenery in Montana and home to the Big Hole River, a renowned trout stream. Or you could head east on I-90, turn south at Whitehall, and you'll hook up with US 287, which will take you through the fascinating historic mining towns of Nevada City and Virginia City. Or you might pick the shortest path, via I-90 and 287 through Ennis, which adds up to about 264 miles of panoramic pulchritude. Now, try covering it on a bicycle. Been there, pedaled that, you say? Perhaps you zipped along the smooth asphalt on your 22-speed Urgestalt, which barely weighs 15 pounds with its carbon fiber frame, tubeless tires, and integrated headset. Still, this ride is still no mere spin around the block—we're talking one mile of total elevation gain. Montana's notoriously unpredictable weather will almost certainly play a part, especially when you get into the mountains. Rain, wind, hail, even snow can blow in at any time, any month of the year.

Now, imagine making the same trip on a single-gear bike weighing more than twice as much. First, though, load that baby up with 60 pounds of gear. And don't bother looking for your friction-free bib shorts or clip-in cycling shoes. No, you'll be dressed in full leather boots with gaiters, heavy canvas pants, a flannel shirt over a thick undershirt, and a big, floppy leather hat. Sounds crazy, right? The Buffalo Soldiers Bicycle Corps didn't think so. Based in Fort Missoula, the regiment of all-Black US Army soldiers pedaled and pushed their way during the summer of

1896 to Yellowstone and back, a 10-day round trip. And that was just a shakedown cruise for an even longer journey.

Three developments converged to inspire the legendary trip that would take eight soldiers of the 25th Infantry on a gut-checking ride to America's first national park. First, the Buffalo Soldiers had been scattered to posts across the West after the Civil War, ostensibly to provide them opportunities for adventure and career advancement not available to them in the South. These African-American soldiers were given their moniker in the western territory due to their dark complexion and nappy hair. Black soldiers knew they'd have to work twice as hard as their white counterparts to gain acceptance, and they took their service seriously, frequently leading the Army in reenlistment rates. They also had the lowest number of deserters.

Second, while the Buffalo Soldiers were drilling, practicing war games, and performing other duties at the Montana forts that had popped up all over the West during the gold rush and westward expansion, a new bicycle craze was sweeping the country in the late 1880s. The so-called safety bike, a diamond-frame cycle with two wheels of equal size, was quickly gaining favor over the penny farthing, the old-timey bike with a tall front wheel and tiny rear wheel. By the early 1890s, the potential for the bicycle to be an effective means of moving regiments of soldiers across great distances more quickly and efficiently than on horseback caught the imagination of the Army's commanding general, Nelson A. Miles.

Third, in the mid-1890s Second Lieutenant James A. Moss, a recent West Point graduate, had been assigned to the 25th Infantry at Fort Missoula, one of the Army's more remote outposts. The Louisiana native was a bicycle nut. He sent his plan for an all-bicycle regiment to General Miles, and the experimental Twenty-Fifth Infantry Bicycle Corps was approved on May 12, 1896.

Their first priority was securing some bikes. Although the popular safety bikes were fine for pedaling down to the corner store for a package of Wrigley's Baking Soda (maybe just to get the free Juicy Fruit chewing gum in every can), the Bicycle Corps would need a much more robust rig. The A.G. Spalding Company of Chicopee Falls, Massachusetts, was up to the task. The business that made its name manufacturing the first big league baseballs and gloves agreed to build a beefed-up bike to Moss's specifications. With steel wheels, double spokes, steel chain cover, an all-steel frame, and reinforced forks, the bikes were designed to withstand the punishing rides the Corps would make across the Mountain West. The puncture-proof tires proved to be that in name only, but at the end of the 19th century, these bikes were cutting edge. Fully loaded with gear, provisions, and ammo, each bike weighed in at 80 pounds.

Moss and his eight-man Corps began making forays farther and farther from Fort Missoula, pedaling as much as 40 miles per day. They drilled between trips, riding through obstacle courses, crossing streams, climbing the bikes over barriers, and riding in formation. In early August Moss and a six-man squad loaded their knapsacks with provisions and equipment and struck out for McDonald Lake, near St. Ignatius, 42 miles north of Missoula. The late summer rains muddied up much of the roads and trails, and the men frequently rode along the railroad tracks rather than slog through the slop. Even though they walked more than they rode, Moss considered the trip a success and immediately began planning their next journey.

On August 10, they would set out for Yellowstone National Park, a round-trip journey of nearly 800 miles. This juggernaut would require a hefty amount of supplies and gear, which the men split up and carried on their bikes.

It's been said that an army travels on its stomach, and the Bicycle Corps was no exception. Their provisions list was lengthy:

5 lbs. prunes

25 lbs. flour

14 lbs. sugar

4 lbs. ground coffee

16 lbs. bacon

18 lbs. canned syrup

4 cans baking powder

10 lbs. bologna

5 lbs. rice

5 lbs. salt

The list also included cans of beans and corn, small cakes of chocolate, beef extract, and other sundries. They brought medicines such as Jamaican ginger, C.C. pills for coughs and cold, quinine pills in case they somehow encountered malaria in the Rocky Mountain West, camphor pills to treat insect bites and rashes, and a bottle of something called Squib's mixture to control diarrhea.

They also carried tents, poles, blankets, extra clothing, cooking utensils, pans, a large coffee pot, and individual cutlery. To keep the bikes in working order, Private John Findley, the Corps mechanic, carried a large wooden box attached to his handlebars that contained extra spokes, nipples, two cyclometers, one pair of tires, two pedal cranks, spare axles, chain links and bolts, and a variety of bike tools.

Add their rifles and pistols, ammunition, personal effects, and various odds and ends, and each man and his bike were loaded down like pack mules. When Moss had hand-picked the soldiers to serve in the Bicycle Corps, he chose athletic men of smaller stature as he thought they would be better at handling the bikes than the lankier guys. Private Findley was the heaviest at 186 pounds, and with the 86 pounds of gear and provisions on his bike and his back, he and his rig weighed in at a whopping 272 pounds.

The bike squad benefited from the added leadership of Sergeant Mingo Sanders, who'd already served for 16 years and was reliable, knowledgeable, and well liked among the men. Blind in one eye, he'd wanted to enlist so badly that he obtained an exemption. He proved to be a valuable asset to the Bicycle Corps, and served as Moss's right-hand man.

Fully outfitted and properly trained, Moss and the soldiers headed northwest to Fort Harrison, near Helena. En route, one of the men, a musician named Brown, fell ill, his guts in a knot from eating wild fruit and drinking tainted water. His condition worsened after he took Moss's remedy of ginger and Epsom salts, so Moss distributed the stricken fellow's gear among the others, gave him $6, and told him to take the train ahead to Fort Ellis, near Bozeman, where he could rejoin the regiment.

The soldiers trekked on, the muddy roads forcing them to retreat to the elevated railroad beds as they zigzagged their way along the route. Occasionally they would stop at a settlement, trading flour for fresh milk and eggs. Progress was slowed by frequent stops to repair leaky tires and broken chains, all of which were handled by Private Findley. The 4 years he'd spent working at Imperial Bicycle Works in Chicago provided him the know-how to keep the wheels turning. Once they turned south from Fort Ellis, they pedaled and pushed their bikes through rain and strong winds, up steep grades and along dusty cattle trails full of troublesome prickly pear.

At one point, the squad encountered a flock of chickens meandering near the road. They dismounted, surrounded the fowl, and at Moss's command, fired their rifles at their potential dinner. These men, unfortunately, were not crack shots. In the lieutenant's journal, he acknowledged his company's poor marksmanship: "As far as we know all the chickens were still living." They had Army bacon for dinner.

When they rode through towns, they always drew stares from the locals, as the sight of a pack of Black soldiers on gear-laden bicycles, rifles strapped across their backs, was not something that appeared every day. The soldiers stopped and answered questions and received plenty of encouragement from the curious residents. They also suffered occasional barbs of racist antagonism, something they could never entirely escape, even in the wide open environs of the Mountain West. In one small town, the soldiers stopped at a blacksmith shop to have two seat springs made. Although they were accommodated, the blacksmith demanded $2 for the 25 cents' worth of parts. "Fine example of one man taking advantage of another man's misfortune," Moss wrote.

While bigotry permeated the postbellum Army—a vainglorious dandy by the name of George Armstrong Custer had always refused to ride in any regiment that contained Black soldiers—the bike corps encountered many instances of goodwill on their journey that helped ameliorate these instances of racism. After passing Fort Ellis, the corps rode west through Rocky Canyon before turning south into Paradise Valley and following the Yellowstone River upstream. It was here that they encountered another squadron of Buffalo Soldiers, a cavalry unit out of Fort Assiniboine, traveling with an infantry platoon on a march. On horseback, riding with the cavalry, was famed western artist Frederic Remington, who seemed to be having the time of his life. He would later recount his adventure for *Cosmopolitan* magazine. "I have never found anything else so fascinating," he wrote of the experience. "The soldiers like it too, for while it is set, in its way, it is vagabonding never the less. I have often thought how fortunate it is that I am not the secretary of war, because I should certainly burn or sell every barrack in the country and keep the soldiers under canvas and on the move."

Finally, the Bicycle Corps rode into Fort Yellowstone at Mammoth Hot Springs, and were greeted by the 1st US Cavalry. The Yellowstone unit had already spent 10 years patrolling the vast national park to protect its resources. Among them was another group of fellow Buffalo Soldiers. Tired but triumphant, the Missoula soldiers rested up and spent a day and a half resting and posing for photos at the Fort before replenishing their rations, mounting up and wheeling south into the park. Moss was always at the ready with his Kodak, and the men were also photographed by Yellowstone photographer F. J. Haynes, including the accompanying photo of the Bicycle Corps posing with their bikes carefully arranged across Minerva Terrace in Mammoth Hot Springs. It's a shocking image, viewed in this modern era when visitors are discouraged from even touching the delicate formations in the terraces, let alone pushing an 80-pound bicycle across the travertine.

They bade farewell to their brothers in arms at the fort and rode south on the rutted road along the park's west side. As with their trans-Montana route, they drew stares from groups of tourists they passed along the way, marveling at the Golden Gate, Roaring Mountain, Obsidian Cliff, and other points of interest. It was the geyser basins that finally slowed them down. Firehole Lake left them speechless, and they reached the Great Fountain Geyser in time to see it erupt, witnessing the "sublime spectacle," Moss reported. "A furious boiling, a rumbling, awe-inspiring noise and then enormous volume of seething water and steam shoots up a hundred feet or more into the air."

The soldiers wheeled their way to the geyser basin at West Thumb, where they admired the deep, colorful pools and the bubbling steam burping from the depths of Yellowstone Lake. From there they headed north toward the Grand Canyon of the Yellowstone, stopping at the Continental Divide to pose for the camera of Lieutenant Moss. They got right into

The Bicycle Corps of Fort Missoula's 25th Infantry poses with their trusty steeds on Minerva Terrace in Mammoth Hot Springs after riding to Yellowstone Park from Missoula. The Buffalo Soldiers' ultimate test would be a bike journey to St. Louis. COURTESY OF THE MONTANA HISTORICAL SOCIETY ARCHIVES

the spirit, lining up with one group of soldiers on the Atlantic drainage side of the imaginary line, reaching across to shake hands with their comrades, lined up along the Pacific drainage side. It's a corny tourist tradition that continues to this day.

After stopping briefly to lay eyes on the Grand Canyon, the Corps rode west past Tower Fall, and left the park by way of Fort Yellowstone, and past the rollicking town of Cinnabar, the terminus of the Northern Pacific's Yellowstone spur. The weather had turned ugly, drenching the men in relentless rain and slowing their progress to a crawl along the muddy road. As they were nearing the site where they'd camp east of Bozeman, two soldiers crashed their bikes into each other, seriously damaging the rim of one of the bike wheels. The rider walked his rig to the campsite, and while the men were trying to figure out a way to Mac-Gyver the rim, a bike tramp rode into camp. He'd been riding around the West for weeks, he said, and was an expert in the field of bicycle repair. He offered to take the damaged rim to Bozeman, track down the parts he'd need to fix it, and have it back to the camp by 6:00 the next morning—all for the low, low price of only $6. By the time he reached Bozeman, unfortunately, the town's only bicycle shop was closed. The determined drifter tracked down the shop owner and was able to procure a rim. By then it was 9:00, so he rented a room and proceeded to attach the rim to the wheel he'd brought from the busted bike. He completed the repair by 4:00 a.m., and returned with the rim to the camp by the appointed time.

Sixteen days after they'd left Fort Missoula, the corps rode back into the post, having covered 790 miles of wildly varying terrain. According to Moss's copious notes, they'd spent a total of 126 hours riding, with an average speed of 6.25 miles per hour. The resourceful unit had proved the point Moss was trying to make with the Army—that bicycles were an efficient alternative to horses for scouting, communications, travel, and many other applications in this time of change for the US military.

But hold up, said Moss, you ain't seen nothin' yet. He'd already hatched a plan for his Bicycle Corps' next move. He set his sights on St. Louis, 2,000 miles from Fort Missoula. Surely the Army could not ignore such an incredible accomplishment, and his assertion that bicycles truly had a place among the military's troop transport methods would finally be accepted.

The following year, Corpsmen Sanders and Findley, along with several other veterans of the Yellowstone trip, would leave June 14, 1897, and ride with Moss through five states to St. Louis. The pair of ten-man regiments was accompanied by *Missoulian* reporter Eddie Boos, who sent dispatches to the newspaper during the trip. Field rations had been cached at 100-mile intervals along the route, and the Bicycle Corps was welcomed into St. Louis by a boisterous crowd after a grueling, 41-day journey. Although Moss wanted to lead his unit on to Minneapolis, he was denied permission and the men returned to Missoula on a train. The bikes were shipped back to Spalding, and any further bicycle experiments were cut short by the US involvement with the Spanish-American War the following year.

Today, the razor-thin shoulders on Yellowstone's Grand Loop Road are a challenge for cyclists touring the park, but for hundreds of bike enthusiasts, it's the only way to see the park. These intrepid two-wheelers can take pride in a shared heritage of their cycling forebears, the disciplined and determined group of Black soldiers of the 125th Infantry Bicycle Corps, who proved emphatically that the Army could go faster, farther, and cheaper, when the rubber meets the road.

28

World Museum of Wildlife Is Truly World Class

IF YOU'RE GOING IN OR OUT OF GLACIER PARK THROUGH WEST GLACIER, you'll pass through the delightful little town of Hungry Horse. It's wedged between the south and middle forks of the Flathead River at the east end of Bad Rock Canyon. Just to the south of town are its namesake reservoir created by its namesake dam, and the area provides incredible views, lots of resources for travelers, and tremendous opportunities for outdoor recreation. Hungry Horse is also home to a unique museum where, for the price of a couple of huckleberry shakes, you can walk among some of the most fearsome, beautiful, and exotic animals on Earth. The World Wildlife Museum offers a close look at a spectacular collection of taxidermy mounts, everything from the smallest marten to a towering giraffe.

Amy Day-Petersen welcomes you with a smile behind the gift shop counter, and indicates a plain white curtain you'll pass through to start the self-guided tour. As you part the fabric and step into the museum, you can't escape an eerie feeling that you're being watched. A hundred pairs of eyes are looking down at you as you enter the main room, where you're confronted by a snarling grizzly bear, a hulking cape buffalo, a 15-foot-long crocodile, and a rock python the length of a Ford Bronco. The snake's thick, muscular body is threaded through a tree, and it seems to be gauging your scent with its forked tongue. They're packed in among dozens of other taxidermy mounts, preserved so skillfully that they look like they might be still alive. Just when you're starting to wonder if you saw something move, you notice a man who has materialized, Jedi-like, beside you. "Do you work here?" you ask.

"I do," he says. "I killed all of these."

Meet Mark Petersen, veteran big-game hunter and the lone provider of the 200 mounted animals that fill the two-story World Museum of Wildlife. Mark and his wife Amy have operated the museum since 2018, and it certainly lives up to its name, with exotic beasts and birds from every corner of the globe, all bagged by Petersen. From the smallest bird, an African blue-bellied roller the size of a crow, to a massive pair of rhinos (white and black), it's a mind-blowing collection of critters. He's brought home trophies from hundreds of hunts. Just don't call him a trophy hunter.

"I think that word 'trophy' has been misused and doesn't really apply to what people think of it when somebody refers to it as 'trophy hunt-ing,'" says the soft-spoken outdoorsman. A compact man in his late 60s, he could pass for 10 years younger. His well-tanned skin crinkles at the corners of his blue-green eyes when he smiles, offering part wisdom, part mischief. He exhibits the calm and deliberate vibe that you'd expect from someone who has spent untold hours in forests and jungles waiting, silent and motionless, for his prey to wander into his crosshairs.

Big-game hunters, he feels, have gotten a bad rap because a few cal-lous individuals drop small fortunes to put themselves in a position to take an easy shot on the most magnificent specimen of a species, just so they can have a photo of them standing over the bloody corpse, and put the mount on display in their mansion or yacht where they regale their friends with the braggadocious story of their Big Hunt. Petersen does bring home trophies from most of his hunts, but he makes it clear that he is not a hunter of that ilk. "A 'trophy' can be a little fork horn mulie deer for a 12-year-old," he explains. "That could be his trophy. A trophy could be a couple of pheasants you get when you're out with your bird dogs. That little 12-year-old shoots their first deer, they're on top of the world. In their eyes, that's the biggest trophy on the planet."

When Petersen is tracking his quarry, be it Austria or the Congo or anywhere in between, he puts a lot of thought into the animals he chooses to hunt. For one thing, he takes the opposite tack of the status trophy hunter, and seeks out the older, slower males of the species. These animals are usually beyond their breeding years, and are already starting to be phased out from their herd. By culling the slow and weak, he may even be contributing to the strength of the herd.

You'd never tell by looking at the specimens in Petersen's museum that these are anything but prime examples of their species, and that speaks to the skill of the taxidermist, Kanati Studio of Myers, Pennsylvania. Wes Good and his team have done the taxidermy on nearly every piece in the museum. From the easily recognizable animals—a honey badger poised to put the hurt on an African porcupine—to the genet, a spotted African carnivore that looks like a cross between a dog and a cat, the mounts are impeccably crafted and naturally posed. Good's taxidermists will start with a commercially made form of the animal, he says, but "we do an extensive amount of reshaping, resculpting and reworking to get it to be the correct size, first of all, then also have the correct body posture and attitude." The giant python was especially challenging, he adds. "We had to completely sculpt that entire form."

Standing between the python and crocodile in the first room is another of Good's favorites, a Lord Derby eland, the largest of the antelope family. With its corkscrew, V-shaped horns, charcoal black stripe down its face, and the large, pendulous dewlap, it's an impressive piece.

You'll see roe deer from western Europe, mouflon sheep from the Middle East, a Siberian bearskin from Russia, and a bongo from the Congo. Petersen has chosen to arrange the pieces aesthetically, rather than bunching them up according to taxonomy or geographic distribution. That's why this might be the only place in the world where you can see a pair of Canadian timber wolves running just a few feet away from an African lion from the savanna swatting at a spotted hyena. Several of the mounts are arranged in such a tableau, like the four springboks, small antelope-like creatures, that appear to be leaping over each other's backs. The national animal of South Africa, they are represented in all four color phases: copper, common, white, and black. Petersen has quite a few examples of different springbok, which inhabit similar terrain to the antelope, and like their Montana counterpart, the pronghorn, are blazingly fast and easily spooked, typically requiring a shot from 300 yards or more. "They are about the fastest thing on the planet once they start running," says Petersen.

Here are just a few of the shockingly lifelike mounts on display at the World Museum of Wildlife in Hungry Horse. Sharp-eyed readers will recognize the striped individual in the center as a bongo from the Congo. AUTHOR PHOTO

One of the interesting—or maddening, depending upon your perspective—things about the museum is that there are no informational signs or tags anywhere that identify the animals or provide any information about their habitat or range. Petersen prefers to provide that information to the tour guests himself, but no one would ever accuse him of being loquacious. He usually doesn't offer to identify the species or share details of the pieces until he's asked. Then, of course, he is happy to give the zoological information, as well as interesting stories about that specific hunt. He has one tale in particular of a hair-raising close call during an elk hunt, where he not only had to shoot a wounded, charging elk as it passed within 2 feet of the tree he was standing behind (from the hip, no less), but also nearly lost all of his toes to frostbite.

So how does a person get safari fever? In Mark's case, his interest was piqued at age 12, and it grew into a full-blown obsession by the time he hit his mid-20s. Growing up in Wisconsin, he was surrounded by sportsmen but his father wasn't a hunter, so Petersen was introduced to the culture by his uncle, who traveled to Hamilton, Montana, each year for the fall hunt and rarely returned empty handed. "I still can see him with an elk hanging behind the shed and I thought that was cool. Looking at the pictures [of Montana] with all the mountains and the pines, and I'd think someday I'd like to do that. When you're 10 or 12 years old you have big dreams for anything."

In his 20s he started deer hunting with his buddies, then one year decided to move up to the next level in a big way. He sold his pickup truck to help raise the $3,000 he'd need for a safari, and has been traveling the world ever since, going to exotic locations to hunt big game. As stated before, Petersen isn't one to shoot an animal on a game farm or indiscriminately take out an important member of the herd. He hews closely to hunting ethics such as fair chase, and once he kills an animal as quickly and humanely as possible, it's turned over to the local tribe for processing. In his hundreds of big-game hunts over 3 decades, he's learned a lot. Not necessarily any foreign languages, though. When asked what languages he might have picked up, he laughs. "Nothin'. But that's really not important. No matter where we have gone, and it can be in Cameroon with the French-speaking pygmies and everything else, basically with hand gestures and five or six words you can communicate with anybody on the planet."

During the offseason, he travels to the various big-game hunting conventions across the country, like Dallas Safari Club or Safari Club International in Las Vegas. "We'll sit down and talk to them about how they run things and what's available, so on and so forth." Once he's chosen his hunt, that's when the research begins. He learns everything he can about his quarry's habitat and behavior, to minimize any surprises and maximize his potential of bagging the animal. Among the 300 or so people who walk through the museum each day in the summer are dozens of hunters, and Petersen enjoys swapping tales with his fellow big-game enthusiasts. What rubs his fur the wrong way, though, are the ones who don't do their research, and blame their subsequent failure on their guide. "There's too many people that come in and tell me about their experiences, and say they shot something that wasn't up to their standards, let's say, and then they'll blame it on the guide: 'Well, he told me to shoot it.' Well, that doesn't hold any water. If you're interested in that particular thing, do some research and know what a good one is. Don't pass the blame on to the guide, because you're the one pulling the trigger."

Petersen brings his experience and knowledge to every excursion. What he doesn't bring is a rifle. Traveling with firearms has become a complicated hassle since 9/11, so he always uses a borrowed gun on his hunts. They range from .22s up to a so-called dangerous animal round, a .416 Rigby. Designed to bring down raging elephants and 2,000-pound muskoxen, a Rigby cartridge is the size of a Sharpie and costs $20 per round. More typically, though, the hunt calls for a .300 Winchester Magnum bolt-action rifle. He has also taken a few of the museum's animals with a bow or crossbow.

Once his party has established camp and he's finally tracking his prey, Petersen has the patience and pragmatic approach that will translate to a successful hunt. Whether sitting, standing, or lying prone, he takes his shot from whatever position is required by his surroundings, be it jungle, forest, prairie, or desert. He'll shoot from as far as 300 yards, he says, but that's rare. The goal is to take the animal with a clean shot, and that usually requires a much closer position to increase the odds. Once they make sure the animal has been dispatched, they wipe it clean of any blood to get a couple of photos. The team takes several measurements and photos for the taxidermist, and then the local tribe moves in to harvest the bounty. "There's not a teaspoon that's wasted," Petersen says. "These people live in the dirt, sleep in the dirt, and mostly live on grits. They go their whole lives without any protein." When Petersen and his safari team donate all the meat to the tribe, they are enriching the lives of the locals. They also provide a major economic boost to whatever area they're hunting by employing guides, packers, cooks, laundry workers, skinners, mechanics, and camp help. "It's a win-win," he adds. "They look forward to it, and a lot of them would give you the shirt off their back. That's the kind of people they are and it just really opens up your eyes."

If you would like to take home a shirt of your own from the museum, Mark has you covered. He is a distributor for King of the Mountain, which manufactures state-of-the-art cold weather outdoor apparel. The brand has a big following, and its Kevlar-and-wool blend material provides tremendous protection from the elements. The Museum gift shop carries a few items, but Mark spends much of his offseason traveling around to hunting conventions and trade shows where, along with website sales, he does the bulk of his business with the outdoors clothing and gear.

You'll find all kinds of quality treasures in the tiny gift shop, ranging from the small pelts hanging inside the front windows—wolverine, fox, lynx, ermine, and more—to sparkling jewelry containing green sapphires created from Mount St. Helens ash. There's a variety of coonskin caps for the Davy Crockett enthusiast, as well as more common tourist fare like huckleberry candy and buffalo jerky. The shop also offers several paintings and other original creations from local artists. One *de rigueur* item they stock for visitors heading into Glacier Park is bear spray. "It's easy to use," says Petersen, displaying a can of Counter Assault pepper spray. "All you have to do is pull the trigger."

By the time the Museum shuts down for the season, usually in mid-October, Hungry Horse may already have seen snow. Mark and Amy get things cleaned up and ready for a winter of dormancy for the museum, but not for them. They stay busy promoting the King of the Hill line, and organizing Mark's upcoming hunts. Once or twice before next June's opening, they will come in and spruce up the pieces, not giving dust or cobwebs a chance to settle. This may include some minor trimming on some mounts if the fur has become unruly here and there. Then it's lights out, and the mouflan sheep, mountain ibex, duikers and klipspringers, olive baboons and South African aardwolf will wait silently in their climate-controlled showroom for the return of Glacier Park's hordes next summer.

29

Lewis and/or Clark Slept Here

No matter what your route between Yellowstone and Glacier Parks, it's a safe bet that you're going to pass some roadside markers with that iconic pose of explorers Lewis and Clark standing together, one pointing off into the distance, the other leaning on his rifle, possibly thinking, yes, that does look like a grizzly bear advancing on us. The most famous explorers in US history entered northwest Montana on April 27, 1805, boating and portaging up the Missouri River with their Corps of Discovery. Their mission, as we all learned in grade school, was to seek a passage to the Pacific Ocean to open up a waterborne trade route from the east. Thomas Jefferson had just signed the Louisiana Purchase, effectively doubling the size of the United States. Although there had been some spotty chronicling of the territory west of the Mississippi, it was mostly uncharted. At Jefferson's behest, Capt. Meriwether Lewis hand-picked a crew of forty-five intrepid outdoorsmen and soldiers to form the Corps of Discovery. With Lewis's good friend Second Lieutenant William Clark as co-commander, the Corps set off from St. Charles in two pirogues and a 55-foot keelboat, laden with supplies and gear, and began working their way up the broad Missouri River.

POMPEYS PILLAR

If you're coming into Montana from the east, whether driving I-90 or flying into Billings, you'll be just a few miles from the only physical evidence left by Lewis and Clark's 2-year expedition. Just 7 miles west of Billings on I-94 along the Yellowstone River is Pompeys Pillar National Monument. "Pomp" was William Clark's nickname for Sacagawea's baby boy,

Jean Baptiste Charbonneau, born during the expedition's trip out west. Upon their return trip in 1806, they split into two parties, Lewis taking a crew down the Missouri, Clark heading south with the rest of the Corps to explore the Yellowstone River. Their plan was to reunite at the confluence, 500 miles to the northeast. As Clark's party crossed the Bozeman Pass and moved from the Rockies into the Great Plains, they stopped and constructed a pair of large dugout canoes, which they lashed together. Once on the water, they encountered a massive sandstone outcropping on the Yellowstone near a natural fording spot known to Indigenous peoples as "the place where the mountain lion lies." While the men were perhaps taking a refreshing dip in the cool waters of the river, Clark hiked up to the 120-foot-high rock and carved his name and date into its soft surface: "W. Clark, July 25, 1806."

It would be more than 50 years before that inscription was seen again by a white man, a prospector named James Stuart who spied the carving while leading a gold-hunting party down the Yellowstone in 1863. Five years later the Crow Reservation was established, and the Pillar was on Indian land. Once the settlers realized the agricultural potential of the fertile Yellowstone Valley, though, Congress once again yanked the rug out from under the tribe, taking back most of the land along the river. After the Huntley Irrigation Project was completed in the early 1900s, the area was quickly settled with white farmers and ranchers.

Pompeys Pillar was designated a National Monument by President Clinton in 2001, and the Interpretive Center opened a few years later, part of the Lewis and Clark Bicentennial celebration in 2006. You can walk a quarter-mile boardwalk today and see Clark's inscription, still there, protected behind shatterproof glass.

LEWIS AND CLARK CAVERNS

File under: Lewis Nor Clark Slept Here. Heading west out of Billings, you can take a 20-mile detour off I-90 and visit Lewis and Clark Caverns State Park. The massive cavern, one of the largest limestone cave systems in the northwest, is definitely worth a tour. Lewis and Clark passed within a few miles of it, but were completely unaware of the caves. The cavern was discovered in the early 1900s by hunters, and later transferred to the state of Montana, which made it part of a 3,000-acre state park with a forty-site campground.

GATES OF THE MOUNTAINS

Those sticking close to the interstates will likely turn north at Butte on I-15, which will take you through Helena and Great Falls. Gates of the Mountains is a series of bluffs along the Missouri River below Upper Holter Lake, about 45 miles northeast of Helena. Tour boats still ply the waters up through the cliffs that seem to pull aside like a doorway, revealing more wilderness and river beyond. Before the river was dammed in 1918, the water was much lower and faster, the cliffs even higher. When the Corps moved through the gorge on July 19, 1805, Lewis wrote in his journal: "The most remarkable clifts [*sic*] that we have seen yet." He estimated the highest cliffs to be 1,200 feet.

TOWER ROCK

Just a few miles downstream from the Gates of the Mountains sits another high rock that Meriwether Lewis scaled to get a view of his surroundings. It had been used for thousands of years before him by the Blackfeet and other tribes who considered this sacred rock to mark the transition from the mountains to the buffalo hunting grounds of the plains. Lewis indicates in his journal that he made it not quite to the top of the 400-foot monolith.

GREAT FALLS PORTAGES (UPPER AND LOWER)

The falls that give the city its name proved to be one of the biggest obstacles the Corps encountered during the 2-year expedition.

It started with what most of the men feared was a wrong turn. On June 3, 1805, the party reached a fork in the Missouri, which later turned out to be the mouth of the Marias River. To a man, the entire company agreed that the north fork, with its chocolate-milk water matching the river they'd been on, was the continuation of the Missouri. Lewis and Clark, both accomplished watermen who knew their rivers, disagreed. The clear water of the south fork meant the river must be running from the mountains, where the headwaters lay. Sacagawea had never been to this area and was of no help. They camped for several days while Lewis led a small party up the north fork, and Clark another detachment up the south fork. No firm evidence was found that could show which was the Missouri, so the leaders stuck to their original decision. It's a testament to the discipline of the Corps that they dutifully followed their superiors' orders to proceed along the south fork, even though they were convinced it was the wrong direction. Clark captained the boats on the water, Lewis paralleled on the shore.

Several days later, after suffering a bout of dysentery, Lewis recovered enough to climb a rise from which he got his first full view of the "beautifull and picturesk" [sic] view of the Rocky Mountains, some 50 or 60 miles distant. He and his men continued up the river, and just as Lewis was realizing, oh, yeah, we have to cross those "beautifull and picturesk" mountains, he began to hear the roar of a waterfall. He wrote, "my ears were saluted with the agreeable sound of a fall of water and advancing a little further I saw the spray arise above the plain like a collum of smoke . . . soon began to make a roaring too tremendious to be mistaken for any cause short of the great falls of the Missouri." Lewis and Clark had indeed chosen the correct fork in the river. The Hidatsa Indians they had wintered with at Camp Mandan in North Dakota had provided them with directions that would lead them to the "great falls." That night his contingent camped, feasting on buffalo tongue as well as a newly discovered species: cutthroat trout. They would get word to Clark and his party, still quite a ways behind them, that they were on the right path.

The following morning Lewis hiked up past the falls to scout out a route for the easy portage the Hidatsa had said lay above the great falls. He walked past some rapids. And more rapids. For 5 miles, nothing but rapids. As if this wasn't concerning enough, he encountered a second set of falls. Seven miles later, he saw three more falls. He should have asked those Hidatsa how many falls were in the great falls.

He returned to the island camp, narrowly escaping a grizzly attack along the way. Clark had stopped the flotilla 5 miles short of the falls, sure they would have to portage from there. Now they had to set about the task of building some crude wagons to haul the boats and supplies the grueling 18 miles around the great falls.

Lewis and a group of men had brought to the "upper portage" camp the iron keelboat frame he'd had fabricated in Harper's Ferry before the expedition. The frame was heavy and cumbersome, but the plan had been to use it after the great falls, on the presumed home stretch—what they thought would be a relatively easy portage over a pass in the Bitterroots, down to the Columbia River, and on to Portland. They sewed together an outer skin of hides, and Lewis prepared to waterproof the seams with pitch from pine trees. Unfortunately, on the islands where they'd camped there were no pines, only cottonwoods. Lewis was undaunted. While the rest of the expedition moved supplies up to their camp from Clark's "lower portage" camp, his men worked on several concoctions containing beeswax, ash, whatever natural materials Lewis could think of to try and make his boat waterproof. After using up several valuable days of the summer season, they finally thought they'd hit upon a successful goop, and coated the entire outside of the craft with it. They launched the boat, which floated "like a perfect cork," wrote Lewis. The crew placed the oars and loaded the *Experiment*, as she had become known. Before they could shove off, a thunderstorm ripped through the area, forcing them to offload some of the cargo that was becoming drenched. When the storm passed they discovered that the *Experiment* was leaking like a cardboard kiddie pool.

Lewis was acutely aware that the days were getting shorter and they needed to get across the Rockies before the snows came. In his journal, he acknowledged the great disappointment of abandoning his precious keelboat, but he never mentioned it again.

Now without the expected carrying capacity of the *Experiment*, the Corps once again felled enough big cottonwoods to carve out several canoes. They had been stuck below the great falls for nearly a month. Finally, on July 15, the Corps of Discovery was able to resume their journey up the Missouri River, toward their rendezvous with Sacagawea's people, the Shoshone.

Lewis and Clark National Historic Trail
Interpretive Center

This gorgeous facility, clinging to a cliff overlooking the "Mighty Mo," is the epicenter of Montana's Lewis and Clark Trail. The Center packs a lot into its 25,000 square feet, including a 158-seat theater, where you can start your tour with a 30-minute introductory film by Ken Burns.

Another, 20-minute film covers the aforementioned portage ordeal around the Great Falls.

There's also a permanent exhibition hall full of displays featuring dress, equipment, and many of the plants and animals that were studied and chronicled by the explorers, most never before seen by European Americans. And you can't miss the life-sized diorama of a team of Corps members pulling a wagon-mounted canoe up a steep slope. You can almost see the sweat.

One of the best features is a generous helping of Native American cultural materials, and some tribal stories of the incredible amount of help and support the expedition received from the Indigenous peoples who had already been living in this "uncharted land" for more than 12,000 years. An undertaking as ambitious and dangerous as this expedition absolutely could not have succeeded without some help from the home team.

CAMP DISAPPOINTMENT

Between Shelby and Browning on US 2, you'll pass by Camp Disappointment. While William Clark was busy defacing Pompeys Pillar in July of 1806, Meriwether Lewis and his party returned to the mouth of the Marias River, the fork they had chosen not to follow on their trip up the Missouri. His aim this time was to determine if the Marias ran north of the 49th Parallel, which would extend the boundaries of the Louisiana Purchase. He was also looking for a portage between the Marias and Saskatchewan Rivers, with the hopes of establishing a northwest trade route between Canada and the Missouri. Constant cloud cover prevented Lewis from obtaining any celestial navigation, and hostile Blackfeet warriors were not shy about protecting their territory. Having failed to establish any of his goals, Lewis named their last bivouac Camp Disappointment, and they headed back to the Missouri.

MISSOURI HEADWATERS STATE PARK

Back on I-90, Missouri Headwaters State Park near Three Forks between Butte and Bozeman marks the confluence of the Jefferson, Madison, and Gallatin Rivers. It was here that Clark, on point with a hunting party, arrived on July 25, 1805, and was able to ascertain the existence of three

How many other teams of explorers have an entire set of whiskey bottles made in their likeness? This set of Lewis and Clark commemorative bottles is just one part of a massive collection of Montana historical items on display at the Headwaters Heritage Museum in Three Forks. AUTHOR PHOTO

separate rivers. I tell you, 200 years later, even with the help of interpretive signage, it takes a minute. When Lewis and the rest of the expedition caught up 2 days later, he called the confluence "an essential point in the geography of the western part of the continent." After spending a couple of days exploring the area, they decided to take the southwestern-oriented fork, which Lewis named the Jefferson River in honor of "that illustrious personage," President Thomas Jefferson.

LEMHI PASS

This is probably for the hardcore Lewis and Clark aficionados, because it is pretty far out of the way. Lemhi Pass National Historic Landmark lies in a remote section of the Beaverhead Range, about 3 hours straight south from Missoula. It's on the Idaho border, 30 miles west of the Lewis and Clark Memorial on I-15 at Clark Canyon Reservoir. A dirt road crosses Lemhi

Pass, where the expedition finally met up with the Shoshone Indians on the Continental Divide in August 1805. Lewis and three other men went ahead to cross the pass, where they traded for some horses their expedition would need to help get the people and supplies across the Divide. Sacagawea was reunited with her brother, Chief Cameahwait, and the bulk of the Corps made it across the pass 2 weeks later, finally entering the Columbia River watershed, and what was then considered Spanish territory.

TRAVELERS REST STATE PARK

This is an easy 15 minutes south of Missoula, near the little town of Lolo. Travelers Rest is the last place the Corps would camp before making their way across the treacherous Bitterroot Mountains, a 150-mile journey that would push the men of the expedition to their breaking point. Located on Lolo Creek about 2 miles west of the Bitterroot River, the spot has always been popular with Salish and Pend d'Oreille tribes, a hub for trading, hunting, fishing, and gathering the plentiful camas root, a main staple.

It's also the only site that's provided archaeological evidence of the Corps of Discovery's presence. They stayed at Travelers Rest on their return journey as well. The Corps had likely arranged their camp in a routine military layout according to Baron Frederick William von Steuben's "Regulations and the Order and Discipline of the Troops of the United States," which must have been a sizable book just to accommodate the title. Lead, used to repair weapons, was found, as well as a small bead of the kind the explorers had brought for trading. Also, a trench latrine was located which contained traces of mercury, which was used to treat syphilis at the time. Apparently beads weren't the only thing they brought from the east.

These are just a handful of the dozens of markers and sites along the Lewis and Clark Historic Trail in Montana. While the explorers never set foot in what are now Glacier and Yellowstone National Parks, their expedition, which some call the most ambitious in history, left its permanent stamp throughout our state. In many places, the surroundings are virtually unchanged from the time the Corps of Discovery first passed through there, and you can walk in their footsteps today.

30

Hungry Horse Dam, the Flathead Valley's Hidden Jewel

As you drive through the small community of Hungry Horse on US 2 between Columbia Falls and West Glacier, you'll pass the eponymous store, motel, and supermarket. You might stop to fill your tank at Bob's General Store, or grab a bite at the Elkhorn Grill. You might also spot the Dam Town Tavern. On the way out of town, you might also glimpse a sign that reads, "The Best Dam Town in the West." You might begin to wonder at this point, does Hungry Horse have a damn spelling problem? Nope. What they do have, hidden away in the Flathead National Forest about 4 miles south of the South Fork's confluence with the main Flathead River, is one damn huge dam. When it was built just after World War II by the Bureau of Reclamation, the Hungry Horse Dam was the third highest in the world, at 564 feet. Its spillway is still the highest morning glory structure in the world. What is a morning glory structure, you ask? Well, if you've seen Morning Glory Pool in Yellowstone's Upper Geyser Basin, the shape of this hydraulic wonder will ring a bell. More on that later.

Let's start with the name of the town (technically an incorporated area), which tends to induce the first question. A place with a name like Hungry Horse pretty much has to have an interesting origin story. In this case, the name was inspired by a pair of freight horses named Tex and Jerry that were pulling a logging sled near the Flathead River's south fork during the brutal winter of 1900–1901. Somehow the two animals slipped their yokes, were gripped by a sudden case of wanderlust, and walked off into the forest. They were finally found by loggers a month later, trudging through the belly-deep snow. The fugitive steeds were freezing, exhausted, and, of course, hungry. The pair were nursed back to health and given the nickname "Mighty Hungry Horses."

The area's original name was, in fact, Damtown. Shortly after construction of its namesake dam began just after World War II, county commissioners changed the name to Hungry Horse. Somewhere, Tex and Jerry were smiling.

The area where Tex and Jerry went on the lam in that winter of 1900 had been a well-used human thoroughfare for thousands of years. Bands of Indians from the Blackfeet, Salish, Pend Oreille, and other tribes moved through Bad Rock Canyon on their way to and from the buffalo-rich plains east of the Rockies. By the early 20th century, white homesteaders and loggers who had moved into the area were beginning to eye the South Fork in terms of providing irrigation, hydroelectric power, and flood control. In 1921 the US Geological Survey began a study of the heavily forested area and its suitability for a dam. Meanwhile, the Army Corps of Engineers began studying alternate sites for the same purpose. By 1942 the United States was embroiled in World War II, and the nation was funneling its resources toward supplying the war effort. The increase in productivity required more electric power, and the cheapest way to get there was hydroelectric. Initially, the Corps proposed raising the level of Flathead Lake by 1 million acre-feet to create storage for downstream hydroelectric production. Locals who did not relish the prospect of hosting underwater cookouts put the kibosh on that plan, and the Hungry Horse Dam was proposed as an alternative.

The Bureau of Reclamation arm of the Department of the Interior, which was created in 1902 to manage water and power in the West, officially selected a site in 1944 for the Hungry Horse Dam, and construction was authorized by Congress on June 5 of that year. Just one thing, said Congress in an atom bomb of irony—we can't release the funding to build this dam that will produce the electricity we so desperately need for the war effort until after the war, "as soon as war conditions permit the diversion of materials and manpower for the work."

The budget for construction of the dam was proposed at $43.4 million. Clearing the forest, building roads, diverting the river, and other preparations of the site were budgeted separately.

First the dam drainage area was logged, and about 90 million board feet of timber was harvested. The remaining snags, stumps, and smaller trees proved more of a challenge to remove. Once a road along the South Fork was built that could support heavy machinery, the project shifted into high gear.

In late 1947 the Guy F. Atkinson Company began excavating a diversion tunnel through the right abutment of the dam site to create a channel for the South Fork to carry water during construction. Typically in the Mountain West, construction projects shut down over the winter when snow and subzero temperatures make work all but impossible. The Atkinson Company's determination was impressive, though, as they ignored several feet of snow and 40-below-zero temperatures, working throughout the winter months, even tripling their shifts in February. They had crews working simultaneously at each end of the tunnel, but when fractured rock caused the upstream portal to collapse, they concentrated their efforts on the downstream end.

Clearing of the 20,000-acre reservoir site would prove to be the longest and most difficult aspect of the project, overlapping the construction of the dam. Wixson & Crowe and J. H. Trisdale, Inc. of Redding, California, received one part of the clearing contract. A local company, J.J. Reese of Columbia Falls, was awarded another. Reese's outfit was unprepared, underequipped, and worked with all the speed of an arthritic sloth. After more than a year's efforts, they'd cleared less than half of the expected area and were sacked by Reclamation and replaced by Seaboard Surety Co., which finished their segment of the job just behind schedule. The California crews completed their parts of the job ahead of schedule.

Clearing the waste and uncut trees from the reservoir area posed a particular challenge for the workers. Initially, a pair of bulldozers dragged a 200-foot length of heavy cable between them to lop off the remaining trees, but the cable tended to slide right over the smaller, flexible trees, or get hung up on the stumps that studded the forest floor. John Trisdale, one of the clearing contractors, came up with a solution. They called it "Operation Highball." If you keep your eyes peeled as you drive through Hungry Horse, you'll see a part of the way brute force was applied cleverly to clear large swaths of post-logging debris and trees. Five giant balls, 8 feet in diameter, were fabricated from inch-thick boilerplate, with a heavy chain on opposite sides. As the bulldozers rumbled along through the logged areas, the monster steel ball they dragged between them kept the cable 4 feet off the ground, passing over the stumps as it snapped off the remaining trees in a scenario that must have looked and sounded like a Harry Potter fever dream. The highball method dramatically speeded up the process of clearing several square miles for the reservoir site. The leftover brush and slash that could be pushed by bulldozers was piled up at the bottom of ravines and burned. What remained was buried.

A conglomeration of Seattle contractors, General-Shea-Morrison, was awarded the contract for construction of the dam in 1948. On July 10 a ceremony was staged, where Montana governor Sam Ford, under the watchful gaze of Assistant Secretary of the Interior William E. Warne, twisted the crank on a detonator box and set off the first dynamite blast to initiate construction of the Hungry Horse Dam. General-Shea-Morrison wasted no time, starting work the next day on building a construction camp just south of the existing government installation. This was no two-tents-and-a-saloon gold mining camp. The self-contained community featured houses, a dormitory, a schoolhouse, a mercantile, a grocery store, and a hospital. It was all accessible by an 80-ton capacity bridge across the river leading to the dam site, where a blacksmith shop, machine shop, and compressor house were built. For the next 6 years, thousands of men working for dozens of contractors toiled to build this massive dam between the walls of the narrow Bad Rock Canyon. Three million cubic yards of concrete were poured. Twenty-three men lost their lives in the process. When Harry S. Truman threw the switch to fire up the power generator on October 1, 1952, Hungry Horse Dam, the world's fourth largest, still had some work left to be done. It wasn't until the following year that the dam was finally completed.

"Operation Highball" was a method used by the land-clearing teams who helped prepare the reservoir area for the Hungry Horse Dam, one of the highest concrete dams in the country. These 8-foot steel balls were dragged across the forested land between two bulldozers, snapping off trees while passing over the stumps from previously cut timber. SHANNON THERRIAULT

Hungry Horse Dam's main job is producing hydroelectric power, and it does so via its four generators, which combine for a total capacity of 285,000 kilowatts. In fact, the power plant produced so much energy—much of which was sold back to the government—the Anaconda Company figured it was the perfect place to build an aluminum plant. Spurred once again by wartime production demands, a major construction project got underway in the Flathead. In 1955 the Anaconda Aluminum Company opened at the base of Teakettle Mountain near Columbia Falls, employing 450 workers. The complex features the largest building in Montana. In the years leading up to the plant's opening, locals had begun raising the question of the facility's negative impact on the environment. C. F. Kelley, chairman of the Anaconda Company's board of directors, was adamant in his assertions that the aluminum plant would leave no lasting scars on the land or its people, vowing to run the facility "so that no damage of any kind will result from its operation." The abundant power it would need, as well as the incredible amount of water used to manufacture aluminum, were readily available, and the company took off, driving the Flathead Valley's economic engine for 30 years. Aside from Glacier Park tourism, it was the area's top industry.

In 1969 the first studies were published indicating air pollution from the company was poisoning area wildlife. In 1970 a class-action lawsuit was filed, but was dismissed in 1973. Over the next decade the company would spend tens of millions of dollars to bring their harmful emissions under control. By some estimates they were cut by 90 percent. The fly-ash used in the mixture of the dam's concrete, which enabled the cement to harden underwater, had been found to cause health issues in the workers who'd breathed in its dust. Still, AAC soldiered on. In the mid-70s the Anaconda Aluminum Company was the Flathead Valley's largest employer, with 981 workers on the payroll.

Over the next few decades the company struggled, fending off increasing attention from the state Department of Environmental Quality and the Environmental Protection Agency while demand for their product began dropping. Energy prices were creeping up, aluminum prices were going down, and the company changed hands in a messy, lawsuit-strewn battle for control. In 2015 the plant closed for good. The following year it was officially declared a Superfund site. What had begun as a benefactor of the dam's power production ended under a cloud of environmental disaster.

While the region is still working to recover from the gut-punch to its economy, the Hungry Horse Dam continues to quietly do its job, holding back 3.5 million acre-feet of cold mountain water, while the outflow keeps cranking out the kilowatts. Tours no longer take visitors down inside the structure, but the Bureau of Reclamation offers a guided walking tour during the summer season and there is a video tour you can watch online. The dam features an excellent visitor center full of historical photos and plenty of facts about the dam's construction, its role in controlling the occasional floods, and its part in the hydroelectric network of the Columbia River system.

Of course you can drive across the dam (and around the entire reservoir) for a firsthand look. You might see water flowing into the dam's most distinctive feature, its bell-mouth spillway. Sometimes called a morning-glory spillway for its resemblance to the flower, this one is called by locals (mostly with a straight face) the Glory Hole. At 490 feet, it is the world's highest morning-glory spillway, although not its widest. That distinction belongs to Geehi Dam in New South Wales, Australia, at 105 feet across. Hungry Horse Dam's spillway hole is basically a 64-foot-wide drain topped with a 12-foot-high concrete ring. When the reservoir tops its capacity, water starts to funnel uncontrolled into the ring and pours down into the spillway, as fast as 225,000 gallons per second. That would fill an Olympic swimming pool in about 3 seconds. The Glory Hole is located quite close to the dam, and when the water is flowing into it, usually at full pool level in July, it's worth a stop at the overlook. It's not every day you see a lake with a hole in it.

Acknowledgments

Setting sail on a project of this magnitude, which would require lots of travel, interviews, and time spent in research centers, museums, libraries, and, of course, coffee shops, was a challenge I happily endeavored. To make this journey during a worldwide pandemic, though, created some rough seas indeed. I took a lot of deep dives in this book, and wound up over my head many times, so I leaned on my network of friends, family, and associates who were there to bail me out when I asked. Wow, you'd think it was a book about the ocean.

First, my unending gratitude to my editor at Rowman & Littlefield, Sarah Parke. Her enthusiasm and vision for *Big Sky, Big Parks* were matched by her patience and guidance—she knew exactly when to give me a gentle prod, and when to just let me roll (which was most of the time).

My wife and partner in adventure (and life), Shannon, as always, was an indefatigable source of encouragement—always ready with great suggestions and solutions when we were on the road. And she will happily turn the car around so I can get a goofy photo or read some roadside historical marker.

Tim Ryan, the Cassady to my Kerouac (sometimes vice versa), opened my eyes long ago to the fact that any story of North America can't honestly be told without at least acknowledging the lives, history, and culture of its original inhabitants. The SKC is lucky to have him looking after the tribes' cultural preservation. Lemlmtš, Tim.

Thanks to Montana poet Philip Burgess for instilling in me a respect and affection for Montana's history that is as important as my curiosity about it.

A big thank-you goes to the staff at the Montana Historical Society Research Center in Helena for all their help and resourcefulness. Y'all obviously love what you do and it shows.

Thanks to Anya Helsel at the Glacier National Park Library archives for her tireless work on the Whitehead brothers' story.

Thank you to former library director Honore Bray, and Karl, Robert, and the rest of the cheerfully helpful staff at Missoula's fabulous new public library. It's truly a magnificent place to research, write, read, and wonder. Also, Karl, thanks for your Sperry stories. I know you're not Yellowstone people. Thank you to Sue Orr, James Reber, Russell Malahowski, Kelly Rosenleaf, and all the Buttians who shared their memories of Columbia Gardens with me. Thank you to Eric Barsness, B. J. Barsness, Kris Barsness, Stacey, Roger, Robert, Catherine, and the other Virginia City Players veterans for their stories. Thank you, Sandy Eckart, for relating your experience during the Yellowstone flood of 2022.

I'm grateful to Tom France, Hank Fischer, Ray Aten, Chris La Tray, Larry Evans, Ed Stalling, Caroline Keys, Mark Petersen, Bob Jones, and Cerisse Allen for sharing with me their knowledge and insight into various areas of history, science, aviation, sports, mycology, wildlife biology, and Indian heritage.

Thanks for your ongoing moral (and otherwise) support and encouragement: John and Jody Wrigley, Stephen Bierwag, Ranger Pete, Ron Clausen, Jonathan, Chip, Chris and Robin, and everyone else who helped me out with ideas and leads during the research phase.

Finally, I extend my gratitude to and deep respect for Yellowstone historian Lee Whittlesey. Your depth of knowledge about Yellowstone is matched only by your obvious love of the park, and your fierce advocacy for presenting only the verifiable truth has become a prime motivation in my own writing. Your work has shown me that history can be presented as an interesting narrative but it must deal in facts, not assumptions or conjecture. Your standard is a high one, sir, and I strive to reach it.

Apologies to anyone I may have forgotten to name here, but know that your contributions to this book are appreciated.

Any errors, omissions, and other factual blunders are my own.

FURTHER READING

I believe that, in order to write a great book, you have to read a lot of great books. Naturally, I pored over such boilerplate tomes as *Undaunted Courage* by Stephen Ambrose and *The Yellowstone Story* (Vols. 1 and 2) by Aubrey L. Haines, both must-have titles in any Yellowstone/Glacier/Montana aficionado's library. The titles listed below were also key resources and were crucial to my understanding of the subjects at hand, but beyond their research value I found them especially compelling and enlightening. In particular, *Empire of Shadows* and *Wonderlandscape*, two very different but equally outstanding works, forever changed the way I regard Yellowstone National Park.

All That the Rain Promises and More: A Hip Pocket Guide to Western Mushrooms by David Arora. Ten Speed Press, 1991.

Butte's Pride: The Columbia Gardens by Pat Kearney. Skyhigh Communications, 1994.

The City That Ate Itself: A Social and Environmental History of Butte, Montana and Its Expanding Berkeley Pit by Brian James Leech. University of Nevada Press, 2019.

Dark Life: Martian Nanobacteria, Rock-Eating Cave Bugs, and Other Extreme Organisms of Inner Earth and Outer Space by Michael Ray Taylor. Scribner, 1999.

Death & Survival in Glacier National Park by C. W. Guthrie & Dan and Ann Fagre. Farcountry Press, 2017.

Empire of Shadows: The Epic Story of Yellowstone by George Black. St. Martin's Griffin, 2013.

Fort Yellowstone by Elizabeth A. Watery and Lee Whittlesey. Arcadia Publishing, 2012.

Gateway to Yellowstone: The Raucous Town of Cinnabar on the Montana Frontier by Lee Whittlesey. TwoDot, 2014.

In Search of Mycotopia: Citizen Science, Fungi Fanatics, and the Untapped Potential of Mushrooms by Doug Bierend. Chelsea Green Publishing, 2021.

It Happened in Glacier National Park by Vince Moravek. Globe Pequot, 2014.

People Before the Park: The Kootenai and Blackfeet Before Glacier National Park by Sally Thompson. Montana Historical Society Press, 2014.

A View Inside Glacier National Park: 100 Years—100 Stories, Ed. by Kassandra Hardy. The Glacier Association, 2009.

Witness to History: The Remarkable Untold Story of Virginia City and Nevada City, Montana by John David Ellingsen. Montana History Foundation, 2011.

Wolf Wars: The Remarkable Inside Story of the Restoration of Wolves to Yellowstone by Hank Fischer. Fischer Outdoor Discoveries, 2003.

Wonderlandscape by John Clayton. Pegasus Books, 2017.

Yellowstone Mileposts: The Visitor's Point-by-Point Guide to the World's First National Park by Thomas P. Bohannon. Hayden Publishing, 2014.

Index

Note: Page numbers in parentheses indicate intermittent references.

A

Absaroka Lodge, 158
Absarokee, Montana, 198
accommodations
   Babb, Montana, 4
   Cody, Wyoming, 88, 89, 90
   Cooke City/Silver Gate,
      Montana, 94
   East Glacier, Montana, 6
   Gardiner, Montana, 92
   Polebridge, Montana, 9–10
   Saint Mary, Montana, 5
   West Glacier/Coram/Hungry
      Horse, 7, 8
   See also specific sites
Amsterdam, Montana, 198
Anaconda Aluminum
   Company, 278
Anaconda Mining Company, 218,
   220–22
Anaconda Smelter Stack State
   Park, 242
Anderson, George, 103

B

Babb, Montana, 3–4
Barcus, Mark and Lori, 89–90

Barness, B. J., 234, (235–38)
Barness, Dori, 233, 234, 235, 237
Barness, Eric, (235–37)
Barness, Kris, 235–37
Barness, Larry, 234, (235–37)
Beanery Queens, 91
beans, Jersey Lilly, sheepherder's
   hors d'oeuvres and, 57–58
bears. *See* grizzly bears
Beartooth Cafe and Miner's
   Saloon, 94
Beaver Hill State Park, 241
Beckler, Elbridge H., 72–74
Beebe, Chauncey "Chance," 29
Beebe, Eve, 33
Belfry, Montana, 198
Ben Rover cabin, 9, 155–56
Benson's corn, 59–60
Big Sandy, Montana, 198–99
Big Timber, Montana, 199
biking. *See* cycling
Billings, Montana, 199
bison and buffalo
   Big Medicine (26 years
      old), 228
   distinctions between, 225
   at edge of extinction, 37

fascination of, 230
as food, 56, 90, 115
fugitive bull, 37, 39
in Glacier, 4, 50
jerky, 56
life span, 228
massive herds to near extinction, 229–30
on open range (*See* Bison Range)
returning after fire (Waterson Bison Paddock), 36–38, 39–40
true protection of, 228–29
white/albino buffalo, 207, 228
in Yellowstone, 97
Bison Range, 224–30
about: overview of, 224
bacterial infection concerns, 229
control struggles, 224, 226–27
Hellgate Treaty and, 226–27
initial herd, 225–26
location and size, 224
National Bison Range (NBR) and, 225–26
origins of, 225–26
terrain and wildlife profile, 227–28
viewing, driving through, 228
water compact, 227
Yellowstone compared to, 228–29
Blackfeet guardian sculpture, 6

Blackfeet Nation/Agency, 4, 72, 73, 85, 112, 196, 200, 209, 267, 270, 274
Bone, Ben, 234
Bovey, Charlie and Sue Ford, 233–34
Bowman Lake, 9
Brett, Lieutenant-Colonel, 173
Brock, Tom, 175–76, 178, 180, 182
Brooks, James P., (26–29)
Buffalo Bill State Park, 88
Buffalo Bill's Antler Inn, 88
Buffalo Soldiers Bicycle Corps, 249–57
about: cycling in 1890s vs. today, 249–50
biking adventures to/through/from Yellowstone, 252–56
photo in Mammoth Hot Springs, 255
prepping for Yellowstone trip, 251
provisions list, 251–52
reasons for biking to/from Yellowstone, 249–50
Second Lt. James A. Moss and, 250, (251–54), 256
securing bikes to ride, 250–51
2,000 mile ride to St. Louis, 256–57
weight of laden bikes, 252
Butte, Montana, 216–23
copper mining and, 216–17
Irish Butte pasty, 62–63
melting pot facts, 217

nicknames, 217
wooden arch, 222, 223
See also Columbia Gardens

C

Camp Disappointment, 270
Camp Sheridan, 138–39
campgrounds, "The Wylie Way" at
    Yellowstone, 161–68
Cattle Baron Supper Club, 3
caverns. *See* Lewis and Clark
    Caverns State Park
cemetery, at Fort Yellowstone, 140
cherries, Flathead, 63–64
Chewing Black Bones
    Campground, 4
Chippewa Indians, (207–15)
Chittenden, Hiram H., 97–98,
    102, 103–5, 131, 141, 142
Chittenden Bridge, 171, 172
Clark, William A., 217, 218
clearing forest with "Operation
    Highball," 275–76, 277
Cody, William F. "Buffalo Bill,"
    (88–90)
Cody, Wyoming, 88–90
colors in hot pools/streams. *See*
    thermopiles
Columbia Gardens
    Anaconda Mining Company
        and, 216–17, 218, 220–22
    attractions, appeal, and vitality
        of, 218–20, 223
    attractions relocated, 223
    creation and opening, 217–18

declining vitality to closure,
    220–21
fire, destruction, suspected
    arson, 221
happiest place on earth, 223
mining effort at, 221–22
wooden arch relocated, 222, 223
Conway, James "Jimmy," plane
    crash, 65–70
Conway, Judith, 65, 67, 68, 69
Conway, Leo, 65, 67, 68, 69
Conway, Shirley, heroism of, 65,
    67–68
Cook, Charles, 98
Cook City General Store, 94
Cooke City/Silver Gate, Montana,
    93–94, 98–99, 100, 105, 199
Coolidge, Calvin, 26, 28
Coram, 8
corn, Benson's, 59–60
Crown of the Continent, 11–12,
    17, 26, 73
cycling
    Giant Springs State Park, 246
    GTSR and, 11–17
    "refrigerator effect" and, 12–13
    today vs. yesteryear, 249–50
    Yellowstone Grand Loop Road
        and, 257
    See also Buffalo Soldiers Bicycle
        Corps

D

dam, Hungry Horse, 7, 273–79
Dante's Inferno, 135

Daugherty, Harry, 30
Day-Petersen, Amy, 258, 259, 264
Demon's Cave, 135
devil in Yellowstone names
    about: overview of, 131
    Dante's Inferno, 135
    Demon's Cave, 135
    Devil's Cut, 131
    Devil's Den, 132
    Devil's Frying Pan, 136
    Devil's Hoof, 131
    Devil's Kitchen, 133
    Devil's Laundry, 132
    Devil's Slide, 133–34
    Devil's Stairway, 134
Dixon melons, 61–62
Doane, Gustavus, 131, 146. *See
    also* Washburn-Langford-
    Doane expedition
driving
    in Bison Range, 228
    between East Glacier and West
        Glacier, 71
    between Glacier and
        Yellowstone, VII–VIII,
        XI–XIII
    Grand Loop Road origins/
        construction, 97–105
    GTSR and, 12, 71
    playlists for the road, 106–13
    top sites in Glacier, 71

E
Earthquake Lake, 91
earthquakes, 91, 105, 123, 126–27,
    142, 173, 186

East Glacier, Montana, 5–6
Eckart, Sandy, 185
Eddies Corner, Montana, 199
electric production, of Hungry
    Horse Dam, 277, 278–79
elk
    Bison Range and, 227, 229
    disease carried by, 229
    Jackson, Wyoming and, 95–96
    National Elk Refuge, 95–96
    Petersen, Mark and, 261, 262
    precarious hunting incident, 261
    wiped out in 1870s, 115
    wolves and overpopulation
        of, 116
    in Yellowstone, 116, 119–20
Elk Island National Park, 38, 40
Endangered Species Act, 118–19
Essex, Montana, 80, (81–85), 200
Everts, Truman C., 131
Everts, Truman C., adventures and
    survival of, (145–53), 162

F
fires, Glacier
    Kenow fire, bison returning
        after (Waterton Bison
        Paddock), 36–38, 39–40
    Lake McDonald Lodge and, 19
    Sperry Chalet (phoenix of
        Glacier) and, 19–24
    Sprague Creek fire, 19–21, 22
Fischer, Hank, 118
Fishing Bridge, 157
Flathead cherries, 63–64
Flathead Indian Reservation, 111

Flathead Indians and Reservation, 72, 111, 224, 226, 227
flood, Yellowstone (worst in history), 93
food
  about: between Glacier and Yellowstone, XII
  Babb, Montana, 3
  Cody, Wyoming, (88–90)
  Cooke City/Silver Gate, Montana, 94
  East Glacier, Montana, 6–7
  Gardiner, Montana, 92–93
  Jackson, Wyoming, 95
  Polebridge, Montana, 9
  Saint Mary, Montana, 5
  tasty state treats to try, 56–64
  West Glacier/Coram/Hungry Horse, 7, 8
forest, clearing with "Operation Highball," 275–76, 277
Fort Yellowstone, 137–44
  Army's role in managing Yellowstone and, 138–39, 143–44
  Bicycle Corps to, 254–55
  building, Camp Sheridan and, 138–40
  buildings today, 144
  cemetery at, 140
  Chittenden, Hiram and, 141, 142
  funding maintenance of, 103
  Judge Meldrum and, 143
  reasons for building, 137–38

soldiers and lifestyle at, 140–43
stone mansion built at, 141, 142
structure and functions of, 139–40
Freeze, Hudson, 176, 180
fry bread/Indian taco, 58–59
fungi, mushrooms, 48–55, 56, 57
Fyant, Shelly, 227

G
Gardiner (town) vs. Gardner River, 92
Gardiner, Montana, 91–93, 158. See also flood, Yellowstone (worst in history)
Gardner River, 128, 152, 183, 184
Garrison, Lemuel A., 173
Gates of the Mountains, 267
Gateway Arch. See Yellowstone Gateway (Roosevelt) Arch
gateway communities, defined, 7. See also Glacier National Park, gateway communities; Yellowstone National Park, gateway communities
General-Shea-Morrison, 276
Geraldine, Montana, 200
geysers in Yellowstone
  Fort Yellowstone to protect, 138
  history and discovery, VIII–IX
  Pink Cone, 125
  Pork Chop, 127
  reading room overlooking, 156
  spiritual perspectives, VIII–IX
Giant Springs State Park, 246–47

Glacier National Park
  about: overview of, IX–XI;
    reservations for, 4
  age of, X
  climate change and glaciers, X
  creation of, IX–X
  Essex and, 80, (81–85), 200
  forgotten hero, 65–70
  missing persons (Whitehead
    brothers), 25–33
  mountain goats in, 41–47, 84
  mushrooms in, 48–55, 56
  plane crash, heroism and death
    in, 65–70
  precautions, X–XI
  reading rooms, 154–56
  reminiscences of growing up
    around, 79–85
  size and magnitude of, IX,
    X–XI
  time to see, XI, XII–XIII
  traveling between Yellowstone
    and, VII–VII, XI–XIII
  vehicle reservations for, 4
  visitors per year, IX
  visitors to Yellowstone and,
    VII–VIII
  wildlife of, X
Glacier National Park, gateway
  communities
  about: road conditions and,
    5–6, 9
  Babb, Montana, 3–4
  East Glacier, Montana, 5–6
  Martin City, Montana, 7
  Polebridge, Montana, 9–10

  Saint Mary, Montana, 4–5
  West Glacier/Coram/Hungry
    Horse, 7–8
Glacier Park Lodge, 6, 26
goats, mountain, 41–47, 84
Going-to-the-Sun Chalet, 26
Going-to-the-Sun Road (GTSR),
  4–5, 8, 11–17, 22, 29, 66–67,
  69, 71
Grand Loop Road, origins and
  construction, 97–105
Granite Park, 27, 29, 30
Granite State Park, 141–42
Great Bear Lodge, 5
Great Falls Portages (Upper and
  Lower), 267–69
Great Northern Railway, 8, 21,
  80–81, 82, 83, 200. *See also*
  Stevens, John F.
Greycliff Prairie Dog Town State
  Park, 158–59
Grizzly and Wolf Discovery
  Center, 91
grizzly bears
  attacks, X
  food for, 64
  in Glacier, 16, 50–51
  Ol' Snaggletooth, 91
  ranchers losing animals to, 197
  western Montana and, 196–97
  wolves and, 120
  in Yellowstone, 91, 116,
    120, 140
  See also World Museum of
    Wildlife

Grizzly Grille, 93
Guy F. Atkinson Company, 275

H
Haskell, Charles, 73, 74
Hellgate Treaty, 226–27
Heritage and Research Center, 92
hero, forgotten (in Glacier), 65–70
heroism, after plane crash, 65–70
highways between Glacier and
    Yellowstone, VII. *See also*
    driving
Hill, James J., 80–81
Historic Yellow Bus, 91
Hoover, J. Edgar, 31, 33
hors d'oeuvres, sheepherder's,
    Jersey Lilly beans and, 57–58
horses and horseback
    exploring Yellowstone, 162
    horse-drawn vehicles, 162,
        163–64, 168
    losing horse in Yellowstone,
        147, 149
    Remington in Yellowstone, 253
    search for Whitehead
        brothers, 27
    Sperry Chalet and, 21
huckleberry products, 64
Hudson's Bay Fur Brigade Trail,
    38–39
Hungry Horse Dam, 7, 273–79
Hungry Horse (town), 7, 273–74

I
IMAX theater, 91
Indian taco/fry bread, 58–59
Indians and Indian reservations
    about: overview of, XI–XII
    buffalo and, 37
    fry bread/Indian taco and,
        58–59
    between Glacier and
        Yellowstone, XI–XII
    Hellgate Treaty, 226–27
    Heritage and Research Center
        and, 92
    Nehiyaw Pwat confederacy,
        208–9
    reviving buffalo population,
        37–40
    See also specific tribes
interpretive pullout, first ever, 101
Irish Butte pasty, 62–63
Irma Hotel and Restaurant, 89, 90
Iron Horse Bar & Grill, 93
Izaak Walton Inn, (80–83), 156

J
J. H. Trisdale, Inc., 275. *See also*
    Trisdale, John
Jackson, Wyoming, 94–96
jerky, bison, 56
Jersey Lilly beans and
    sheepherder's hors d'oeuvres,
    57–58
Jessup, Jack, 29–30
Joliet, Montana, 200
Jones, Bob, 79–80, 83, 84, 85

Jones, C. J. "Buffalo," 140
Jones, Deane Sterne, 79, 80

K
Kaparich, Chuck, 219
Keys, Caroline, 15–17
Kingman, Dan, 102–3
Kootenai tribe, 72, 73, 111, 226, 227
Kremlin, Montana, 201

L
Lake Hotel, 157
Lake McDonald, 12, 14, 18, 52
Lake McDonald Inn, 154
Lake McDonald Lodge, 19, 27
Langford, Nathaniel P., 98, 131, (146–48), 162
Leland, Rod and Tracy, 35
Lemhi Pass, 271–72
Leopold, Aldo, 117
Leopold, Nathaniel, 117
Lewis and Clark Caverns State Park, 243, 266–67
Lewis and Clark National Historic Trail Interpretive Center, 269–70
Lewis and Clark, on massive buffalo herds, 229
Lewis and Clark, sites and anecdotes connected to, 265–72
    about: overview of, XII, 265, 272
    Camp Disappointment, 270

Gates of the Mountains, 267
Great Falls Portages (Upper and Lower), 267–69
Lemhi Pass, 271–72
Lewis and Clark Caverns State Park, 243, 266–67
Lewis and Clark National Historic Trail Interpretive Center, 269–70
Missouri Headwaters State Park, 158, 244–45, 270–71
Pompeys Pillar, 265–66
Tower Rock, 267 (*See also* Tower Rock State Park)
Travelers Rest State Park, 272
Lewis Hotel, 27, 29–30
Little Shell Tribe (Chippewa), 207–15
    history and fight for recognition, 208–13
    long hard fight of the Métis and, 207–13
    Nehiyaw Pwat confederacy and, 208–9
    official recognition as nation, 207–8, 213–14
    Red River Cart and, 209, 211
    today, 214–15
    Turtle Mountain Reservation and, 208
    white/buffalo and, 207, 228
Livingston, Sacajawea Park, 160
lodging. *See* accommodations
Loeb, Richard, 117
Logan Pass, 11, 12, 43, 50, 85

Logan Pass Visitor Center, XIII
Lolo, Montana, 201
Lost Creek State Park, 242–43
Lyford, Bob, 29–30

M
Madison Buffalo Jump State Park,
  243–44
Malahowski, Russell, 221
Manhattan, Montana, 201
Many Glacier Hotel, 27
Marias Pass Memorial Park,
  71–78
  about: overview of, 71
  engineering of, Stevens, John F.
    and, 72–74, 76, 77, 81
  McCarthyville and, 77–78
  Mini-Me Washington (T.
    Roosevelt) Monument, 71,
    72, 77
  Roosevelt, Theodore and, 74–76
  Roosevelt Memorial, 72, 77, 78
  "Slippery Bill" Morrison and,
    76–78
Martin City, Montana, 7
Maxville, Montana, 201–2
McCarthyville, 77–78
McDonald Creek, 12, 27, 29
McKinley, William, 74
Meldrum, John W., 143
melons, Dixon, 61–62
Métis. See Little Shell Tribe
  (Chippewa)
Milltown State Park, 240

Mini-Me Washington
  Monument, 71, 77
Minor, Kate, 23
missing persons
  perilous adventures of Truman
    C. Everts in Yellowstone,
    (145–53)
  Whitehead brothers (Joseph
    and William) in Glacier,
    25–33
Missoula Public Library, 160
Missouri Headwaters State Park,
  158, 244–45, 270–71
Montana
  beautiful places to read (See
    reading rooms)
  colorful towns and origin
    stories, 198–206
  tourism importance, VII–VIII
  See also specific town/community
    names
morel mushrooms, 51, 57
morning glory spillway, 273, 279
Morrison, Dan, 243
Morrison, William "Slippery Bill,"
  76–78
Moss, James A., 250,
  (251–54), 256
mountain goats, 41–47, 84
Mowry, L. C., 27, 28
Mullis, Kary, 180–81
Museum of the Yellowstone, 91
museum of wildlife. See World
  Museum of Wildlife

museums, between Glacier and
 Yellowstone, XII
mushrooms, 48–55, 56
music, playlists for the road,
 106–13

N
Norris, Philetus W., (99–103), 131

O
obsidian and Obsidian Cliff,
 99–100, 101, 128, 129
Ojibwa bands, 208
Ol' Snaggletooth, 91
Old Faithful Inn, 5, 157
Old Faithful Snow Lodge, 156
Olson, Karl, 22
"Operation Highball,"
 275–76, 277
Opportunity, Montana, 202
Orlich, Don, 221–22
Orr, Sue, 218
oysters, Rocky Mountain, 61

P
Park Cafe and Grocery, 5
Perry, Pat, 235, 236
Petersen, Mark (description, p.
 258, bottom), 259–64
Pink Cone Geyser, 125
Pitcher, Major, 171–72
plane crash, heroism and death in,
 65–70

playlists for the road, 106–13
Polebridge, Montana, 9–10. *See
 also* Ben Rover cabin
Polebridge Mercantile (the Merc),
 9, 10
Pompeys Pillar, 265–66
Pork Chop Geyser, 127
Power, Montana, 202–3
Pray, Montana, 203
Prince of Wales Hotel, 35, 36
Prudhomme, Gabriel, 211

R
Radersburg Cemetery, 159
Ranger Station at Saint Mary, 5
Rapelje, Montana, 203
reading rooms, 154–60
 Glacier, 154–56
 Montana (other), 158–60
 Yellowstone, 156–58
Reamer, Robert, 5
Red Lodge, Montana, 93, 99,
 189–90
Red Rock Point, 12
reward for Whitehead brothers,
 30–31, 32
Richardson, H. F., 170–73
Riel, Louis, 211
Ringling, Montana, 203
roads between Glacier and
 Yellowstone, VII
Rock City, Montana, 192–97
Rocker, Montana, 204

Rocky Mountain oysters, 61
Roosevelt, Theodore
    conservation and other
        contributions, 74–76, 105,
        130, 225–26
    memorial to, 72, 77, 78
    National Bison Range and,
        225–26
    National Bison Range (NBR)
        and, 225–26
    Nobel Peace Prize, 75
    Panama Canal and, 76
    youngest president, 74
Roosevelt Arch. *See* Yellowstone
    Gateway (Roosevelt) Arch
Roosevelt Memorial, 78
Roscoe, Montana, 204
Rosenleaf, Kelly, 219–20, 221

S
Sacajawea Park, 160
Saint Mary, Montana, 4–5
Salish tribe, 72, 111, 226, 227,
    240, 272
Scout Saddle Company, 89–90
Sheepeater Cliffs, 128
sheepherder's hors d'oeuvres, Jersey
    Lilly beans and, 57–58
Sheridan, William, 138
Sholly, Cam, 185, 187, 188
Silver Gate, Montana. *See* Cooke
    City/Silver Gate, Montana
Slippery Otter Pub, 90
Sluice Boxes Primitive State Park,
    245–46
Smith, Doug, 119, 122

Southern Cross, 159–60
Sperry Chalet, 19–24
Sperry Lodge, 154
Spring Meadow Lake State
    Park, 248
Stalling, Ed, 13–14, 15, 17
Stanford, Montana, 204
state parks. *See specific park names*
Stevens, John F., 72–74, 76, 77, 81
Swiss chalets, 8, 21

T
temperature, colors in hot pools
    and. *See* thermopiles
tent camping, "The Wylie Way,"
    162–68
testicles, Rocky Mountain
    oysters, 61
thermopiles, 175–82
    Brock, Tom and, 175–76, 178,
        180, 182
    at center of myriad research
        fields, 179–80
    color brilliance in hot pools/
        streams and, 177–80
    extremophiles and, 179–80, 182
    Freeze, Hudson and, 176, 180
    life survival temperatures and,
        175–76, 179–80
    "new" bacterium and, 176
    PCR test, COVID-19 and,
        180–82
    tardigrade, 179–80
    as viruses, bacteria, archaea, and
        eukarya, 177–78
Thronson's General Store, 4

Thronson's Motel, 4
Tower Rock State Park, 245, 267
Trail of the Cedars, 53
trails
   notorious Uncle Tom's Trail,
     170–74
   range of length, 169
   Thorofare, 169
Travelers Rest State Park, 272
Trisdale, John, 276. *See also* J. H.
   Trisdale, Inc.
Truman, Harry S., 276
Tuff Cliff, 129
Tumbleweed Bookstore and
   Cafe, 93
Turtle Mountain Chippewa. *See*
   Little Shell Tribe (Chippewa)
Two Dot, Montana, 204–5
Two Medicine Lake, 154–55
Two Medicine River, 193,
   (194–96)
Two Sister's Café, 3

U
Uncle Tom's Trail, 170–74
University of Utah Seismograph
   Stations (UUSS), 126, 127

V
Virginia City, Montana, 205, 231,
   232–33
Virginia City Players, 231–39
   about: overview of, 231
   Amateu Dramatic Association's
     first performance, 232

   evolution of, 235–39
   gold boom giving rise to,
     231–32
   origins and development,
     231–35
   players/productions, roles, and
     skills, 233–34, 235–38
   today, 239
visits to Yellowstone
   affordable, "The Wylie Way,"
     161–68
   "carriage trade" dominating, 162
   horse-drawn tours, 163–64, 168
   See also driving
volcano, Yellowstone as, 123–30
   ancient supereruptions, 124
   caldera, (123–25), 129–30,
     135, 148
   chances of erupting, 123–24,
     129–30
   evidence of volcanic activity
     forming Yellowstone, 127–29
   false fears of, 123–26
   history of, 124
   hydrothermal activity/
     explosions and, 126, 127–28
   Lava Creek Eruption, 124, 129
   seismic activity, 126–27 (*See also*
     earthquakes)
   as "supervolcano," 123–24
   West Thumb and, 123, 128
   Yellowstone Volcano
     Observatory, 126

W

Walton (town), 81–82

Walton, Sir Izaak, 200. *See also* Izaak Walton Inn

Washburn, Henry, 131, 146

Washburn-Langford-Doane expedition, 98, 133, 134, 146–47, 157, 199. *See also* Everts, Truman C., adventures and survival of

Waterloo, Montana, 206

Waterton Bison Paddock (return after fire), 36–38, 39–40

Wear, David, 138

West Glacier/Coram/Hungry Horse, 7–8

West Yellowstone Historic Center, 91

West Yellowstone, Montana, 90–91

Wharton, J. R., 217–18

Whilt, Jim, 29

Whitehead, Dora, (26–33)

Whitehead brothers (Joseph and William), 25–33

wildlife

exotic museum with all exhibits hunted by owner (*See* World Museum of Wildlife)

Jackson, Wyoming and, 95–96

National Museum of Wildlife Art, 96

See also bison and buffalo; elk; grizzly bears; mountain goats; wolves

Withrow, Ray and Maude, 81–82, 85

Wixson & Crow, 275

wolves

Bison Range and, 229

grizzlies and, 120

Grizzly and Wolf Discovery Center, 91

ranchers losing animals to, 197

white, in Stanford, Montana, 204

wolves, reintroduction to Yellowstone, 114–21

about: overview of, 114–15

Cinderella and, 119, 120, 121

Crystal Creek pack, 114, 119

depletion of wolves prior to, 115–17

drawing worldwide attention, 119–20

Druid pack (Druids), 114, 119–21

Endangered Species Act and, 118–19

expansion of packs, 120–21

livestock industry opposing, 118

murderous reputation of wolves and, 115–16

number of wolves today, 122

ongoing controversy after, 122

poisoned bait ban and, 117

waking up to wolves' value and, 117–19

Wonderland Cafe, 92–93

Woodering, Sam T., 173

World Museum of Wildlife, 258–64

Wylie, Mary Ann, 163, 168

Wylie, William Wallace and Wylie Camping Company, 162–68

Wylie Permanent Camping Company, 167

Y

yellow bus, historic, 91

Yellowstone, fort. *See* Fort Yellowstone

Yellowstone Gateway (Roosevelt) Arch, 75, 92, 105, 142

Yellowstone Lake, volcanic activity and, 127–28

Yellowstone National Park
   about: overview of, VIII–IX
   brilliant colors in hot pools/ streams (*See* thermopiles)
   Buffalo Soldiers bike trip to/ from (*See* Buffalo Soldiers Bicycle Corps)
   building, philosophy guiding, 101
   building Grand Loop Road, 97–105
   early Army post in, IX
   first national park, VIII
   flood (worst in history), 93, 183–90

perilous adventures of Truman C. Everts, (145–53)
   protecting, Fort Yellowstone and, 137–38
   reading rooms, 156–58
   size and magnitude of, VIII, XI
   time to see, XI, XII–XIII
   traveling between Glacier and, VII–VII, XI–XIII
   uniquenesses of, IX
   visitors per year, IX
   visitors to Glacier and, VII–VIII
   volcano of (*See* volcano, Yellowstone as)

Yellowstone National Park, gateway communities
   Cody, Wyoming, 88–90
   Cooke City/Silver Gate, Montana, 93–94
   Gardiner, Montana, 91–93
   Jackson, Wyoming, 94–96
   West Yellowstone, Montana, 90–91

Yellowstone National Park Protection Act, 162

Yellowstone Trading Post, 94

Yellowstone Volcano Observatory, 126

Yellowstone-Glacier Bee Line Highway, VII

About the Author

Ednor Therriault has spent more than 20 years exploring Montana from corner to corner. He's authored two editions of *Montana Curiosities*, and revised two editions of *Montana Off the Beaten Path*. His other books include *Yellowstone Myths and Legends*, *Haunted Montana*, and *Seven Montanas*. He is also a frequent contributor to *Distinctly Montana* and *Mountain Outlaw* magazines.

Therriault brings the wit of a humorist, the fact-finding tenacity of a journalist, and a deep Montana pedigree to his work. His great-great-grandparents homesteaded along Douglas Creek in the Flint Valley in the late 1800s, and his grandfather mined for gold in Garnet, now Montana's best-preserved ghost town. His father, a decorated Marine pilot, was born in Missoula. Ednor also studies Native American history, and recognizes the importance of including Indian culture and narratives in his writings of the complex history of Montana.

As Bob Wire, Ednor has written and recorded six albums of original music, and has been performing live shows all over the West for 30 years.

He lives in Missoula with his wife, Shannon.